Kotahitanga

Kotahitanga
The Search for Māori Political Unity

Lindsay Cox

Auckland
OXFORD UNIVERSITY PRESS
Melbourne Oxford New York

Oxford University Press, Walton Street, Oxford OX 2 6DP
Oxford New York Toronto
Delhi Bombay Calcutta Madras Karachi
Kuala Lumpur Singapore Hong Kong Tokyo
Nairobi Dar es Salaam Cape Town
Melbourne Auckland Madrid
and associated companies in
Berlin Ibadan

Oxford is a trade mark of Oxford University Press

National Library of New Zealand
Cataloguing-in-Publication Data
Cox, Lindsay, 1960–
Kotahitanga : the search for Maori political unity / Lindsay Cox.
1v.
ISBN 0-19-558280-0
1. Maori (New Zealand people)—Politics and government.   2. Maori
(New Zealand people)—Ethnic identity.   I. Title.
323.11994093   (305.8994093)   zbn93–036165

Cover designed by Nikolas Andrew
Typeset in Māori Bembo by Egan-Reid Ltd.
Printed in Hong Kong
Published by Oxford University Press
1A Matai Road, Greenlane
PO Box 11-149, Auckland, New Zealand

Contents

Foreword

During the decade prior to 1990 the Treaty of Waitangi began to acquire a stature it had never hitherto known. For the Māori this had little to do with the sesquicentennial commemorations proposed for that year. Rather, it was about the newly found relevance of the Treaty for their place in the life of this country.

And so 'new' words came into colloquial—and official—use. There was, for instance, tribal or iwi identity, rangatiratanga or kin-based leadership, taonga or elements of heritage—all having key points of reference in the Treaty, all therefore capable of qualifying relations with the Crown, and all inviting response from Māori people anywhere.

This book is a part of this new activity, and it leads us ultimately to one major response, the National Māori Congress. On the other hand to see the Congress only in contemporary terms would be to distort the Māori people's search for sovereignty that has its roots in the first settler contacts.

Lindsay Cox has been fortunate in his Māori ancestry and his scholarly interests to be able to record the beginnings of the Congress and to set it in the context of a history of Māori endeavour to achieve a voice independent of European aspirations and ambition. Beneath the author's careful analysis of action and reaction, of process and form, lies a saga of spirit and spirituality without which nothing truly Māori can ever flourish. Yet for the latest Kotahitanga movement to succeed it seems that even more has to be called forth: stamina, imagination, perhaps the charisma of heroes.

I commend the book for what it is: a sensitive study of a striving for unity among the Māori people confronted with challenges to their identity. And I commend it in particular to those who would add to their understanding of rangatiratanga. Na reira, kia ora mai tatou.

I. H. Kawharu

He Kupu Whakatau

Tini whetū ki te rangi, ko Tāne-nui-a-rangi ki te whenua.

Tihei Mauri Ora.

Ko te mea tuatahi, te mihi atu ki tō tātou Kaiwhakaora. Ko Ia te putaketanga o ngā mea katoa. Nāna e homai, Nāna hoki i tango atu, nā reira ka mihi atu, ka whakamoemiti atu ki a Ia.

Ka huri ngā whakaaro ki ngā tini aitua kua hinga mai nei, kua hinga atu ra. Nā reira, haere atu ra koutou, haere, haere, hoki atu. E Te Reo, e te kaiwhakapiripiri, e te whaea i hapaingia te kaupapa o te Māngai, haere, haere, haere atu ra. Haere tahi atu i a Tā Hemi. Hoki atu korua ki a rātau i takahia tērā huarahi i mua atu ra. Hoki atu ki Tawhīti Nui, ki Tawhīti Roa, ki Tawhīti Pamamao, Te Hono ki Wairua. Hoki atu korua, koutou katoa, ki te mīnenga i tū ai kei tua o te arai. Āpiti hono tatai hono, rātau ki a rātau. Āpiti hono tatai hono, tātau nei ngā hunga ora ki a tātou.

E Te Ārikinui, Te Atairangikāhu, tēnā rawa atu koe. Tēnā hoki koe e te Āriki o Tūwharetoa, ko koe tēnā e tā Hepi. Nā tō korua mahi, ā, koutou ko Te Reo Tahupōtiki Wiremu Rātana Hura, i tūwhera ai te Whakamīnenga o Ngā Iwi o Aotearoa i te kotahi tekau ma whā o ngā ra o Here Turi Koka, i te tau 1990. Nā reira tēnā koutou katoa ngā rangatira o te motu. Tēnā koutou, tēnā koutou, tēnā koutou.

He mihi hoki kia koe e Tā mo to aroha mai ki ahau, me ngā kupu whakatau nou i tuhituhi mo te tīmatanga o tēnei pukapuka. He mihi hoki ki a koe e Te Ranginui i tautoko mai koe i tēnei kaupapa. Nā reira ka mihi atu ki a koutou katoa o te Tari Māori o te Whare Wānanga o Tamaki Makaurau. A, ka mihi atu hoki ki ngā hoa mahi i awhina mai nei, no te Tari Māori o te Whare Wānanga o Manawatu. E hara i te mea ko te pukapuka i puawai nei, he hua nōku anake, engari, nō mātou katoa.

Na reira, tēnā koutou e panui mai nei, tēnā koutou, tēnā koutou katoa.

viii

Preface

Late in June 1989 a national Māori leadership hui was called at short notice by Sir Hepi Te Heuheu. Interested in political developments occurring among and between iwi, and also eager to hear and perhaps meet some of the notable rangatira of the nation, I welcomed the opportunity to accompany the Rangitāne and Ngāti Raukawa delegations which travelled to Turangi on the morning of 23 June. I sensed that something very important was about to happen and the chance to be a part of it was indeed a rare one.

The debate concerned the formation of a congress: a National Māori Congress (NMC). This was an issue of considerable moment. The speakers and participants included several dames and knights of the realm, spiritual and political leaders, senior Māori academics, as well as kaumātua and kuia from many iwi. Surely this was a milestone in Māori development: history in the making—a hui which would set in motion something beneficial, something powerful, something for future generations.

Later, at Rātana, in August of that year, the Department of Māori Studies from Massey University undertook to record the proceedings of the follow-up hui. Again the rangatira of the four winds attended, this time in even greater numbers. The collation of reports and documenting of historic events was stimulating. Observing the interplay and protocol as elders formulated opinions and expressed a desire for unity was not only educational, but also allowed a degree of participation, albeit at that stage peripheral.

Momentum for a Congress grew in early 1990 and I was fortunate enough to assist Professor Mason Durie, the Secretary of the Whakakotahi Taskforce (and later of the National Māori Congress) in his work. Concurrently, I enrolled in a masterate programme at Massey University. As the year passed, and consideration was given to a possible thesis topic, the new Congress emerged as a challenging and timely subject for study.

The thesis itself grew from there but, in order to contextualize Congress and provide a framework for analysis, it became clear that a historical and philosophical overview would be necessary. Following the completion of the thesis, opportunity for discussion arose with Ms Anne French of the Oxford University Press, and the thesis was accepted for publication.

Chapter One of this resultant book explores the British concept of sovereignty and the effect it has had upon Māori. It is submitted that kotahitanga movements—whether spiritual, political, social, economic, or all of these—are, at least in part, manifestations of Māori desire to exert Māori sovereignty, or are a reaction to the impact of European administration (kāwanatanga). The eventual outcome of this desire is categorized according to three themes, outlined later in this preface, each of which is explored chronologically through case studies.

Chapter Two provides a brief background to Māori social organization and leadership, with a particular emphasis on the capacity for interaction within and between discrete kin-based units: forerunners, so to speak, of kotahitanga. Examples of cooperation in military or economic ventures are used to illustrate purposeful inter-tribal unity.

The third chapter outlines the Treaty of Waitangi and explores some of the early colonial administrative instruments through which the principle of kāwanatanga was expressed.

The next three chapters deal with the three themes that form the basis of this analysis of Māori political unity:

- the theme of 'He Whakaminenga o Ngā Hapū' (Chapter Four) examines unity based upon tribal constructs
- in 'He Iwi Tahi Tātou' (Chapter Five) the focus shifts toward unity based upon notions of assimilation and amalgamation
- in 'He Paihere Tangata' (Chapter Six) the thrust for unity is seen to stem from a particular sectarian interest.

A history and analysis of the latest kotahitanga movement, the National Māori Congress, forms the basis of Chapter Seven, and the conclusions are brought together in Chapter Eight.

Much of the information used to illustrate the case studies covered in this work is derived from secondary sources which are referenced in the text. The subject of Māori political unity has been dealt with by many leading authorities from within the disciplines of History and Anthropology as well as Māori Studies, and I am humbled by the significance and depth of those earlier writings and the chance to comment on them.

Some data were obtained through perusal of published minutes of various hui associated with the Pāremata Māori, whereas other material derives from the Irish University Press Series, *Great Britain Parliamentary Papers*.

Contemporary bodies such as Māori committees and district councils have been experienced at first hand. While details of meetings and personalities involved at this level are not directly relevant to this study, and are not included here, direct participation has enabled a degree of familiarity to develop.

As one of the five delegates to Congress from Te Runanganui o

Rangitāne and a member of the NMC Operations Committee, I have been able to sit among the representatives from other iwi at Congress Executive meetings and at various committee meetings, as well as the hui-a-iwi convened occasionally to respond to government policy initiatives. This opportunity to be part of the movement and to spend time with leaders and workers of the NMC has been invaluable in researching kotahitanga as it emerges in the 1990s.

Perhaps the most valuable outcome of this association has been the realization that unity does not happen just because people are willing to act in concert; the momentum for unity, all too often taken for granted, must be actively maintained and pursued. This insight, while superficially quite obvious, emerged gradually, and is perhaps an aspect of kotahitanga which is not as apparent to those who are involved at other levels.

This book is neither the first nor the last word on Māori unity. If it contributes to the understanding of kotahitanga and provides an accurate record of the formative years of the National Māori Congress, then it will have achieved its purpose.

Heoi ano, e whakamatau ana e mātou ki te whakawhānui, ki te whakamārama hoki, nga mahi o mua ra, a, o inaianei, mo rātou, nga Rangatira mo Apopo.

Naku noa iti.

Lindsay Cox

Chapter One
The Emergence of Māori Sovereignty

> . . . we acknowledge New Zealand as a Sovereign and independent State, so far at least as it is possible to make that acknowledgment in favour of a people composed of numerous, dispersed, and petty Tribes, who possess few political relations to each other, and are incompetent to act, or even deliberate, in concert. (Lord Normanby's instructions, 14 August 1839)[1]

Normanby's observations have proven to be superficial and misleading. Political relations between tribes were in fact long-standing, complex, and expressed as concerted action as the need arose. The potential for unity among and between iwi and hapū, discussed in Chapter Two, was manifested only occasionally and only for specific purposes. Motivated either by warfare or by socio-economic necessity, unity attained by Māori did not reach, or even aspire to, the national level. Nonetheless, periodic short-term, cooperative activities demonstrated a capacity to act in unison. The formation of a national body politic was a novel concept to Māori, but by 1830 the increasing impact of alien technological, religious, and economic influences had wrought much change in Aotearoa[2]. Contact with external nationals and the need to interact with them caused Māori to rethink their relationship with other tribes. Perhaps for the first time, Māori saw themselves as more like each other in comparison to the newcomers. As the untoward effects of colonization grew, so grew a sense of nationhood among Māori.[3]

The introductory quote from Lord Normanby's instructions demonstrates a willingness on the part of the British Colonial Office, by 1839, to recognize and assign to Māori the sovereignty over Aotearoa. In the years preceding this official stance, Māori had begun to explore models of unity: models which would enable international intercourse; models which focused on political unity by accommodating tribal differences; models which approached the recently introduced political notion of Māori nationhood; models which reached out and embraced the significance of sovereignty. An analysis of European ideas on sovereignty and of indigenous reaction to it will further provide a context for the topic of kotahitanga.

Sovereignty: The British View

A State may be deemed sovereign when it can be demonstrated that it is free from external control,[4] and is governed by its own laws and authority. Even at this stage, one might commence a debate as to what constitutes a law and whether that law needs to be codified to have status. The traditional practices of a group, bound together in common cause (defence or economic advancement), constitutes that group's customary rules. This body of practices is their manifestation of their laws and as such merits recognition at least in the eyes of Western jurisprudence as a part of natural law. The absence of a central body politic and a codified set of statutes does not negate the significance of the laws observed by that group. This position is discernible in the policies and practices of the British Colonial Office, where treaties were used to cede sovereignty to the British Crown.[5] By the 1830s, tribes in Africa, in the Americas, as well as in the Pacific were consistently attributed sovereignty as a prelude to seeking their consent for cession to the British Crown. Their sovereignty was based on their undisputed title to the soil,[6] their own laws of land tenure, and the social constructs that determined authority and control.

Andrew Sharp[7] offers a detailed description of sovereignty through an analysis of Thomas Hobbes's *Leviathan* (1651). The following hallmarks, derived by Sharp from Hobbes (Ch. 18), are given as 'the essential governmental powers of sovereignty'. They are:

• the right to make laws
• the right of judicature
• the right to make war and peace
• the right to appoint office holders
• the right to honour subjects with titles and dignities, and
• the right to regulate what opinions are allowed to be propagated in public.

Together these form the basis of Sharp's 'Doctrine of State', the absence of which implies a state of chaos. Māori obviously possessed a clear social, political, and spiritual corpus by which affairs were ordered. Even in the absence of a corporate body politic it is clear that a state of chaos did not exist prior to contact with Europeans. Since there was a lack of chaos it was not difficult to assign sovereignty and nationhood to tribes of Aotearoa, and to recognize the chiefs, Ngā Rangatira, as the guardians of that sovereignty.

Chapter 18 of *Leviathan*, however, gives a somewhat different impression of sovereignty. For Hobbes, it is essential that a supreme source of judgement resides in a position of authority over the State:

. . . yet if their actions be directed according to particular judgements, and particular appetites, they can expect thereby no protection neither against a Common enemy, nor against the injuries of one another.[8]

The Reverend Samuel Marsden, in a letter to the Reverend J. Pratt (4 June 1824) on the viability of forming a settlement in Aotearoa, expressed a similar view to Hobbes.[9] Concerned about the governance of settlers in the absence of an effective administration to compel lawful behaviour (particularly in regard to inter-ethnic relationships), he suggested the establishment of a Māori king. The need for a source of authority, a power, resident above European and Māori alike, was seen as a vital prerequisite for stability in the event of colonization. Māori were quick to realize this wider aspect of sovereignty hitherto missing from their experience of tribal control and authority. There was a need to create new alliances so that tribes were protected from internal and external predation: a protection derived from the combined mana of rangatira; a protection for Māori from Māori as well as from Pākehā. The need for some form of national government was thus highlighted as an intrinsic element of sovereignty.

Fundamental to the concept of sovereignty is the acknowledgment of that sovereignty, from both within the community and without. It is essential that members of a population act in accordance with the designated administration and adhere to its direction. Further, sovereign bodies must accept each other's autonomy and authority. Thus sovereignty may be rendered as the acknowledged political power of a social group acting in concert for their mutual welfare and security.[10]

Regarding recognition, Joe Williams[11] parallels the situation in the Aotearoa of 1840 with relationships between the United States of America and the native American Nations of the early 1800s. Chief Justice Marshall,[12] in the Supreme Court decision *Worcester* v. *Georgia*, talks of the Indian tribes as being

> . . . distinct, independent political communities, retaining their original natural rights, as the undisputed possessors of the soil from time immemorial . . .

They were thus recognized by each other and by the colonizing power with whom they had contact.

For the Māori, the parameters of sovereignty needed to be defined. Rangatiratanga, as exercised on behalf of hapū, conformed well to the notion of sovereignty at a tribal level, but, lacking a unified political authority, could Māori as a whole be described as a sovereign people? Could a group of autonomous tribes, each with its own individual status, be deemed sovereign? By at least 1840 it is clear that the British Colonial Office were prepared to treat rangatira as though, when acting in concert, they exercised some measure of sovereign authority in New Zealand, even in the absence of a central body politic. The second draft consular instruction to Captain Hobson (8 March 1939)[13] indicates this acceptance:

> Her Majesty's Government acknowledge in the Natives of New Zealand an independent and national character as far as is possible that such a character should be attributed to a collection of separate tribes occupying so extensive a Territory, without any definite union between the different Tribes . . .[14]

An area of sovereignty which needs to be clarified is where, for the British, does such sovereignty reside? It appears that for the United Kingdom (if not for the British Empire) the notion of sovereignty has remained constant since Victorian times. Nominally the Queen is sovereign; in reality it is the Queen in Parliament that is the supreme source of law.[15] It seems likely that Māori, seeing Queen Victoria, her predecessors, and successors as the head of the State and of the Church, did not fully appreciate that the actual law-making and unmaking powers rested with a group of elected representatives. Māori were much more comfortable with the vision of a wise and all-powerful sovereign.

Sovereignty is deemed to be incommunicable and inseparable. The sovereignty of the British Crown over its territories is 'exclusive and exhaustive' and 'indivisible'.[16] McHugh (1989, p. 41) reiterates that a 'constitutional monarchy . . . requires all legal sovereignty to remain in the Crown'. By 1840, a cession of sovereignty from Māori to the British Crown was proposed in the English version of the Treaty of Waitangi. The Māori version, on the other hand, appeared to reinforce the powers of tribal sovereignty. Unwittingly (or perhaps wittingly if the motives of Henry Williams are to be credited with vision)[17] the Treaty had confused issues of sovereignty, at least in Māori eyes.

Māori Nationalism

It was this confusion and the settler government's subsequent (i.e., post-Treaty of Waitangi) dismissal of Māori views that played an important role in the desire for a unified Māori body which would be able to parallel the Crown's exercise of an unqualified and seemingly unjust demonstration of sovereignty.

The continued search for Māori unity, as manifest by a series of political, religious, and social movements, might be referred to as a search for sovereignty: a search for an equal voice in national affairs—a voice distinctively Māori and independent from European aspirations and ambitions.

This book explores kotahitanga: the concerted operation of rangatira to give effect to a developing notion of collective Māori sovereignty.

The Basis for a Thematic Approach

Exploration of the complex and developing subject, kotahitanga, requires a suitable framework. When formulating this strategy, a number of definitive categories were considered. A purely chronological development was not favoured since it conveyed little of the dynamic interaction within kotahitanga movements and the changes, over time, that have characterized particular institutions. A simple sequential treatment did not allow for the grouping of similar approaches, which supports the hypothesis that Māori unity was, alternately, actively promoted and just as actively discouraged according to the prevailing philosophy of successive national administrations. Some movements were perceived as against the national (colonial) interest (Pāremata Māori, Kīngitanga: see below) whereas others were promoted to enhance government control of Māori (Sir George Grey's rūnanga district, Kohimārama, and the Māori Councils of 1900: see Chapter Two).

A second approach, also rejected in part, was to use the structural–organizational substrate to differentiate movements. The earliest expressions of unity were firmly based in peculiarly Māori constructs. Later movements adopted structures derived from European models. Some were an amalgam of both traditions. What emerged during preliminary consideration was a picture of hierarchical models largely similar in form. Any apparent differences reinforced the alternating pattern mentioned above, with Māori initiatives displaying Māori structures and government proposals exhibiting European traits. As colonization spread and Pākehā influences increasingly pervaded Māori society, a discernible mingling of the two systems developed. Mere structure, then, was an inadequate vehicle for elucidation. A combination of structural and chronological influences failed to simplify the inquiry.

The possibility of using the impetus for each movement as a means of categorizing and then analysing kotahitanga arose. The themes explored in this book emerged from this line of enquiry. The pattern of Māori-derived initiatives, Crown reaction, and subsequent Māori response could also be incorporated in this approach.

Preliminary research resulted in a list of '*supra*-tribal' movements and a list of bodies seeking to represent Māori at a national or at an international level. Formative impressions on the impetus for each, their organizational structure, and the source of their authority, were compared using a chronological table (Table 1). This table, while comprehensive, is by no means exhaustive.

Table 1: Parameters of Māori unity: a chronological overview

Date	Body or Movement	Organizational Structure	Event or Impetus	Source of Authority
1816	Kohuiarau (Ko Huirau or Ko Huiaroa)	Iwi-based, through marriages and defence networks	Terehou (of Ngāi Tūhoe: successful military campaign	Iwi
1831	United tribes	Iwi-based (Northern)	Petition to William IV	Iwi
1835	Confederation of United Tribes	Iwi-based	Declaration of Independence	Iwi: appeal to British Crown
1858	Kingitanga	Iwi-based (Waikato)	Māori Sovereign	Iwi
1861	District rūnanga	Hundreds, District rūnanga	Government regulation of Māori activity	Legislation
1892	Kotahitanga	Paremata Māori	Rangatiratanga and Treaty of Waitangi	Iwi
1900	Council	District councils, Central coordination	Māori Councils Act 1900	Legislation
1925	Te Iwi Morehu, Te Maramatanga o Ihowa	Elected President, Church executive. District council. Apotoro and local church committees	T W Ratana, Tahupotiki Wiremu	Atua/Tumuaki
1940	Māori War Effort	Iwi, regions, central control	World War II	Iwi and Parliament;
1945	Tribal Committees	Tribal committees in regions, regional tribal executives	Māori Social and Economic Advancement Act	Legislation
1953	Māori Women's Welfare League	Branches, regional executives National Council	Māori Community and Department of Māori Affairs	Māori women
1962	New Zealand Māori Council	Local committees, District Councils, regional executives, National Council	Community Development Act	Legislation
1990	National Māori Congress	Iwi delegates, Executive, presidential leadership	Tino Rangatiratanga and Treaty of Waitangi	Iwi

The Framework

Three themes, each of which are developed chronologically and through case studies, were derived from an analysis of Table 1. Column 4, 'Event or Impetus', was rejected as a means of categorizing the investigation because no clear parameters emerged. Each item indicates that Māori are reacting to external influences, and are thus very similar. The framework adopted examines Māori unity according to the underlying philosophy, purpose, structure, and ownership manifest by the various movements which had Māori unity as a goal. By exploring the relative influence of three themes it became possible to classify and discuss the respective movements and to offer comparisons between them. Examples from history, each illustrating a particular theme, formed the prelude to an analysis of a contemporary movement, the National Māori Congress.

Theme One: He Whakaminenga o Ngā Hapū

The first theme developed in this book has been named 'He Whakaminenga o Ngā Hapū' in memory of the first recorded national Māori movement: the United Tribes of 1835. The protection of the mana of each constituent iwi is a clear goal of organizations which epitomize this theme.

Theme one examines unity based upon tribal structures and deriving from iwi initiatives. Typical of these movements, which uniformly sought to affirm Māori sovereignty—or 'Tino Rangatiratanga' as it is termed in the Treaty of Waitangi—is a perceivable parallel theme of external threat. As outlined in Chapter Two, the forerunners to unified political action among Māori were motivated either to achieve mutual material advantage, or to counter a recognizable external menace, both of which could only be attained through unity of action.

The 1831 petition to King William IV and the Declaration of Independence of 1835 are both manifestations of insecurity among iwi invoked by the perception of potentially aggressive, external nations. Subsequent movements (Pāremata Māori and Kingitanga) are symptomatic of disaffection stemming from a loss of Māori sovereignty. Both the Imperial Parliament in London and Colonial Ministries onshore implemented legislative, judicial, and executive mechanisms which excluded Māori input or led to the alienation of tribal lands. (These are covered in Chapter Three.) Tribal leaders, concerned to protect traditional authority, to assert their mana over their resources, and to maintain the well-being of their people, found common cause which eventually developed into national Māori bodies politic.

Theme Two: He Iwi Tahi Tātou

In the second theme developed to examine Māori unity, 'He Iwi Tahi

Tātou',[18] a noticeable shift in emphasis is observable and State initiative and sponsorship supplants iwi-derived structures. It will be shown that the Crown has imposed upon Māori structures which were designed to give a semblance of autonomy while in fact they have allowed the State to direct and focus activity. In the development of these structures, consultation with tribes tended to be secondary to the perceived need for efficient administration, and traditional boundaries, inter-tribal animosities, and Māori aspirations were often ignored. A clear goal of unification couched under this rubric is the assimilation of Māori into the predominate culture. While ostensibly designed to allow Māori a mechanism for input into the governance of the nation, or at least of their own affairs, structural impediments, economic hegemony, and colonialist policies made them a tool for the manipulation of political energies to suit State agendas.

It can be seen that the acquisition of land or the control of Māori disaffection was behind these movements. A further hallmark of these attempts to unify Māori was the solicitation of Māori support. Leaders who were prepared to cooperate with the State were chosen, and those who were less amenable were ignored. While this pattern may have altered during recent times, the tendency to set up a power base, a limited Māori voice, and then to use that base to direct affairs, remains evident. Emphasis is usually given, not always directly, to the provisions of Articles I and III of the Treaty of Waitangi, namely the State's right to rule and the protection of Māori interests. Indeed, the Treaty itself, with its promises of State protection and of citizenship, can be seen to conform to this paradigm. Finally, it will be shown that these measures were adopted to counteract burgeoning Māori sovereignty. Just as the Treaty might be seen as a reaction to the 1835 Declaration of Independence, the 1900 Māori Councils Act was conveniently timed to detract from the operation of the Paremata Māori established in 1892.

Theme Three: He Paihere Tangata

The third theme explored in this book is 'He Paihere Tangata', under which heading are grouped national Māori bodies that seek to unite Māori people on the basis of common ethnicity. This section, therefore, emphasizes pan-tribal movements that focus on particular sectoral interests.

The structures developed by each movement do not as a group conform to a specific pattern. Some are distinctly Māori while others echo a European approach; often a combination of the two provides a framework to give effect to the interests of a given organization. The tendency has been to aggregate the most effective methodologies from each cultural strand into an effective system for the group. The decision to consider these bodies as a group is not based upon the mechanisms by which goals are attained, but rather upon the common desire of each body to pursue a defined goal.

One feature encountered when analysing interest-centred groups, as Kawharu terms them,[19] is that often they are more concerned with local affairs and tend not to form national movements. Kawharu outlines some areas of interest observed operating in Auckland. He assumes that they would have counterparts in most large urban centres. These are:

- welfare: the promotion of socio-economic development (Māori committees and women's welfare league organizations)
- religion: major denominations as well as Rātana movement, Mormon, and others;
- youth and sports groups, which may include 'concert parties'
- marae development: Akarana Marae Society;
- national political party involvement
- 28th (Māori) Battalion Association.

This is by no means a comprehensive list of the activities which might cause Māori to congregate as Māori in an urban setting. Kawharu presents it merely to indicate some of the pursuits which cut across tribal affiliations and provide opportunities to come together outside traditional, kin-based groups. These associations tend to be of more recent vintage and are often strongly tied to an urban environment. As such, they may be aptly perceived as a reaction to modern social influences and as a result of relocation away from tribal territories. At least initially, in the absence of iwi members, Māori sought out other Māori, as they were more like themselves than Pākehā.

In regard to the first category, 'welfare', Māori committee structures will be dealt with in Theme Two, while the Māori Women's Welfare League (MWWL) will be covered in Theme Three.

The major Christian sects are not covered here, even though some have separate Māori structures. These structures are adjuncts to their European counterparts, and are not designed to unite Māori at a national level, but are rather aimed at bringing Māori into the Church. As such, they are outside the purview of this book. A possible exception is the new structure being proposed currently in the radically altered Constitution of the Anglican Church. Since the turn of the century Māori have sought equality and autonomy within the Church, only to be rebuffed. It was not until 1928 that Bishop Fredrick Augustus Bennett was consecrated as an Anglican Bishop. The Catholic Church was even less willing to concede to Māori demands: Bishop Takuira Mariu was not elevated until 1988.

The Rātana movement differs from these other institutions as it is a deliberately pan-tribal movement; it is discussed below. Sporting and youth groups tend to focus on local and regional activities, as do Māori culture groups. While these activities do at times bring people together for national competitions, the thrust of these encounters is temporary and lasting structures tend not to develop.

Political parties are again specialized in their membership. Although a national thrust is often envisaged, these activities are particular to the adherents of that political organization, and, like mainstream churches, membership is not predominantly Māori. The Mana Motuhake Party is something of an exception to this formula and is further analysed in Theme Three.

Endnotes

1.   Lord Normanby's instructions to Captain Hobson are included in the *Report of the Waitangi Tribunal on the Orakei Claim* (November 1987), p. 137–40.
2.   Ian Pool, (1991), *Te Iwi Māori*, pp. 35–58, discusses the impact of disease and technology on the Māori population up to 1840. See also A. T. Ngata, (1928), 'Anthropology and the Government of Native Races in the Pacific', *The Australasian Journal of Psychology and Philosophy*, 6, p. 5, in which he details the impact of firearms upon Māori.
3.   Ngata, *op cit.*, p. 6, expresses doubt as to whether a central government would have evolved but for the imposition of British rule.
4.   D. A. de Smith (1979), *Constitutional and Administrative Law*, 3rd edn, p. 63.
5.   For details of colonial treaties in other parts of the world, see P. G. McHugh, (1989), 'Constitutional Theory and Māori Claims', in I. H. Kawharu (ed.), *Waitangi: Māori and Pākehā Perspectives of the Treaty of Waitangi*, pp. 30–3.
6.   The doctrine of aboriginal (or native) title is now firmly a part of international law. Much enlightening material appears in Kawharu, (1989), *op cit*. See especially, McHugh (pp. 50–3), Brookfield (pp. 10–11), and Williams (pp. 84–9).
7.   A. Sharp, (1990), *Justice and the Māori*, Ch. 13, pp. 249–51.
8.   Thomas Hobbes, (1651), *Leviathan*, p. 87.
9.   R. McNab (ed.), (1908), *Historical Records of New Zealand* 1: 327–630.
10.   McHugh, in Kawharu, (1989), *op cit.*, p. 28.
11.   J. Williams, (1989), 'Towards a Treaty Driven Society', p. 3.
12.   (1832), 31 US, (6 Pet), 350.
13.   See note 1 above.
14.   McHugh, (1989), *op cit.*, p. 31, quotes this extract from Consular Instructions, 2nd draft, 8 March 1839, CO 209/4, pp. 221, 226–7.
15.   de Smith, *op cit.*, p. 64.
16.   McHugh, in Kawharu, (1989), *op cit.*, p. 39.
17.   Henry Williams and his son Edward received and translated the English Treaty into the Ngāpuhi dialect on 4 February 1840. Their limited qualifications and other possible translators are discussed in C. Orange, (1987a), *The Treaty of Waitangi*, pp. 39–43.
18.   The words used by Hobson after each chief signed the Treaty of Waitangi on 6 February 1840.
19.   I. H. Kawharu, 'Urban Immigrants and Tangata Whenua', in E. Schwimmer (ed.), (1968), *The Maori People in the 1960s*, pp. 184–5.

Chapter Two
Tribal Unity: Cultural Predeterminants

Ma Pango Ma Whero Ka Oti[1]

. . . it does not appear to be at all difficult for Strangers to form a settlement in this Country; they seem to be too much divided among themselves to unite in opposing, by which means and kind and gentle usage the Colonists would be able to form strong parties among them. (Captain James Cook, 31 March 1770)[2]

This assessment of the capacity for unity amongst the tribes of New Zealand more accurately reflects the nature of Cook's understanding than Māori ability to unite. While certainly there was a predilection for Māori to maintain autonomous tribal groups, under particular circumstances inter-tribal cooperation was not uncommon. Cook based his opinions on occasional contacts with coastal dwellers. The transient nature of his encounters led to this simplistic view and displayed an ignorance of the extensive alliances that operated in peace and in war.

An examination of Māori society and the socio-political structures prevalent in pre-contact times is therefore a necessary prelude to the topic of kotahitanga. A description of the hierarchical structures preferred by Māori follows. It explores leadership patterns and roles, and provides specific examples of situations where these structures were expanded to facilitate corporate effort at an inter-tribal level.

Sources

The issue of sources of material relating to Māori will be dealt with first as it has an affect on all that follows.

Of considerable importance to any understanding of Māori society is the reliability of available sources. Three main avenues of investigation are available to the student of ancient Māori society: Māori oral tradition, early

11

European writings, and archaeological evidence. Whereas an in-depth analysis of the relative merits of these is not appropriate here, the following comments are pertinent.

Oral Tradition

Sir Peter Buck (Te Rangihiroa),[3] maintains that traditional accounts from pre-literate societies ought to be regarded as history. He highlights difficulties which beset those dependent on written records when they deal with orally transmitted information, and makes the point that little reliance is given by them to such data. Dependence on retrievable records diminishes the need and therefore the faculty to memorize ('even for the passing of examinations, memorisation is of a transient nature', Buck, 1926: 181). The highly developed mnemonic capacity of scholars trained in oral history has astounded counterparts from other traditions. That much of this material cannot be verified from independent sources, however, is a further cause of dilemma among Western scholars,[4] and may be used by them as a reason for avoiding oral sources.

In a recent chapter on New Zealand prehistory,[5] Anderson postulates two drawbacks to the use of tribal traditions (in regard to determining a suitable name for the earliest settlers of Aotearoa). The first of these is the lack of specific detail about that period. The second, which could be seen as a further attempt to invalidate Māori knowledge, is an asserted misconception among historians about the nature of these records. Anderson introduces the idea that whakapapa was subject to manipulation in order to support particular assertions of power by leaders. There could be some truth in this notion, and his suggestion that tribal traditions need to undergo some serious contextual analysis to allow the emergence of a 'genuine historical narrative' has some merit.

Many traditional accounts of events could be said to have been embellished over time. The imagery and power of many legends render them fantastic to academics, and they are viewed with scepticism. Tales of taniwha left by their masters to guard particular locations hold little authenticity for many. But the matter is really one of abstraction. In the legend of Kupe, known to many Māori and most New Zealanders, the taniwha Arai Te Uru was left to guard the entrance to Hokianga Harbour.[6] Superficially marvellous and perhaps of little moment, there is nonetheless another level of meaning contained in this story. Elsdon Best writes that Te Uru Te Ngangana married Hine Turama, a sister of the better-known Hine Titama, and their offspring are recounted as being Ngā Whetu, the stars.[7] Ara is the word for a pathway. Thus the name of this leviathan might be rendered as 'Pathway in the Stars'. Polynesian navigational methods relied heavily upon an intimate knowledge of celestial bodies and so this part of the tale is now less elliptical than it once was. The legend of the Tākitimu canoe mentions Arai te Uru as one of the taniwha which guided this tapu vessel to Aotearoa[8]— another concealed reference to the navigational techniques of the Māori. If tradition as historical evidence is limited, then the limitation is perhaps more in the intellectual tradition and training of the student than in the tale itself.

It is important to remember that oral tradition has not ceased just because a more 'acceptable' alternative is available. Māori continue to store, maintain, and transmit historical details orally. For Māori, this information is vital to the social, economic, and political well-being of groups, and is consequently a dynamic resource. The same events in which many ancestral figures have played a part are retold through waiata (songs),[9] whakatauaki (proverbial expressions), whakapapa (genealogical tables), and whaikorero (formal speeches). Each telling is designed to accommodate the audience at hand, while the overriding theme of the teller will cause certain details to be emphasized and others to be played down. The descendants of each participant in any given scenario will possess the version of history which best suits the maintenance and reproduction of their kin unit. That these versions will differ in style and content is essential to the dynamism of Māori history and therefore of Māori society. The Western historical tradition is broadly perceived as being static. Once recorded, reinterpretation of events and their outcomes, while continuous, has an intrinsic delaying mechanism: the creative written word. These records also serve the needs and aspirations of their adherents. In New Zealand it is these records which are relied upon by the majority as authentic. Any variation from them tends to be viewed with suspicion, although this attitude is currently and constantly subject to review,[10] and is no longer universally accepted by historians.

Early Writings

Some caution must also be exercised, however, when dealing with written records from the early contact period. While probably accurate in many respects, mere recording does not guarantee validity. Material from Cook's journals, for instance, requires careful consideration. As Colenso[11] points out, only some places were visited by the *Endeavour* and only at particular times of the year. Whilst his specific concern was with statements on the horticultural expertise of the Māori, the point is illustrative. Cook's visit to Uawa (Tolaga Bay) coincided with the end of the kūmara planting season: a time of scarcity of this cultivated food. His encounters in various other locations where cultivation did not take place caused him to draw inaccurate assumptions. Had he arrived in the same place four to six months earlier a very different impression may have been recorded.

Add to this Janet Davidson's point regarding communication,[12] which was impaired by linguistic and philosophical differences between the newcomers and tangata whenua. All societies acculturate their members with a peculiar set of moral, ethical, and spiritual beliefs. When encountering another group whose basis for understanding the world is not only unknown, but also in part unfathomable, the observer's tendency will be to overlay their thought patterns on the other's manifest activities. Comparison with other groups who are perceived as being at a similar level of development might also be attempted. In any event, a broad and perhaps imprecise impression might be recorded as a statement of fact. These early records, then, are limited and subject to cultural bias. Any attempt to build a valid body of knowledge around them is unlikely to produce a comprehensive and authentic document.[13] There is a high probability that extrapolation of this data will generate flawed information.

A further caution centres on the skill level of some early writers. Mariners, whalers, explorers, and missionaries have all contributed to our views of the 'Māori as he was'. The introduction of the musket, potato, livestock, and Christianity, for example, considerably altered the situation for Māori in New Zealand. Contact records, therefore, provide valuable insight into an ethnic group which experienced an accelerated technological development. Still they were as often as not recorded by people untrained in observation and in analysis of social settings. Language, philosophical difference, and cultural bias were barriers that often led to simplistic conclusions and the promotion of Māori society as romantic, apolitical, and rigidly tribal.[14]

The interpretation of early writings is further complicated by the dubious motives of the authors. Hanson[15] explores this theme with particular reference to writings produced near the end of the nineteenth century. He asserts that much of what has come down as Māori culture is in fact a constructed orthodoxy which primarily served the ends of colonialist regimes. The methods of conversion of 'pagan' peoples to Christianity have often involved a setting down and adaptation of their traditions. For this process to be successful the seeds of a similar dogma must either be inserted into the myths, or points of commonality emphasized at the expense of balance.

Archaeological Evidence

Evidence gained from archaeological investigations is most useful in the consideration of lifestyles dating back to early periods of habitation. Early investigation of ancient sites in New Zealand, however, initially concentrated upon the bones of moa (*dinornithiformes*)[16] and later on other extinct birds. The presence of a living, recently Neolithic 'race' created an atmosphere in which study of ancient relics associated with these people was seen as of little value.

Sir Richard Owen, an English anatomist, came into possession of a single large bone in 1839, and because of its size and composition determined that it belonged to an extremely large bird. His proclamation of this new species sparked an interest in moa and New Zealand that would last for a considerable period. This interest predetermined the focus of archaeological research in this country and resulted in the destruction of other valuable evidence which was not recognized as useful at the time.[17] Such material would be of substantial value to researchers into prehistory today, because modern theory and practice has developed to accommodate and incorporate multiple evidence.

Archaeological data, when combined with oral traditions and early writings, can provide highly plausible images. Links with other related Polynesian cultures can be drawn, and reasonable approximations reached. (Linguistic comparisons are particularly useful in this regard.) When used in combination with advanced scientific methods, including radiocarbon dating,[18] X-ray florescence analysis,[19] and biochemical techniques, a comprehensive scenario can be constructed. Many sites which may have been particularly illuminating are now less useful as clues to the lifestyle of their inhabitants, and are either no longer in existence or have been relocated from their original positions. Meticulous scrutiny is therefore needed to extract from excavated material the threads of truth which might be woven into a tapestry of the past.

A further legacy of the early preoccupation with the collection and sale of moa relics, and the less sophisticated training of researchers, is the rise of a phenomena known as fossicking. This is the casual discovery and removal of evidence in the absence of systematic data recording, appropriate analysis techniques, and suitable extrapolative theory. This may not only render sites useless, but also has the potential for the misunderstanding of evidence and a subsequent need for the re-analysis of resultant theory. Indeed, this is currently a matter consuming much of the energy of the Historic Places Trust.

The understanding of Māori society which emerges from these three investigative processes is one of variation. The nature of this variation has implications for this thesis and will be covered below.

Regional Variation

The modes of production, the nature of resources, and the social constructs which rested upon these elements varied geographically and over time. Climate and geology were also influential. Janet Davidson highlights the theme of regional diversity and provides much archaeological data to support her view.[20] The obvious differences between the observable lifestyles of Te Taitokerau (Northland) and Murihiku (Southland) have long been recognized. Davidson maintains that regionally discrete patterns of subsistence have been ignored. The case studies below illustrate this economic diversity and provide some insight into the underpinnings of social diversity.

According to Atholl Anderson,[21] the people of the far south, Murihiku, developed socio-economic systems based on the resources available to them. He constructs three distinct time periods during which the economy and social orientation of that population varied quite markedly. These eras he called simply: 'The Early Period'—AD 900–1350; 'The Middle Period'—AD 1350–1550; and 'The Late Period'—AD 1550–1800.

Anderson maintained that the southern climate, unsuitable as it was for the propagation of imported Polynesian food crops (kūmara, taro, uhi), created a greater dependence upon the available mammals and avifauna than experienced elsewhere. As food sources declined through exploitation and environmental changes, settlement patterns and economic activity adapted. Fishing replaced hunting as the economic mainstay of Murihiku. The concomitant technological and demographic changes caused by this new economic thrust are amply evidenced in his archaeological data. Thus, while large social groups may once have gathered seasonally to slaughter and preserve moa,[22] concerted economic activity declined over time. Groups became smaller and more mobile, ranging over wider areas to utilize a multiplicity of resources. A dispersed social system had developed in response to changing economic circumstances. Regular contact with other sections of the broader social group became constrained by logistic reality. Wider familial networks, whilst extant, were similarly de-emphasized.

The manifest diversity disclosed through a comparison of material evidence from the early period and observation of contact society was great enough to support the fallacious concept of pre-Māori habitation of New Zealand. This population supposedly consisted of a race which was widely thought of by early commentators as being non-Polynesian in origin.[23]

Teone Tāre Tikao (1850–1927) provided Herries Beattie with much anecdotal material regarding the tradition and custom of the central and northern regions of Te Waipounamu (the South Island).[24] A traditional political leader trained by the prominent tohunga of his people, Tikao is a source for the history and lore of that region who has no peer. He mentions horticulture as one means of food production. The need to tend and defend crops lends itself to a sedentary lifestyle.[25] Tikao details many battles and paints a picture of endemic warfare, especially in the pre-contact and early historical period. His material lends credence to a picture of society as defence-oriented and also sedentary.

Much material on the variety of birds, animals, and fish gathered in this area is also included. This colours the view of this region to some extent. The pursuit of these food supplies requires some mobility. We can assume, therefore, a semi-nomadic lifestyle with a series of defensible bases as being the norm.

Evidence supplied by Atholl Anderson to the Waitangi Tribunal while they were dealing with the Ngāi Tahu claim gives a clear indication of regional variation in Te Waipounamu. His evidence indicates that in the Otago peninsula during the late seventeenth and early eighteenth centuries the barracouta (maka) formed an economic mainstay for that portion of the Ngāi Tahu people. Although this particular species may have been harvested elsewhere, the evidence shows that it was only a significant resource in Otago. Other regions relied upon other resources.[26]

While exact demographic statistics are unavailable, a population density greater than that for Murihiku can be postulated. Such a scenario suggests a more closely bound social structure. The proportionally higher rate of military engagements implies a need for greater interdependence of groups—particularly political defence-oriented alliances.

The south-eastern corner of Te-Ika-a-Māui (the North Island), especially that region known today as Palliser Bay, provides us with firm archaeological evidence regarding kūmara cultivation—evidence relied upon to discount theories of a 'hunter-gatherer' society which pre-dated Māori horticulture.[27] Davidson[28] cites the work of Helen Leach in this region, which establishes settlement of the area at around 1100AD. For this study it is the type of settlement that is of interest.

> The people lived in small settlements near river mouths close to their gardens and hunted, fished and gathered shellfish as well as gardening . . . (Davidson, 1983: 294)

In the more populous northern parts of the North Island where climatic conditions allowed an increased reliance upon horticultural pursuits, settlement patterns became ostensibly more uniform. The pattern of temporary fortified pā and associated mara, tauranga ika, and kāinga is well documented and is often perceived as traditional Māori culture. It is not possible, however, to identify a single unified 'traditional society' among the Māori. The discussion below is based upon what has become the 'orthodox' version of traditional Māori society.

Social Organization

According to early commentators (Best, Firth, and Buck), the whānau was the principle economic unit, especially in regard to food production and social organization. The hapū functioned in situations requiring a larger labour force with a particular suitability for military operations, the development and maintenance of marae and pā, and, for some groups, large-scale economic pursuits. The iwi was less significant for everyday activities and is seen primarily as a political unit called together in times of particular stress.[29] Ties between iwi which stem from the ancestral canoes (waka) which brought the Māori to these shores were activated periodically for a short duration and only when mutual advancement was anticipated.

Leadership

For most of these groups, leadership roles were determined according to primogeniture in the male line.[30] It is clear that ability, inclination, and the provision of a successful and effective administration were, and indeed still are, co-requisite qualities for authority. Senior males therefore provided leadership of the whānau (extended family group), of the hapū (clan), and ultimately of the iwi (tribe). Rangatira (the term applied to these men), ever mindful of the need to ensure popular support, especially for actions outside the ambit of daily existence (for example, military campaigns), were well versed in whakapapa (genealogy), were skilled orators, and led, in the main, by example. This was true for economic, social, political, and spiritual pursuits and required a detailed knowledge of associated atua (deities), karakia (ritual), and tikanga (practice). Such knowledge was acquired through instruction (the institution of whare wānanga was important)[31] and experience.

The transmission of leadership roles is discussed in the *Report of the Waitangi Tribunal on the Orakei Claim*, a claim which was filed by Joseph Parata Hawke on 7 April 1986.[32] The Tribunal concluded that, unlike the feudal hereditary right to rule relied upon by Europeans, heredity among Māori merely conferred upon a potential leader the chiefly traits of his forebears. Descent, while an important factor, must be coloured by a display of the appropriate attributes of leadership. Importantly, these qualities must be identified by the kin group which will eventually confirm that leader's position.

The basis of this leadership was mana, a term used to denote social status, influence, worth, and respect. It had several sources: mana ascribed by birth and thus resting upon the prestige of ancestors and through them to the pre-human deities from whom authority and power flowed (mana atua); mana deriving from the land and the special relationship which has developed over generations of occupation and control (mana whenua); and mana which comes from the support of one's people and requiring their active cooperation (mana tangata). Iwi are ever mindful of protecting and enhancing these qualities in all areas of activity. Māori Marsden explains mana as a 'spiritual power and authority as opposed to the purely psychic and natural force ihi'.[33] This dualism of power and authority incorporates the notion that not only is a rangatira the 'lawful' agent and leader, he is also spiritually empowered to direct the affairs of his people. It is important to realize that just as mana is increased through the provision of successful leadership and through excellence, it might equally be diminished through failure. Another integral aspect of leadership in traditional Māori society is therefore a requirement to achieve.

The term Rangatiratanga expresses the operation and application of this leadership. A given iwi or hapū acts as an autonomous unit whose principle aim is the preservation and welfare of the group. The rangatira of each discrete community are the repositories of that community's mana, which they are bound to serve and protect in both the secular and the spiritual dimensions.

Ross Bowden[34] highlights the distinction between the spiritual and the secular realms, and maintains that 'leadership in Māori society was not a single or unitary phenomenon . . .'. Ritual authority was based upon seniority of descent, ideally patrilineally, and was operationally distinct from the exercise of political power. The paramount exponents of ritual, 'tohunga ahurewa' were often the final arbiters and policy-makers for a hapū because of the level of training that they had received. While the daily exercise of political power may have resided with rangatira, the need to mediate with Atua during all-important phases of the economic, social, and military cycles required the attention of tohunga. Thus it is more accurate to cast Māori leadership patterns in a dualistic rather than a unitary mode.

Militarism as a Catalyst for Unity

E hara taku toa i te toa takitahi, engari he toa taki tini.[35]

That iwi came together to participate in large-scale military operations is evidenced by such battles as Hingakaka (The Fall of the Bright Plumaged Parrots). Both Kelly and Te Hurinui document this conflict between the Waikato confederation and an extremely large force from the southern and eastern districts. Some variation as to the year of this encounter exists (dates range from 1780 (Percy Smith) to 1807 (Kelly)) but there is agreement regarding the scale of this engagement. Three thousand Waikato warriors took the field under Te Rauangaanga against the 10,000 of Pikauterangi in what is remembered as the largest pre-musket encounter in New Zealand. It appears that, at least for those allied with Ngāti Toa under Pikauterangi, the desire to extract vengeance for previous defeats, both recent and of long-standing, provided a strong catalyst for unity, while kinship ties were secondary and perhaps more a device employed in oration to solicit support.

Vengeance also spurred the renowned Tairawhiti leader, Tumoana Kotore I Whakairia Oratia, who while seeking utu for the death of his grandfather, Poroumata, melded the various iwi and hapū of his time into a network of support for his campaigns. His marriage to Ruataupare, the much-admired daughter of Te Aotakī, provided him with the nucleus of his forces. Adopting a strategy of alliances and subjugation he ensured that his home, Kawakawa, was a safe haven. It was vital that those surrounding his kāinga remained either neutral, supportive, or otherwise unable to threaten his plans. It is said that some thirty years elapsed from the time he left his father's people at Opotiki until he settled his account with Ngāti Ruanuku in the battle of Hikutawatawa.

His career did not end here, however, and through a series of significant marriages he established his offspring at key points in the territory. Through alliances with other hapū and by conquest he extended his sway over much of the East Cape. Since his time, the people of Ngāti Porou have exercised mana whenua in this region, but over the generations since then the exertion of rangatiratanga by hapū within the iwi may have led to a diminution of cohesion amongst his descendants.

Concerted Economic Activity

The previous discussion of instances where iwi Māori would cooperate for a mutual advantage may create the impression that warfare alone was sufficient reason for Māori to unite. That this was most certainly not the case is illustrated by the case studies below. The first concerns an annual shark-fishing venture undertaken in the Muriwhenua. The other details the taking of titi (mutton birds) in Murihiku.

Muriwhenua

By the time Matthews read his paper 'Reminiscences of Māori Life Fifty Years Ago' before the Auckland branch of the New Zealand Institute on 22 November 1910, twenty-five years had elapsed since the fishing venture he described had last occurred.[36] This decline in interest he attributed to the participation of younger men in economic activities such as gum digging, and to a change in the dietary preferences of his contemporaries.

The article specifically refers to the taking of kapetā (dogfish) in the far north of the North Island, Te Taitokerau at Rangaunu Harbour. In 1855 this activity was restricted by custom and native practice to two days in January each year. The first day, or rather night, was Rākaunui (two nights after the full moon) and consisted solely of night fishing. The second day on which the kapetā might be taken, called Pakoki, was two weeks later and fell just after the new moon (Whawha-ata) had risen. Fishing was then conducted in daylight hours only. The relationship between economic activity and the phases of the moon is deliberate, the result of generations of experience. It is well-known that the moon controls the tides. The Te Rarawa fishermen are also aware that the size of the tide has a direct bearing on the number of kapetā entering their harbour and upon the distance that they travel upstream. This relationship determined the most propitious times for taking the fish, and it was strictly forbidden to take them outside these two days. Any transgressor would be subjected to a muru raid.[37]

Further, Matthews reports that to commence fishing before the signal to begin would result in the offender having his canoe split up. The gravity of this punishment in part reflects the mana of the rangatira whose role it was to determine when fishing would commence. The philosophy behind this practice was pragmatically economic. To commence fishing together would ensure that the greatest possible catch would be obtained. To jump the gun, as it were (the signal to start was indeed a gunshot in Matthews's time), would risk alarming the fish prematurely, thus endangering the continued well-being of the gathered tribes.

It can be seen that the occasion of taking kapetā served not only to consolidate the position of the rangatira who controlled the harbour, but also to renew the traditional ties between participants. The event is portrayed by Matthews as being primarily recreational. In his view, the obvious economic importance is given lower priority. This is an example of an important economic event misinterpreted by the observer because of the differing cultural perspectives and ways of conducting affairs.

Large numbers of Te Rarawa tribesmen and related hapū and iwi would gather to undertake the catch. The report indicates that often fifty canoes, each holding twenty men, would participate each year. The iwi would gather up to a week prior to the designated night, bringing with them their wives and families. The mouths of the three main rivers—the Awanui, the Okuraiti, and the Pukewhau—were the traditional rendezvous points for the fishing parties.

Although it appears that the fishing was principally the domain of the men, wives and kuia did not come to the maunga (the local word for the event) in a purely spectator capacity. Indeed, preparing harakeke (*Phormium tenax*, native flax) and making the necessary cordage were among the tasks they performed. Another was the gathering, cooking, and drying of pipi (a bivalve mollusc) to supplement the winter diet. Prior to the actual fishing, the preparation of waka, matau, and other associated equipment was required. Fish for bait and to feed the encampment was also needed, giving lie perhaps to Matthews's impression that the affair was some sort of carnival or holiday. No doubt much excitement and pleasure attended the gathering of tribes, as would be expected when kin come together, but economic necessity ensured that it remained an extremely serious undertaking.

In assessing the economic importance of these fishing ventures, the figures Matthews quotes relating to catch sizes are relevant. On the day he attended the maunga in 1855, the vessel he was on captured 180 kapetā. The total catch of all canoes over the two days of fishing was 7000 fish. In 1875, one large canoe is recorded as having landed 265 sharks weighing six tons in total.

The bodies of those sharks which were not eaten immediately were hung by the tail from a tārawa to enable the wind and sun to dry the flesh. Once dried, they were stacked on elevated platforms (whata) until needed. Variously cooked in chunks in a hangi, in strips over hot rocks, or chewed in small quantities without further preparation, dried shark was an important component in the diet of many iwi. The oil derived from the liver of a shark also had many uses, including the anointment of the hair and body. Mixed with kōkōwai (red ochre), this oil was used as a paint for carvings and canoes, as well as for mortuary and other ritual purposes. It was an important resource in itself, and had some potential as a trade item.

Ngāi Tahu

Herries Beattie,[38] in a paper read before the New Zealand Institute (9 December 1919), provides much information regarding the hunting and fishing practices of Māori from Otago and Southland. In his section on the catching of kanakana (piharau or lamprey) he mentions annual gatherings of hapū on the Karoro River. While this activity was undertaken by individual groups at traditionally defined locations, the notion of peaceful cooperation for mutual benefit is present. Beattie included some anecdotal evidence . recorded by an N. Chalmers, who is said to have witnessed the fishing for kanakana and its attendant ritual in November of 1853.

The recent Waitangi Tribunal Report[39] on the claim lodged by Ngāi Tahu gives an indication that at least one economic activity served to unify the iwi. In the region of Te Ara a Kiwa (Foveaux Strait), titi (mutton birds) were, and indeed still are, a major economic resource. Titi were taken during the autumn and winter months but remained a food source for much of the year. Dr Edward Shortland recorded in 1851 the use of pōhā titi in which these birds were preserved.[40] Composed of rimurapa (bull kelp), the pōhā was a seaweed sack made prior to the birding season. When a suitable plant was located at low tide among the rocks, it was pruned to the required length (about one metre was usual). The parts which formed the vessel were left adhering to the rocks, and over time the severed portion grew together to form the base of the pōhā. When that had occurred, the seaweed was removed to the kāinga, and the pōhā were constructed.

It was a relatively simple task to split the kelp and separate the two sides by inserting a hand or a stick into the open end. The bag was then inflated, tied, and left to dry. When it hardened, the pōhā became a watertight container in which the birds were stored. The titi were grilled over the embers of a fire, and the fat produced in the process was collected. When cooked, they were stacked in the pōhā and the fat was poured in on top. This acted as a sealant and as a preservative. So effective was this method that the birds remained edible for up to two years. The kelp bags themselves were not particularly resilient, and were often wrapped in totara bark to strengthen them.

In *The Ngai Tahu Report*, it is stated that titi were of importance to the whole of Ngāi Tahu and that the iwi would gather from as far afield as Kaikoura to participate in the harvesting and preservation of the birds. Whether or not these activities were conducted as a large-scale corporate activity or were carried out by individual whānau and hapū is not clear. What is clear is the propensity of Māori to unite to pursue economic as well as military goals.

Specificity of Purpose

Just as the hapū is most accurately perceived as an amalgam of interrelated whānau, so the iwi is a coalition of hapū united by an apical ancestor. This pattern of incorporating related kin groups through a commonality of descent provides a template for inter-tribal unity. Situations in which Māori seek unity involve common purpose. Variously militaristic, political, or socio-economic, these purposes have traditionally allowed Māori to activate other culturally appropriate institutions and to pursue the common end.

The promotion of mutual security, as illustrated by the military pursuits mentioned above, has long been a priority. The internal integrity of large, cognatic descent groups rests in part upon the need for numeric strength for the defence of the tribe. The warriors of each constituent whānau of a hapū cooperated to defend the corporate territory. In times of greater threat, hapū similarly formed defence alliances. Te Rauangaanga was able to achieve success through uniting related iwi to defend the larger region. During the conflagration known to Māori as Te Pakanga Tuarua,[41] Te Hokowhitu a Tu brought this theme to a pinnacle. The defence of the realm, indeed of the empire, brought Māori together as no other military encounter had. Importantly, this cooperation extended far beyond the battle front. Recruitment, support (both in Aotearoa and abroad), and, in the fullness of time, repatriation, united iwi to a significant level.

It would be erroneous, however, to assume that the external threat motive alone galvanized Māori into action. A strong and recurrent military theme, evidenced by the tale of Tuwhakairiora, was utu, the active seeking of redress for past wrongs. Other instances of warfare were induced by the need to secure access to resources, territory, and/or the crops of another community. Thus, unity of this sort was more than merely reactive—there was a strong proactive theme as well.

Economic and social advancement are also influential in traditional manifestations of unity. While individual whānau utilized specific resources for daily needs, large-scale economic activity occurred at the hapū level. Food production was effected by economies of scale. Downes comments upon the eeling practices among the people of the Whanganui River.[42] During the tuna heke (seasonal eel migration), large-scale hapū-level activity was undertaken. The aforementioned mutton-birding and shark-catching activities demonstrate an even broader level of economic cooperation. The building of pā were conducted by hapū, as were marae construction and maintenance, the reception and hosting of manuhiri (visitors), and the development of social policy.

Endnotes

1.   'By black and red it is finished.' A proverbial expression indicating the need for both workers (symbolized as black) and chiefs (red) acting together to accomplish the group's desires.

2.   J. C. Beaglehole (ed.), (1955), *The Journals of Captain James Cook*, Vol. 1, p. 278—a comment upon settlement in New Zealand. See also, A. H. and A. W. Reed (eds), (1969), *Captain Cook in New Zealand*, p. 141.

3.   Sir Peter H. Buck, (1926), 'The Value of Tradition in Polynesian Research', in *Journal of the Polynesian Society*, 35: 181.

4.   In fact, oral material is not a major source in this book. Where traditional views are used they are quoted from early writers.

5.   A. Anderson, 'The Last Archipelago: 1000 Years of Māori Settlement in New Zealand', in David Green (ed.), (1989), *Towards 1990: Seven Leading Historians*

Examine Significant Aspects of New Zealand History, GP Books, Wellington, pp. 1–19.

6.   A. W. Reed, (1977), *Treasury of Māori Exploration: Legends Relating to the First Explorers of New Zealand*, A. H. and A. W. Reed, Wellington, p. 36.

7.   E. Best, (1976 edn), *Māori Religion and Mythology, Part I*, Government Printer, Wellington, p. 125.

8.   A. W. Reed, *op cit.*, p. 193; see also, D. R. Simmons, (1976), *The Great New Zealand Myth*, p. 115.

9.   A generic word for song. Various subgroupings of song exist for Māori, many of which are specifically concerned with the transmission of oral tradition. Oriori, 'lullabies', are perhaps most important. See *Nga Moteatea*, Vols. I–III for examples.

10.   Judith Binney, (1987), 'Maori Oral Narratives, Pakeha Written Texts', *New Zealand Journal of History*, 21 (1): 16–28, presents an important comparison based on this theme.

11.   W. M. Colenso, (1880), 'On the Vegetable Food of the Ancient New Zealanders before Cook's Visit', *The Proceedings of the New Zealand Institute*, 13: 3–4.

12.   J. Davidson, (1984), *The Prehistory of New Zealand*, Longman Paul, Auckland, pp. 10–11.

13.   The apparent misrecording of Tolaga Bay is one example; see A. Salmon, (1991), *Two Worlds: First Meetings Between Maori and Europeans*, Viking/Penguin, Auckland, p. 169, for details. Her later comments on the role of women at Uawa are also pertinent—see p. 181.

14.   In a history workshop at Massey University (2 May 1991), Dr Peter Brown discussed the journals of Jules Durmont D'Urville. It is possible to discern this sort of treatment in his works.

15.   Allan Hanson, (1989), 'The Making of the Māori: Cultural Invention and its Logic', *American Anthropologist*, 91, pp. 890–902.

16.   See Barney Brewster, (1987), *Te Moa: The Life and Death of New Zealand's Unique Bird*, Nikau, Nelson, p. 54, for a 'Moa family tree'.

17.   Ibid., pp. 37–53, describes the development of interest in this bird among Europeans.

18.   G. Caughley, (1988), 'The Colonisation of New Zealand by the Polynesians', *Journal of the Royal New Zealand Society*, 18: 245–55, explains the method and presents some of its drawbacks. He also explains and contrasts the principle theories based on radiocarbon dates—see pp. 253–7.

19.   A. Fox, (1978), *Tiromoana Pa, Te Awanga, Hawke's Bay Excavations 1974–5*, Department of Anthropology, Otago University, Dunedin, p. 46, gives details of this technique and its application.

20.   J. Davidson, (1984), *op cit*.

21.   Atholl Anderson, (1983), *When All The Moa Ovens Grew Cold: Nine Centuries of Changing Fortune for the Southern Māori*, Otago Heritage Books, Dunedin.

22.   Ibid, see Anderson's comments on the Early and Middle Periods.

23.   The convolutions of early theories on Māori ethnicity are explored in M. P. K. Sorrenson, (1979), *Māori Origins and Migrations: The Genesis of Some Pakeha Myths and Legends*, Auckland University Press, Auckland, pp. 11–34. See also J. Davidson, (1983), 'Māori Prehistory: The State of the Art', *Journal of the Polynesian Society*, 92: 291–307.

24.   Herries Beattie, (1939), *Tikao Talks: Ka Taoka o te Ao Kohatu: Treasures from the Ancient World of the Māori*, 1990 edn, Penguin, Auckland, pp. 139–40.

25.   Support for this can be gained from other writers, e.g., Colenso, *op cit.*, p. 6.

26. Waitangi Tribunal, *Wai 27, The Ngai Tahu Report 1991*, Waitangi Tribunal, Wellington, pp. 195–8.

27. Julius Haast—(1872), 'Moas and Moahunters', *The Proceedings of the New Zealand Institute*, 4: 67–9—parallels contemporary discoveries of *pachydermata* bones and associated human relics and formulates a theory of pre-horticultural hunter-gatherer societies in Europe. Transposition of these notions gave rise to a similar belief in New Zealand.

28. (1983), *op cit.*, pp. 294–5.

29. In the Treaty of Waitangi, the word hapū is used to denote tribes: '. . . nga Rangatira me nga hapu . . .'.

30. A. Mahuika—(1977 edn), 'Leadership: Inherited and Achieved', in M. King (ed.), *Te Ao Hurihuri: The World Moves On*, Hicks Smith/Methuen, Auckland, Ch. 4, pp. 62–85—discusses exceptions to this rule from within Ngāti Porou of the East Coast.

31. E. Best, (1974), *The Māori School of Learning: Its Objects, Methods, and Ceremonial*, Government Printer, Wellington.

32. Waitangi Tribunal, *The Report of the Waitangi Tribunal on the Orakei Claim*—November 1987, Waitangi Tribunal, Wellington, pp. 131–4—provides a useful discussion of this matter. Te Rangikaheke's comments are on p. 132.

33. M. Marsden, (1975), 'God, Man and the Universe', in King, (1977), *op cit.*, p. 145.

34. Ross Bowden (1979), 'Tapu and Mana: Ritual Authority and Political Power in Traditional Māori Society', *Journal Polynesian History*, 14: 50–61.

35. 'My prowess as a warrior rests not upon my individual strength but rather upon the concerted action of my people.'

36. *The Proceedings of the New Zealand Institute*, (1910), 43: 598–605. An extensive extract from this article is reproduced in Waitangi Tribunal, (1988), *The Report of the Waitangi Tribunal on the Muriwhenua Fishing Claim*, Waitangi Tribunal, Wellington, pp. 68–74.

37. Muru is a ritualized stripping of property from a kinsman who negligently or deliberately endangers the well-being of the tribe. A. Ward—(1973), *A Show of Justice: Racial Amalgamation in Nineteenth Century New Zealand*, Auckland University Press, Auckland, pp. 8–9—provides a description of this social mechanism.

38. H. Beattie, (1920), 'Nature Lore of the Southern Māori'*The Proceedings of the New Zealand Institute*, 52: 53–4.

39. *Wai 27, The Ngai Tahu Report 1991, op cit.*, p. 196.

40. 'Southern Districts of New Zealand', referred to in E. Best, (1942), *Forest Lore of the Māori*, p. 285.

41. World War II saw the formation of the 28th Māori Battalion. Its structure was tribal, and many perceive this to be the basis of its success. The Māori War Effort Organisation also grew from this conflict, and is discussed in Chapter Three.

42. T. W. Downes, (1918), 'Notes on Eels and Eel-weirs', *The Proceedings of the New Zealand Institute*, 50: 296.

Chapter Three
Kāwanatanga: A Catalyst for Kotahitanga

Ko Te Tuatahi
Ko nga Rangatira te Wakaminenga, me nga Rangatira katoa hoki, kihai i uru
ki taua Wakaminenga, ka tuku rawa atu ki te Kuini o Ingarani ake tonu atu te
Kawanatanga katoa o o rātou wenua. (Article the First, Treaty of Waitangi,
1840)

The Treaty of Waitangi

Signed at Waitangi on the 6th day of February 1840 by the Crown
representative, Captain William Hobson (1793–1842), and by forty-three
Māori on behalf of their hapū, the Treaty became the founding document of
New Zealand. As has been amply discussed elsewhere,[1] there are two distinct
versions of the Treaty, one in Te Reo Māori and the other in English (see
Appendix Two). It was the Māori language version which most Māori signed;
Captain Hobson, as the Queen's Consul, signed the English version, as did
thirty-nine Waikato leaders at various hui at Manukau and the Waikato
Heads.[2] That these two treaties were and are understood differently, and in fact
vary quite markedly, is the issue which has caused unrest at a tribal and at a
national level.

Before considering the Treaty and its impact, it will be enlightening to
examine and define the word 'treaty'. J. Williams concludes that the Treaty of
Hopewell between the United States of America and the Cherokee was
characterized as an international agreement. Williams asserts that this is
because the Cherokee were perceived as a distinct, independent, political
community. It is therefore significant that the word 'treaty' was also applied
at Waitangi because it shows clearly that the situation was deemed to be
international, and that the parties were 'distinct and sovereign political
entities whose rights as against each other fell to be regulated by agreement'.[3]
This had been made abundantly clear in Lord Normanby's instructions to
Captain Hobson. In 1840 we can at least assume that rangatira and the iwi/
hapū for whom they stood held legal title and were presumed to exercise

both legislative and judicial functions of government.

Benedict Kingsbury,[4] after an examination of the contemporaneous British policy toward indigenous peoples, of the various instructions issued to British negotiators of the period, of French and American attitudes to British involvement in New Zealand, and of subsequent international arbitral decisions, maintains that:

> The Treaty was a valid international treaty of cession, and the parties in 1840 were recognised as having the necessary legal capacity to enter into such a treaty.

The Treaty of Waitangi is fundamentally an exchange written in five parts (a preamble, three articles, and a postscript). As consideration for the cession to the British Crown of sovereignty ('kawanatanga'—Article the First) and the pre-emptive right to purchase land (Article the Second), Māori would receive British protection from both foreign and internal aggression (both Māori and Pākehā) and lawlessness (Preamble). Further, Māori authority ('rangatiratanga'—Article the Second) would be guaranteed over things Māori ('te Tino Rangatiratanga o o rātou wenua o rātou kainga me o rātou taonga katoa')[5], and Māori people, as individuals, would acquire the rights and privileges of British subjects (Article the Third). These rights were to be additional to those guaranteed in Article Two.

Two distinct classes of tribe are recognized in Article the First of the Treaty: those affiliated to the United Tribes of New Zealand, as outlined above, and those whose independent leaders had not entered into that declaration. That these leaders were deemed competent to transfer sovereignty to the Crown is perhaps the clearest indication of the British acceptance that, together, rangatira constituted the sovereign power in the State of New Zealand. This recognition of both independent and United Tribes was an attempt to create at least a semblance of solidarity and of unanimity of consent at a national level. Indeed, Lord Normanby required Hobson to obtain the free and intelligent consent of the Māori people as reflected by the words 'having been made fully to understand the Provisions of the foregoing Treaty' (Preamble). Hobson himself commented that of the forty-three foundation signatories, twenty-six had also signed the Declaration.

It is less clear whether tribes regarded unanimity at a national level as a prerequisite for sovereignty. Indeed, the guarantee of tino rangatiratanga acknowledged their independent tribal sovereignty. Māori could not be regarded as homogeneous. That point appears to have found little support once the Treaty was signed.

Another issue for consideration is the position of iwi, hapū, and whānau who either elected not to concede to the Crown's request for kāwanatanga, or did not receive the offer of citizenship.

Non-Signatory Tribes

Many rangatira, then and since, have seen the Treaty as being a 'Ngāpuhi affair', an agreement undertaken by iwi of Te Taitokerau, and of little significance to themselves. Tuwharetoa, Te Arawa, Rangitāne, and Kati Mamoe are known not to have signed the Treaty. Tuwharetoa actively refused to subsume their mana to the English Queen and it is likely that Te Arawa, because of close genealogical and political connections, supported their stand. Te Wherowhero (later known as King Pōtatau) had entered into the Declaration of Independence but refused to sign the Treaty (although other Waikato chiefs signed). The Ngāi Te Rangi leader, Tupaea, and others under his influence, would not sign. Te Kani a Takirau, son of Te Hinematioro and acknowledged leader of Ngāti Porou, although he offered hospitality to Williams when the latter conducted hui at Uawa, and did not impede others who chose to sign, would not sign himself. It is possible that some rangatira were overlooked by Hobson's emissaries in their quest for support, and did not sign for that reason.

Wīremu Tamihana Tarapipipi Te Waharoa, also called 'The Kingmaker', second son of Te Waharoa and principal chief of the Ngāti Hauā (an iwi affiliated to the Waikato Confederation) is said to have made this clear statement regarding his position under the Treaty:

> I am chief of Ngāti Hauā, which is an independent tribe: my father, Te Waharoa, was chief before me; neither he, I, nor any of my people signed this treaty, therefore we are not bound by it.[6]

Wīremu Tamihana also expressed concern over the way in which signatures were obtained. The presentation of gifts and blankets to chiefs as an inducement to sign the Treaty is highlighted as one area which concerned him.[7] That the free and informed acceptance of the Treaty was to be obtained, with a concomitant level of understanding, seems not to have figured significantly in all dealings with iwi on this matter.

McLintock (1958: 146) records a similar statement by the Ngāti Tamatera leader, Taraia, wherein he disclaimed Crown jurisdiction over his recent affray as no Europeans were affected. That other iwi (including Tūwharetoa and Ngāi Te Rangi) maintained a similar position raises the question of the legitimacy of Crown action on their behalf or against them. Effectively, opposition to the Treaty, although significant to Māori, amounted in real terms to nought. Governor Hobson's proclamation of sovereignty through a treaty of cession can have but limited validity.

When on 21 May 1840 Hobson proclaimed sovereignty over the North Island by right of a formal treaty of cession it can be assumed he was including all Māori and their lands—those reluctant, those unapproached, as well as those willing. That this was contrary to his instructions and more than slightly dubious has been amply discussed elsewhere.[8]

In 1843, in a memorandum to the Acting Governor, Willoughby Shortland, regarding the outbreak of hostilities between Ngāti Whakaue and Ngāi Te Rangi, William Swainson, the first Attorney-General, maintained that the Crown did not have sovereignty over non-signatory tribes. This opinion, if widely accepted, would mean that Māori could only be regarded as British subjects and thus bound by colonial law through an express act of consent. Many iwi in the early 1840s would, under this interpretation of the Treaty's effect, have been subject only to traditional laws and practice, as their leaders had not been party to the Treaty. George Clarke (Protector of Aborigines) opposed the use of force on the 1843 occasion because it would be construed by Māori signatories and non-signatories alike as a breach of faith. He agreed, however, with Colonial Treasurer Shepherd and with Governor Shortland Willoughby, who argued that it would be

> an act of humanity to both natives and Europeans to consider the whole of the tribes of New Zealand as British subjects.[9]

Analysis of the terms of the Treaty reveals that it contains reciprocal bilateral obligations,[10] which for Māori have not been kept. This is well-documented and remains very much a live issue. It is this aspect of the Treaty that has caused leaders to gather and discuss issues, the ramifications of which can be seen to affect not only their own iwi and hapū, but also the wider spectrum of Māori constitutional and political activities.

This book explores a common theme: the theme of injustice—a theme which has been addressed by iwi individually and collectively since the Treaty was signed—a theme which has caused Māori to create mechanisms to implement and assert their tino rangatiratanga.

The Treaty is a solemn agreement between Māori and the Crown for the administration of these islands. It prescribes and affirms the position of and operational spheres of both parties. The Crown was to exercise, initially through the Queen's governors, the legislative, judicial, and executive powers epitomized as kāwanatanga, while reserving unto and guaranteeing to iwi their tino rangatiratanga. A constitutional model from which a system for sharing power might have developed is thus set down in the Treaty. The failure on behalf of the Crown to attempt to realize this fundamental precept, as epitomized by other breaches of the Treaty, has given rise to prolonged dissatisfaction among iwi—the fruits of which have found expression in many forms, some violent and destructive, others more gradual and constructive.

The following outline of constitutional developments which did occur in the colony illustrates the Crown's failure to include Māori both in the development of government structures and in participation in the parliamentary process. These failures eventually forced Māori to construct their own mechanisms for exercising the tino rangatiratanga guaranteed by the Treaty.

Constitutional Abrogation of Tino Rangatiratanga

Prior to the New Zealand Constitution Act 1852,[11] a British statute which introduced a two-tier system of government within New Zealand, the administration of the Crown colony was maintained through the Colonial Office in London and executed by various governors on location. According to McLintock,[12] political appointments to the Colonial Office held little prestige and were looked upon as a stepping stone to greater power. Colonial affairs were of slight interest to the majority of the voting public and were consequently afforded scant regard by the politicians of the realm. Apparently, although Cabinet approval was mandatory, colonial matters did not particularly divert their attention. Responsibility fell, therefore, upon the Secretary of State for War and Colonies[13] or the Colonial Secretaries as they were popularly known.

Immediately following the signing of the Treaty, 'local' control was exercised by the Governor-in-Chief, Sir George Gipps, from New South Wales, while the Legislative Council of that colony was empowered to enact laws for New Zealand. Lieutenant-Governor Hobson, although allowed considerable discretion, was fettered by the need to relay all correspondence through the New South Wales administration—an arrangement irksome to both parties but eventually remedied to some degree through the issuing of Letters Patent on 16 November 1840. It can be seen that this earliest period in the constitutional life of the nation held no place for any input by Māori at a legislative level. That the exercise of rangatiratanga had been as yet uncurtailed by the machinations of Crown control is significant in that it did not present Māori leaders with an immediate focus for disaffection, either collectively or individually. The Treaty, in recognizing the responsibility of rangatira to control the destiny of their people, at least in the Māori version, created an obligation upon the Crown to develop mechanisms whereby that responsibility could be incorporated into and given effect by the constitution of the fledgling nation.

The Charter of 1840

Letters Patent issued under the authority of the Imperial Parliament established New Zealand as a colony in its own right. The Charter of 1840, as it became known, set the new colony's boundaries and provided new names for the three principal islands. Te Ika a Maui became New Ulster, Te Waipounamu, New Leinster, while Rakiura was named New Munster. Perhaps these names, transplanted as they are from turbulent Ireland, premeditated a similar unilateral approach to government for New Zealand. The template for governmental process contained in the Charter created the positions of Colonial Secretary, Attorney-General, and Colonial Treasurer, who, constituted as the Executive Council, were required to advise the Governor. It was envisaged that these three officers would assume roles appropriate to their titles: the Colonial Secretary would work on a colonial code; the Treasurer would address the fiscal security of the colony; while the Attorney-General would implement the measures to ensure the protection of property and the prevention and punishment of crime. That this remained an exclusively European body again points to the lack of provision for Māori contribution to affairs of State. A Legislative Council, consisting of this executive body together with three Justices of the Peace, was also provided for and empowered to enact laws (to be known as Ordinances). The Charter did not come into effect until May 1841.

In a recent essay, David Williams maintains that the sole reference in the Charter regarding the indigenous peoples of Aotearoa is clause 15, which states:

> And we do further enjoin and command you not to propose or assent to any Ordinance whatever, by which persons not of European birth or descent might be subjected or made liable to any disabilities or restrictions to which persons of European birth or descent would not also be subjected or made liable.[14]

This clause might equally refer to indigenous American, African, or Asian persons settling in New Zealand, and it recalls some contemporary debates in which multicultural and indeed bicultural perspectives are advanced without reference to the guarantees of the Treaty.[15] The European ethnocentric perception of others, upon which they justified their colonial expansion, is evidenced in this passage. There was to be no attempt to assimilate themselves into the existing Māori patterns of behaviour, legislative processes, or mechanisms for the prosecution of justice. Notions of indigenous custom, process, and law are absent from the Act. It was not envisaged that they would be allowed to continue to operate, let alone be encouraged or actively protected. The earliest legal instruments by which the colony was established were heavily biased toward British concepts of sovereignty, and excluded a Māori perspective.

According to Walker (1990: 98) the Governor was given wide powers to survey the whole of the country and to divide it up into 'districts, towns, townships, and parishes'. The notion of 'wastelands' is also contained in the Charter. These were presumably tracts of Māori land which to English eyes, as they remained uninhabited and undeveloped, were under-utilized and therefore free from ownership. The Governor was instructed by the Charter to make grants of these lands to individuals for their use or to corporations for development as public assets. Walker makes the point that rangatira were not privy to these acquisitionist provisions and that, had they been so, the nation of New Zealand may have foundered before it had been properly formed. Land, and especially the alienation of land, can be identified, even at this early stage, as the potential bone of contention between iwi and tauiwi (foreigners). Indeed, as will be shown, it was the Pākehā attitude to acquiring land, and the institution of policies and practices, which, by ignoring the protection promised in the Treaty, most disaffected Māori—a disaffection which provided a powerful catalyst for unity at a pan-tribal level— nourishment to the developing sense of nationhood among Māori.

Demands for Representative Government

Māori were by no means the only ones discouraged by the constitutional developments of the 1840s and 1850s. The logistics involved in the implementation of the Colonial Office, policy developed half a world away in London, created significant delays and required the Governor to operate with a high degree of personal latitude. The early insolvency of the colonial administration, which developed under Hobson and which was not alleviated by Shortland's brief reign as Acting Governor, did little to secure settler support. The diminishing revenue generated through the resale of land, combined with the cumbersome bureaucracy which had evolved to facilitate these transactions, meant that demand for land far exceeded supply. The shortfall was highly vexatious to entrepreneurs whose schemes were thus jeopardized. Settlers, disenchanted with government land transfer mechanisms and by the autocratic approach of early governors, sought an avenue for representation. Appeals to the Imperial Parliament eventually materialized in the shape of the New Zealand Government Act 1846.

1846: A First Constitution Act

Enacted by an English House of Commons, for whom the rights of British nationals were superseding earlier humanitarian impulses towards indigenous peoples, the New Zealand Government Act 1846 sought to provide an acceptable avenue for settler participation in the governance of New Zealand. An ambitious three-level system of colonial, provincial, and municipal bodies based upon boroughs was suggested.[16] The bulk of the Act, to which McLintock gives extensive coverage (1958: 285–8) directs itself to these ends and includes crucial provisions for the acquisition of 'wastelands' by the Crown.[17]

These provisions are contrary to Article Two of the Treaty which

> guarantees to the Chiefs and Tribes of New Zealand and to the respective families and individuals thereof the full exclusive and undisturbed possession of their Lands and Estates Forests Fisheries and other properties which they may collectively or individually possess so long as it is their wish and desire to retain the same in their possession . . .[18]

This was seen by Governor Grey as a suitable mechanism to forestall the implementation of the Act. Whether out of a concern for the consequences of thus alienating Māori land, as discussed by Hackshaw,[19] or for his own ends (see McLintock: 291–2), Grey secured the enactment of a suspending bill in December 1847 which effectively halted the proposed constitutional reforms.

Had this Act come into effect, most Māori would have been excluded from the franchise by a provision which required voters not only to occupy a tenement (i.e., a Crown grant), but also to be able to read and write the English language. While generous and indeed at the forefront of constitutional development in European terms, this arrangement signalled a reluctance to take seriously the implied partnership contained in the Treaty.

One path whereby this implied partnership may have been better realized was the discretionary power of the Governor to set apart aboriginal districts, Chapter 14 of the Act, within which

> the laws, customs and usages of the Aboriginal Inhabitants, so far as they are not repugnant to the general principles of humanity, shall for the present be maintained.[20]

This provision was also contained in the New Zealand Constitution Act 1852 and will be discussed below.

The Constitution Act 1852

Passed by the Imperial Parliament on 30 June 1852, sections of the New Zealand Constitution Act 1852 remained a part of the constitutional fabric of

New Zealand until repealed by the Constitution Act 1986. The bulk of the Act, like the 1846 enactment, established a hierarchical framework of councils. Two tiers were envisaged: one a supreme legislature, the General Assembly or Colonial Parliament (comprised of an elected House of Representatives and an appointed Legislative Council), the other a series of six subordinate Provincial Councils, the elected bodies being selected by land- or leaseholders who were over twenty-one and male. Franchise was further qualified by the requirement of individual title to property (£50 freehold, £10 leasehold, £10 p.a. rental urban, or £5 p.a. rental rural).[21]

Map 1: Provinces established under the Constitution Act 1852

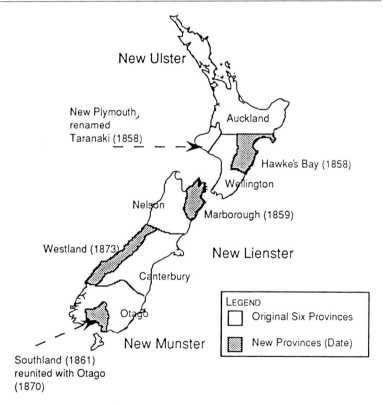

Derived from Olssen and Stenson, 1989: 144

This clause again militated against participation by Māori in the political life of the colony, since land was traditionally vested in the hapū, the iwi, or in some instances was held collectively by the whānau.[22] This device, superficially liberal, eliminated effective Māori input into the formulation and direction of State policy.[23] When drafting this constitution, however, some consideration was given to the inclusion of a Māori franchise, but it was thought prudent to omit such a clause. Earl Grey, the former Secretary for War and Colonies, had felt that in the fullness of time Māori would become sufficiently acculturated to European modes of operation to take advantage of the property franchise contained in the constitution.[24]

This theme of waiting for Māori to adjust to the new order is also obvious in the establishment of four Māori electorates in 1867.[25] These were to be a temporary measure to allow Māori input into the electoral system. Instituted by the Maori Representation Act 1867, the four seats were an expedient to provide a franchise for Māori until they were sufficiently assimilated and had individualized their land titles. When this enlightened day dawned, they would be eligible to vote under the franchise laid out above. Apparently, this day is yet to dawn.

Further, Māori mechanisms and processes at the executive and administrative levels were accorded no validity or role in national affairs. John Gorst,[26] for one, maintains that this contributed to the dissatisfaction of Māori leaders and to the rise of the King movement. Frequent local and general assemblies which debated issues that would inevitably affect Māori as individuals and as a group were held: Māori, however, had no voice at these meetings. The realities of kāwanatanga were beginning to be felt whilst tino rangatiratanga was being openly ignored.

Māori response to this rise in the power of colonist-driven Provincial and General Assemblies, which inadequately addressed their own concerns, was to establish councils of rangatira and kaumātua known as rūnanga. The rūnanga heard disputes and initiated codes of civil behaviour to enable their people to cope with the rapidly changing environment in which they found themselves. While operating primarily at the hapū level, attempts to coordinate tribal rūnanga and eventually inter-tribal rūnanga became increasingly evident. The Kotahitanga movement, which found eventual form as the Kīngitanga and as Paremata Māori, can be seen to stem from this period.

Only two out of the eighty-two sections comprising the Constitution Act 1852 dealt directly with Māori matters. One of these, section 73, served to incorporate the pre-emptive right of the Crown to purchase and resell land at a constitutional level. The other, section 71, allowed for the delineation of districts wherein Māori custom and law would continue to be observed. Here again, the imperial legislators displayed a preparedness to give effect to the guaranteed tino rangatiratanga of iwi. Local administrators, however, whose responsibility it was to execute parliamentary will, remained reluctant to grant formal autonomy to iwi. A shared sovereignty was, and perhaps still is, abhorrent to the executive arm of government. Section 71, although it remained a part of statute law until repealed in 1986, and was ideally suited to situations which developed later (the King movement, for example), was never given effect.

Endnotes

1.   See especially, M. P. K. Sorrenson, (1989), 'Towards a Radical Reinterpretation of New Zealand History: The Role of the Waitangi Tribunal', in I. H. Kawharu (ed.), *Waitangi: Māori and Pākehā Perspectives of the Treaty of Waitangi*, Oxford University Press, Auckland.

2.   His plan was to move through the islands convening hui and gathering further signatures. Fifty-six signatures were collected in the Hokianga on 12 February. In all over 500 rangatira signed the Treaty. Olssen and Stenson—(1989), *A Century of Change: New Zealand 1800–1900*, Longman Paul, Auckland, pp. 79–82—cover this ground well and provide a thumb-nail sketch of Hobson's career on p. 72.

3.   J. Williams, (1989), 'Towards a Treaty Driven Society: New Perspectives on the Treaty of Waitangi', New Zealand Planning Council, Wellington, p. 3.

4.   Benedict Kingsbury, (1989), 'The Treaty of Waitangi: Some International Law Perspectives', in Kawharu, (1989), *op cit.*, pp. 121–57.

5.   R. J. Walker—'The Treaty of Waitangi as a Focus of Māori Protest', in Kawharu, (1989), *op cit.*, p. 264—renders this phrase as: 'the full chieftainship of their lands their homes and all their possessions'.

6.   J. E. Gorst, (1975 edn), *The Māori King, or, The Story of our Quarrel with the Natives of New Zealand*, Capper Press, Christchurch, p. 39. The circumstances surrounding this statement are unclear from the context in which it was found and, if this is a translation, the Māori text and translator are not cited.

7.   L. S. Rickard, (1963), *Tamihana, the Kingmaker*, A. H. and A. W. Reed, Wellington, p. 58.

8.   F. M. Brookfield, 'The New Zealand Constitution: The Search for Legitimacy', in Kawharu, (1989), *op cit.*, pp. 4–5.

9.   P. Adams, (1977), *Fatal Necessity: British Intervention in New Zealand 1830–1847*, Auckland University Press/Oxford University Press, Auckland, p. 220. McHugh in Kawharu, (1989), *op cit.*, p. 60, documents several Colonial Office memoranda which indicate that they would not countenance any implied division of British sovereignty.

10.   D. V. Williams, 'Te Tiriti o Waitangi—Unique Relationship Between Crown and Tangata Whenua', in Kawharu, (1989), *op cit.*, pp. 64–91.

11.   A. H. McLintock, (1958), *Crown Colony Government in New Zealand*, Government Printer, Wellington, pp. 417–32, reproduces the Act as Appendix D.

12.   Ibid, pp. 78–9. In Appendix B, McLintock lists the twelve incumbent Secretaries of War and Colonies between 1830 and 1852 (pp. 145–6).

13.   Ibid, p. 76, tells us that this combination resulted from the inheritance by the British of former French outposts following the Napoleonic wars and dates to 1801.

14.   D. V. Williams (1990), 'The Constitutional Status of the Treaty of Waitangi: An Historical Perspective' *New Zealand Universities Law Journal*, 14: (1): 20–1.

15. R. Mulgan, (1989), *Māori, Pākehā, and Democracy*, Oxford University Press, Auckland; see especially 'Part One: Bicultural Concepts'.

16. D. V. Williams—(1990), *op cit.*, p. 21—defines boroughs as 'such parts of the Islands of New Zealand as are or shall be owned or lawfully occupied by persons of European birth or origin'.

17. F. Hackshaw—'Nineteenth Century Notions of Aboriginal Title and Their Influence on the Interpretation of the Treaty of Waitangi' in Kawharu, (1989), *op cit.*, pp. 103–4—indicates that Colonial Secretary Earl Grey developed the principle of 'wastelands' from an article written by Dr Arnold of Rugby in 1831. Arnold maintains that the application of labour to land is causative in establishing ownership.

18. Article Two of the Treaty of Waitangi. See Appendix Four for both English and Māori versions.

19. Hackshaw, *op cit.*, pp. 103–5.

20. D. V. Williams, (1990), op cit., p. 21.

21. M. P. K. Sorrenson, (1986), 'A History of Māori Representation in Parliament', in *Report of the Royal Commission on the Electoral System: Towards a Better Democracy*, State Services Commission, Wellington, B-13.

22. See G. Asher and D. Naulls, (1987), *Māori Land: Discussion Paper No. 29*, New Zealand Planning Council, Wellington, especially Chapter 2, pp. 3–8.

23. It is to be noted that the earlier literacy in the English clause has been deleted. Māori were quick to attain literacy skills in Māori, no doubt a by-product of Christianity, and probably would soon have developed a similar facility in English.

24. Raewyn Dalziel, (1989), 'Towards a Representative Democracy: 100 Years of the Modern Electoral System', in David Green (ed.), *Towards 1990: Seven Leading Historians Examine Significant Aspects of New Zealand History*, GP Books, Wellington, p. 52.

25. M. P. K. Sorrenson, (1986), *op cit.*, B-5.

26. [1864], pp. 73–5.

Chapter Four
He Whakaminenga o Ngā Hapū

Ae, e whakaae ana ahau mo tēnei e haere ake, kia kōtahi anō te kōhao o te ngira e kuhuna ai te miro mā, te miro pango, te miro whero. A muri, kia mau ki te aroha, ki te ture, me te whakapono. (King Pōtatau Te Wherowhero at his coronation, Ngāruawāhia, 2 May 1859)[1]

Characteristics of Theme One

The first theme developed in this book is He Whakaminenga o Ngā Hapū, tribal solidarity. The theme examines unity based upon tribal constructs stemming from Māori initiatives, with a clear goal of protection for mana-a-iwi emerging. Typically, the theme concerns the affirmation or rather the reaffirmation of Māori sovereignty in the face of external threat.

Previous discussion has already examined the origins of unified political action among Māori—motivations being attributed either to common gain or the confrontation of an external threat through united action. The petition of 1831 to King William IV and the Declaration of Independence of 1835 can both be tied to a sense of insecurity brought about by vague notions of foreign interests. Within this theme, later movements can be seen to be a reaction to the abrogation of Māori sovereignty either by legislative instruments passed by the Imperial Parliament in London, or by the settler government in New Zealand—the latter being by far the more incursive (as outlined in Chapter Two).

The loss of tribal lands and the resulting diminished capacity to maintain, reproduce, and direct the community according to traditional patterns can be regarded as a serious external threat. Thus the impact of alienation and diminishing political standing drew autonomous iwi together within a bond of mutual concern.

A definable goal of kotahitanga has been the assertion of Mana Māori Motuhake as a desire to create a Māori vehicle for recognition of Māori in internal affairs. Consistently, the establishment of a Māori bodies politic to develop and advance Māori agendas has resulted.

The maintenance of traditional leadership patterns is a feature of these movements. Customary leaders, whose authority stems from the seniority of their descent, from the recognition and support of their people, and from an association with particular land areas, repeatedly instigated and promoted these movements. They spoke for and on behalf of their people and collectively influenced Māori thinking and aspirations.

Three case studies are employed to investigate this theme:
- the Declaration of Independence (He Whakaminenga o Ngā Hapū)
- the Māori King Movement (Kīngitanga)
- the Kotahitanga movement which led to the formation of a Māori Parliament (Pāremata Māori).

The Declaration of Independence

A Background

The seeds of the Declaration of Independence of 1835 were sown in a climate of external threat. By the early 1820s some iwi, especially those who traded regularly with Europeans, were acquiring not only new crops, livestock, tools, and religion, but also the musket. The balance of power was altered and the desirability of contact with those able to provide weapons and other resources increased. Wards[2] reveals that colonists and traders who where making a profit in the New Zealand market actively sought some level of British intervention. It was thought that an armed presence would not only protect traders from the natives, but would allow control over expatriate Europeans. Anglican missionaries also desired a firm British commitment in order to forestall the efforts of French Catholics under the leadership of Bishop Pompallier.

Māori concern over the increasing lawlessness of Europeans resident among them grew.[3] The accelerating requirement for land generated a growing unity among northern tribes and amplified demands for the Europeans to control their own people. The form this took was influenced to a large degree by missionaries and by James Busby.

The arrival of the French warship *La Favourite* in 1831 inspired the first formal request for British protection in the form of a petition to King William IV drafted by the Church Mission Society on behalf of some thirteen northern chiefs.[4] It seems that the affair was less in the hearts of Frenchmen and more in the minds of the missionaries. Perhaps it served missionary aims to alarm the local chiefs and thus elevate their own position as intermediaries with King William, as well as apply pressure upon the Colonial Office to act.

Figure 1: He Kara, the flag adopted at Waitangi, 20 March 1834

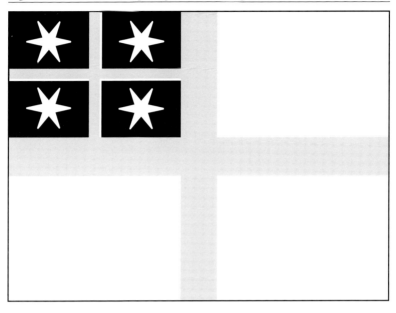

    = Red   = Blue

The tenuousness of their position was no doubt the spur to their hobby-horse. Peter Tremewan, in *French Akaroa*, gives a scholarly account of French attitudes to the annexation of Aotearoa to the French Empire. He provides much evidence supporting a growing French interest in establishing military, economic, and colonial bases in the South Pacific, but emphasizes French unwillingness to ruffle English feathers.[5]

A Māori Flag

Busby, the British Resident in New Zealand (1832–40), was behind the adoption of a national flag[6] by twenty-five northern chiefs on 20 March 1834 at Waitangi.[7] Busby proposed that, as Resident, he would certify ships' registers which were to be provided by rangatira.

Ratification of ships' registers were subject to the adoption of a flag and a concomitant request to the British monarch for it to be respected. Not only did this provide a method of registration for locally built ships, but it was an internationally recognizable symbol of Māori autonomy that premised an emerging sense of nationhood among Māori. The British Admiralty was instructed to recognize the flag and to take cognizance of Māori registers.

For Busby, the seeds were sown for Māori nationhood. He had provided a model for concerted action in the international arena and a possible procedure for national administration—a model he was to develop further through the Declaration of Independence ('He Wakaputanga o te Rangatiratanga o Nu Tirene'—see Appendix One).

The Declaration

On 28 October 1835, Busby, in response to the perceived threat of the French Baron, Charles Philip Hippolytus de Thierry,[8] and in line with Governor Sir Richard Bourke's instructions,[9] persuaded a group of thirty-four northern rangatira to form a confederation of tribes. Styled as the 'United Tribes of New Zealand',[10] they petitioned King William IV 'to be a parent of their infant state . . . its protector from all attempts upon its independence'.[11] Eighteen chiefs, predominantly from the Hokianga (but also including two notable southern leaders, Te Hapuku of Ngāti Te Whatuiapiti and Te Wherowhero of the Waikato), subsequently affiliated to form the Confederation of Tribes referred to in the Treaty of Waitangi. At least in the north, a 'national' Māori movement was under way and a route to a centralized Māori body politic was being explored.

Orange further maintains that Busby saw the creation of a collective Māori body politic as the principle means to the cessation of inter-tribal warfare. A formula for the operation of a legislative assembly of chiefs who would 'meet annually . . . to enact laws, dispense justice and regulate trade'[12] is contained in the third paragraph (there are four in total) of the Declaration. Busby clearly envisaged the 'Congress' established by the document as an embryonic national government: a mechanism for Māori to adapt British practice to their own ends. That these labours were to prove less effective than planned, and that the structure was devised and promoted by the incumbent European authority on these shores, are in themselves significant. The first attempt to unite iwi to control Māori affairs at a supra-tribal level was imposed from without: a recurrent theme in Māori–State relations.

John Ross[13] asserts that Busby's relationship with Thomas McDonnell, appointed Additional British Resident in August of 1835, played a significant role in the formation of the United Tribes. Apart from his initial pique over the appointment, Busby had a distinct personality clash with McDonnell. Further, McDonnell had exercised some powers of arrest which he did not have, and was meeting with some success in influencing the rangatira of Hokianga: most especially the enactment of a prohibition against the landing and sale of liquor in his region. It is significant that this 'by-law' was sanctioned by local rangatira and may in fact be the first expression of legislative authority on these shores. Ross sees this assumption of legislative power by McDonnell as crucial to Busby's efforts to form a Confederation of Chiefs competent to make laws. He hoped to establish a body politic which would be the sole font of law and thus render the Hokianga Liquor Law null and void.

An alternative interpretation of the development of the United Tribes of New Zealand ('Ko te Wakaminenga o Ngā Hapū o Nu Tirene') appears in a submission to the Select Committee on Māori Fisheries from Te Rūnanga Ko Huirau.[14] They maintain they are the lineal descendants of the signatories of the Declaration of Independence and of the Treaty of Waitangi, and are the bearers of the above-mentioned Māori flag which they continue to fly. Further, the submission states that they first met in 1816 and had sent a delegation to the Court of King George IV to negotiate the right to fly a flag. The Māori oral traditions, restated in their submission, give another perspective to the events which history records as the work of Busby. A greater level of Māori participation is indicated and indeed it appears as though impetus for the actions came from Te Whakaminenga. They also maintain that the Confederation was active at Waitangi on 6 February 1840, at Kohimārama in 1860, in the 1889 Kotahitanga movement, and is still active today. (This document may explain the apparent paradox which Busby's unusually hasty actions have left for historians,[15] and also his inability to maintain the momentum of the movement—it was not his and it continued without him.)

This, the earliest attempt at a formal constitutional arrangement for Māori, held some promise: traditional leaders, operating in unison and according to familiar customs, would make and execute decisions for the welfare and advancement of their people. What was new and perhaps the stumbling block was that the leaders would become bound by collective decisions to undertake concerted actions and to adopt a degree of uniformity in their activities. They must first agree to abide by and implement the will of the coalition. Whilst this was possible in the past for limited durations among regional groupings with a common cause or enemy, a sustainable, long-term affiliation to a superior mana would require considerable diplomacy and patience. It was perhaps this traditional tribal autonomy that impeded the development of a national body politic among Māori.

Ko Te Kīngitanga o Aotearoa

Constitutionally alienated from participation in national government, Māori needed to develop their own structures to embody the sovereignty which they were realizing had been lost to them.[16] This realization developed largely as a result of increasing loss of land by the Māori, a diminishing standing in the community, and a decrease in the proportion of the general population of those who were Māori.

The development of a monarchical structure in Tonga, as discussed by Sione Latukefu,[17] was underpinned by the adoption of Christianity. Apart from the inherent pacification of warring factions, the demise of the earlier polytheistic culture is highlighted as being highly influential in this regard. The link between monotheism and monarchy is one which deserves further exploration. Although the Christian ethos was well established in Aotearoa during the period under scrutiny, this hypothesis is too complex to fall within the ambit of this book.

Development of a Māori Monarchy

The notion of establishing a Māori monarch had been discussed as early as 1824.[18] Samuel Marsden perceived the inherently tenuous position which awaited any proposed colony in Aotearoa, and postulated that the creation of a Māori kingdom would enhance the prospect of settlement. His proposal, however, directed to a fellow member of the Church Mission Society, was intended to optimize the position of Europeans. The effect his proposal would have had for Māori, beneficial or otherwise, had little relevance to his scheme. The Kīngitanga which eventually emerged in 1858[19] sought to advance or at least maintain the position of Māori in national affairs. Charles de Thierry also formulated a version of this notion.[20] Of course, his plan was to establish his own hegemony in at least part of Aotearoa. Pei Te Hurinui[21] credits Queen Victoria with the inspiration for a Māori king. During Governor Grey's visit to her Majesty in 1845, the Queen enquired who was most powerful among the leaders of the Māori. Informed that Te Wherowhero of Ngāti Mahuta exercised most authority she is said to have instructed Sir George Grey to elevate him promptly to a regal status.

According to Leslie Kelly,[22] Waikato tradition credits the Te Āti Awa leader, Piri Kawau, with the initial concept of a king for the Māori. Having encountered the pomp and majesty of British royalty during a visit to England, he returned with a desire to assume such a position among his own people. However, he met with no success. John Grace offers another version of Piri Kawau's involvement wherein that chief had observed the plight of indigenous peoples in South Africa while accompanying Sir George Grey to the Cape Colony. He wrote to Wi Tako in 1854 urging the establishment of a king so as to avert a similar relationship with Europeans developing in Aotearoa.[23]

Tamihana Te Rauparaha[24] also imported monarchical ideas from abroad and sought to become the supreme leader of all tribes. The kaumātua (elders) of his people dissuaded him, reasoning that because Kāwhia, the traditional

Figure 2: Mātene Te Whiwhi *(Courtesy of the National Museum of New Zealand)*

centre for his people, was held by another iwi, it would be inappropriate for him to assume such a position.

Te Whiwhi-o-te-Rangi (baptized Mātene Te Whiwhi by Octavius Hadfield in 1843), a rangatira of Ngāti Raukawa at Ōtaki and a close relative of Tamihana Te Rauparaha,[25] then took up the idea. Together they actively promoted the notion among iwi. For Mātene, the protection of Māori land was central to his advocacy of a Māori monarchy. For Tamehana the creation of a unity beyond the tribe was a mechanism whereby law and security for the land and for iwi would be advanced. Later events were to show that both these leaders placed considerable value on the maintenance of law and order and actively discouraged any military activity to resolve Māori grievances— both with Europeans and among Māori.

In 1855 (J. W. Mackay gives 1852)[26] they visited various iwi and laid down the proposition. Taranaki, Whanganui, Taupō nui a Tia, Heretaunga, Te Tairawhiti, Rotorua, and the Waikato all received them and their message.[27] As a result, several leading figures emerged as contenders for the office. Notable among them were Tamihana Te Rauparaha of Porirua, Whitikau of Ngā Rauru, Tamati Hone Oraukawa of Taranaki, Topia Turoa and Te Anaua of Whanganui, Te Kani a Takirau of Uawa, Karauria of Heretaunga, Te Hapuku of Te Hauke, Waka Nene of Te Taitokerau, Taonui Hikaka of Maniapoto, Te Wherowhero of Ngāti Mahuta, and Te Heuheu Iwikau of Taupō.[28]

Mātene Te Whiwhi advised the proponents of Kīngitanga that the services of genealogical experts would be vital to the selection process. In Māori (and European) terms, traditional power is vested in those persons able to trace a direct line back to the foundation leaders of their nation. The rangatira who were suitable for kingship of Aotearoa could all establish distinguished pedigrees and connections to the most exalted lines. According to Te Hurinui, the scrutiny undertaken by Te Hukiki and Whioi,[29] two such genealogical experts, determined that the ancestry of Te Wherowhero equipped him best for kingship.

Although no immediate sovereign emerged, the concept was well received. There were several reasons why Māori were interested in establishing a king. Foremost amongst these would have to be the rapacious acquisition of land by Europeans. The establishment of a recognized institution to control Māori land interests was seen as an effective method to stop the alienation of land. Secondly, the erection of a central authority with power to arbitrate, legislate, and prosecute might eventually terminate inter-tribal bloodshed. Māori recognized that they had been disenfranchised in their own country and were accorded a lower status than Pākehā. Pākehā pre-eminence was ascribed to the unity afforded them by their Queen.[30] To facilitate a similar cohesion among Māori as a precursor to the assumption of an equal position in the nation, Māori were willing to investigate the elevation of a suitable rangatira to the position of king. Among Māori at least, neither subversion nor aggressive intent were contemplated as catalysts for Kīngitanga. As with the instances of inter-tribal cooperation discussed earlier, the existence of a perceived common threat enabled Māori to enter into a common cause. That there would be no diminution of rangatiratanga under the proposed new order would have been a matter for serious deliberation among leaders.

Not all iwi, however, were inclined toward the establishment of a Māori king The Ngāpuhi response chronicled by John Te Herekiekie Grace[31] in *Tuwharetoa* relates their reaction to the suggestion. Having listened 'haughtily' to the proposal at a meeting on the Hokianga River at Opara, the Ngāpuhi rangatira rejected the notion, preferring to maintain relations with the English Queen. It was further expressed that, should they choose to adopt a sovereign, the line of Hongi Hika had a suitable candidate in the form of Matiria. Ngāpuhi, even today, while respectful, do not adhere to the King movement.

James Cowan[32] details a hui held at Paetai on the Waikato River in 1856. Representing the Te Arawa peoples of Rotorua and Maketu, Temuera Te Amohau is said to have rejected the notion entirely. For him, the signature appended to the Treaty of Waitangi by Timoti was sufficient for Te Arawa to be bound to Queen Victoria ('taku kingi ko Kuini Wikitoria').[33] However, many commentators then and since have recorded that Te Arawa, in line with the position adopted by Te Heuheu Mananui[34] of Tuwharetoa, were opposed to the Treaty of Waitangi and had not signed it. Cowan gives no further details regarding the identity or standing of Timoti, nor the contemporary significance attached to his signing the Treaty.

It may well be that either this leader, Temuera Te Amohau, and those who supported him or indeed the whole of the Te Arawa Confederation, were simply against the notion of Kīngitanga. That he, along with Te Haupapa and Te Pukuatua, had earlier refused to sign the Treaty seems not to have been considered during this debate. His advice, should a Māori king indeed be created, was that Te Kani a Takirau would best fit the genealogical criteria for office.

For his part, Te Kani a Takirau was disinclined to assume the position and rejected his nomination with the saying, 'E hara a Hikurangi i te maunga haere'.[35] The authority and prestige which was already his could not be advanced by any further honours. His birthright as the descendant of Hinematioro was superior to any kingship. ('Kua kingi mai ano au i oku tupuna.'[36]) Whitikau is also said to have refused the position. When approached, Topia Turoa declined the invitation, noting that his tribal fisheries would be inadequate to meet the demands of hosting continual hui at a national level. The ability to provide adequate or even sumptuous hospitality is one of the hallmarks upon which the mana of an iwi rests. This aspect would have been considered by all candidates for the kingship. Te Heuheu Iwikau also declined the title and proposed Te Wherowhero as the most suitable candidate for kingship. He accompanied Te Whiwhi to Waikato to make the offer.[37]

According to Te Hurinui, one of the reasons why Te Wherowhero was reluctant was the continuing enmity with Ngāti Hauā over the death of Te Wherowhero's great aunt, Rangianewa, in 1825 at the hands of Ngāti Koroki, led by Te Tarapipipi.[38] This matter was resolved by the politically astute Ngāti Hauā leader when he gave his favourite daughter, Te Raumako, in marriage to Ngāti Apakura.[39] Eager to see an end to the internecine tribal warfare and to protect dwindling land reserves, Wiremu Tamihana Te Tarapipipi became a foremost advocate of Te Wherowhero for the mantle of king.

Figure 3: Wiremu Tamihana Tarapipipi Te Waharoa, the Kingmaker
(Courtesy of the Cowan Collection, Alexander Turnbull Library)

Te Tarapipipi had earlier been thwarted in his attempts to secure representation for Māori in the House of Commons and also in his attempts to obtain the Governor's mandate for a Council of Chiefs to operate under section 71 of the 1852 Act. Consequently, he saw the Kīngitanga as the most appropriate vehicle available for the advancement of Ngāti Hauā in particular and Māori in general. As a result, he channelled his considerable personal talents into the movement as an alternative to his early mainstream efforts.

It must also be remembered that Wīremu Tamihana was a deeply religious man. Although not baptized until 23 June 1839, Tamihana had acquired Christian ideals and education under the auspices of Reverend A. N. Brown at the Church Mission Society mission station established at Matamata in April 1835. His ready grasp of literacy skills enabled him to act as scribe for his father and take the lead in the educational pursuits of his people. His firm Christian leadership of Ngāti Hauā (he succeeded Te Waharoa over his elder brother, Te Arahi, in 1838) is seen as an important influence in the decline in hostilities between his people and their Te Arawa neighbours. Under his leadership, two Christian kāinga were established, as well as a system of justice based on tribal rūnanga. By this means, law and order were maintained among the Ngāti Hauā people, and it was Tamihana's firm belief that, given a suitable administrative structure, the same condition might be brought about for all Māori.

He called and attended several hui, both in the Waikato and nationally, at which he actively promoted Te Wherowhero as the most suitable candidate for king. At one such hui, held at Rangiriri in June 1857, the renowned Ngāti Hauā warrior, Wīremu Nera Te Waitaia of Whaingaroa, spoke against the movement. Nera was a contemporary of Tarapipipi's father, Te Waharoa, and was seen by some as the only possible alternative to Te Wherowhero. It can be seen, therefore, that not all were united in support of Kīngitanga, and that perhaps internal politics at the iwi level had some influence on the major proponents of the movement.

Te Heuheu addressed the gathering and cited Māori grievances as being sufficient cause to adopt an autonomous position in national affairs. In his own speech at this hui, Tamihana proclaimed the need for a Māori king to bring law and order to Māori in light of the government's inability to do so. It seems unlikely, however, that the mere provision of an effective administration and a cessation of tribal warfare imposed by the Crown would have altered the course of Kīngitanga. The symbolic elevation of a king was an act of nationalism on the part of Māori. Māori, feeling the yoke of Pākehā domination, would have been made even more uncomfortable if that yoke had been pulled tighter. Nationalist urges rest heavily upon identity, usually an identity couched in terms of oppression. The Kīngitanga, as with other approaches to political unity, enabled Māori to see themselves as being more like each other than like Pākehā, and to identify as Māori as well as being a member of a tribe. A more effective Crown policy to control and absorb Māori into the State would have exacerbated the already hostile feelings of tribes, and may have precipitated open warfare earlier than did occur, and probably at a greater level.

Another hui, known in oral tradition as 'Hinana ki Uta, Hinana ki Tai',[40] which focused on Kīngitanga, was held on the shores of Lake Taupō. Called together by Iwikau Te Heuheu, tribal leaders gathered at Pukawa, the principle Tuwharetoa pā, late in 1856.[41] Upon the marae stood a tall flag-pole from which flew the Māori flag sanctioned by King William IV. At various intervals along its length flax ropes were suspended. In his whaikorero, Iwikau explained the significance of the pole. It represented Tongariro, the sacred mountain of the Tūwharetoa people. The ropes signified the maunga tapu of each iwi as represented by their rangatira. As each maunga was identified, the appropriate leader demonstrated the adherence of his people by securing the rope to a peg driven into the ground in front of his group.

The central mountain of Te-Ika-a-Māui, supported by the mountains of ngā iwi o Aotearoa me Te Waipounamu, surmounted by a symbol of Māori autonomy, the flag, is a powerful representation of the steadfast support for Kīngitanga which existed by 1857. Ngongotahā (Te Arawa), Putauaki (Ngāti Awa), Tawhiuau (Ngāti Manawa), Hikurangi (Ngāti Porou), Maungapohatu (Ngai Tūhoe), Titiokura (Ngāti Kahungunu), Kapiti (Ngāti Toa), Otairi (Ngāti Apa), Tapuaenuku, Kaikoura, and Aoraki (Ngai Tahu), Paratetaitonga

Figure 4: 'Pukawa' Lake Taupō, pencil and wash by Stevenson Percy-Smith, January 1858 *(Courtesy of the Alexander Turnbull Library)*

(Whanganui), Taranaki (Taranaki, Te Āti Awa, and Ngāti Ruanui), Pirongia and Taupiri (Waikato), Kakepuku (Ngāti Maniapoto), Rangitoto (Ngāti Matakore and Ngāti Whakatere), Wharepuhunga (Ngāti Raukawa), Maungatautari (Ngāti Hauā and Ngāti Koroki), Maunganui (Ngāi Terangi), Te Aroha (Ngāti Tamatera), and Moehau (Ngāti Maru) are the names of these mountains recounted by Te Heuheu Tukino to James Cowan. The other outcome was a decision, agreed to by all, to name Te Wherowhero as king. His own reluctance to assume the throne had prevented him from attending that hui. Michael King (1977: 24) makes the point that some were later to say that authority to make a commitment to Kīngitanga had not been given to all chiefs, or that the support was limited to that time and that place. Be that as it may, a clear mandate emerged from the conference to appoint a king and for that king to be Te Wherowhero.

Te Wherowhero

At this stage it would be appropriate to relate some of the personal and tribal attributes which made this leader a fitting choice for kingship. As detailed above, his father, Te Rauangaanga, was an exceptional war leader. Te Wherowhero was also an accomplished warrior, both as a general and in hand-to-hand combat.[42] His whakapapa linked him to most of the powerful iwi of Aotearoa, and he was the paramount leader (ariki) of the Waikato tribes. His major affiliation went to Ngāti Mahuta, who commanded sway over the mid-reaches of the Waikato river, from Te Kūiti north. Importantly, his son, Te Mātutaera, later to become King Tāwhiao, had married into the Ngāpuhi confederation and established strong links with the principal leaders of Te Taitokerau.[43] These links not only provided a strong economic base from which the Kīngitanga could operate, but also positioned him as a leader suitable to the majority of iwi. Te Wherowhero had also been educated in the whare wānanga of the Tainui people (Te Papa o Rotu) and was recognized as a leading tohunga. The spiritual dimension which he was able to bring to the position of King was of considerable moment in Māori estimation. A further advantage may also have been the cordial relationship he enjoyed with the Pākehā. It is often maintained that his residence in Auckland served as a shield for the State capital, and he was on particularly good terms with Governor Sir George Grey during his first term.

Following the decision at Pukawa, hui were held at Rangiohia and finally at Ngāruawāhia, where the elderly (in his mid-eighties) Waikato Ariki was elected King. Some debate concerning the appropriate appellation to be used to designate the new office ensued. Many leaders preferred a Māori title, such as Ariki Taungaroa, Toihau, Kahutaratara or Matua, but the title King, symbolic of a new order and equal to that used by Europeans, was eventually adopted. The notion that the Māori King and the English Queen would be allied under God was a strong theme of the Kīngitanga, and a clear indication that subversion was not a goal of the movement.

The ritual of elevation was performed by Wiremu Tamihana at Ngāruawāhia in 1858 (Te Hurinui gives 2 May 1859 as the date of coronation). No crown was used in this ceremony—instead, following a ritual anointment of a biblical nature and appropriate karakia (formulaic incantations), a Māori version of the Bible was placed over Pōtatau's head. This same Bible remains in the possession of the Kahui Ariki (the Māori royal family) and has been used by the senior rangatira of Ngāti Hauā in the coronation ceremonies of each of the five subsequent monarchs. Tamihana conducted the tohinga (coronation ceremony) for both Pōtatau and Tāwhiao. His son, Tupu Takingakawa, officiated when King Mahuta and King Te Rata where crowned, while Tarapipipi II, the son of Tupu, conducted the ritual for King Koroki. Te Waharoa Tarapipipi, son of Tarapipipi II, and fourth rangatira to be known as Kingmaker, performed the ceremony for Princess Piki, now known as Kuini Dame Te Atairangikāhu.[44]

A set of laws devised by Tamihana based upon the 'Laws of God', clearly indicating the spirituality of the Kingmaker and of the movement itself, were presented at the coronation of Pōtatau. Tamihana came to realize, however, that the power of the King to coerce his subjects was negligible, and allegiance to him was to some extent limited. Rangatira, traditionally autonomous masters not only of their own destiny but also of that of their kinsmen, simply would not follow the King's council unless it suited their own plans to do so. The actions of Ngāti Maniapoto in supporting their Taranaki allies against the express wishes of King Tāwhiao is illustrative of this.

The institution of a king as a focus for Māori nationalism, however, was effective. In an analogy presented by Tamihana to describe his perception of the relationship between the Government and the Kīngitanga, he described them as being equivalent, but both subject to the laws of God and protected by the mana of the Queen.[45]

Upon his ascension, Te Wherowhero adopted the name Pōtatau Te Wherowhero, but his reign was brief. He died on Sunday, 25 June 1860, after a reign of one year and fifty-four days.[46] He was succeeded by his son, Tukarotu, who had earlier been baptized by Reverend Robert Burrows, an Anglican minister, as Mātutaera (Methusala). The name he took upon his ascension was Pōtatau II. Later, in August of 1864, while visiting the Pai Marire prophet and founder, Te Ua Haumene, at his headquarters in Taranaki, he was given the name Tāwhiao.[47] Tāwhiao and his closest advisers, known as Tekau ma Rua, had travelled to Ahipaipa in company with a large body of Ngāti Maniapoto warriors. During their stay, Te Ua

Figure 5: Tāwhiao Matuteaera Pōtatau Te Wherowhero (second Māori King). Portrait published in *The Maori King* by J E Gorst *(Courtesy of Alexander Turnbull Library)*

Haumene anointed him and foretold that he would overcome his enemies. Before he left for Te Kūiti he promised his support for the prophets Tohu Kakahi and Te Whiti o Rongomai at Parihaka.

Te Ua Haumene

Te Ua founded the prophetic cult known as the Hauhau movement, and consistently stressed the need for passive resistance to the incursions of European colonization. This philosophy gave rise to the name Pai Marire, which Elsmore translates as 'Good and Peaceful'.[48] Seen as the 'first independent expression of Māori Christianity',[49] the Pai Marire faith is a departure from both traditional Māori spirituality and from the contemporary teachings of European missionaries. For the first time, Māori adapted Christian symbolism and to some extent dogma, not only to express a spiritual dimension, but also as a reaction to Western domination. Although initially attracting little popular support, the tumultuous political climate in Taranaki was fertile ground for the prophet's words. Following the outbreak of open hostilities in Taranaki and in the Waikato, considerable numbers joined the faith from both Taranaki and the Waikato, and also from Whanganui. Early in 1865, two groups of evangelical followers left Taranaki and travelled by different routes to Poverty Bay. Their goal was to unite all the tribes of the North Island under the banner of the Pai Marire religion. Here again we see a departure from early religious experience. Biblical and traditional spirituality are being melded to promote a strong pro-Māori message. Political and military unity, directed at the ultimate well-being of Māori as a 'race' rather than at tribal advancement, were only a part of the goal.

James Cowan, in his account of the 'New Zealand' wars,[50] emphasizes, perhaps too strongly, the anti-Pākehā feeling which pervaded the Hauhau movement. Incensed by the loss of life and the raupatu (confiscation of land) which followed the Anglo–Māori wars, an atmosphere of extreme despondency afflicted many tribes. The prophetic pronouncements of Te Ua promised final victory over the Pākehā, and appealed to many who were willing to take up the new faith. Cowan's interpretation of the movement is therefore coloured in hues of hatred and fanaticism. More recent analyses, however, portray Te Ua as a pacifist, passing the responsibility for the outpourings of violence to his lieutenants, who reinterpreted his messages and provoked violence.

What must be emphasized about the Pai Marire religion is its potential for creating and maintaining unity. A mixture of religious zeal and an inbred love of kin and country produced an appeal for many tribesmen which supplanted an earlier commitment to the missionary faiths. The aspiration to regain land recently lost was common to many of the latterly belligerent iwi, and was thus an excellent inducement for unity. Further, adherents and practitioners of the indigenous religion, who had been suppressed by the introduction of the Gospel, now saw the increasing disaffection with Europeans and all that was associated with them as an opportunity to reassert their particular mana. In Cowan's interpretation it was these men who acted as the catalyst for war.

Te Hokioi, E Rere Atu Na

Among the institutions which arose to support the movement was the Māori language newspaper, *Te Hokioi, E Rere Atu Na*. The name translates as 'The

Hokioi (a mythical bird) that flies disseminating information'. Established late in 1861, the broadsheet was printed by two Waikato men, Wiremu Toetoe and Hemara Te Rerehau. In 1859 they had travelled to Vienna and learned the art of printing at the State Printing House. In May 1861 they returned, bringing with them a press gifted by Archduke Maximillian.[51]

Primarily, the newspaper published the Proclamations of King Tāwhiao and informed his supporters of events which transpired. Edited and written by Wiremu Parata Te Tuhi, the newspaper asked probing questions of the Government and advocated a reinterpretation of the Treaty of Waitangi. Te Tuhi was a second cousin to Tāwhiao, and assisted him as an adviser, warrior, and secretary, as well as taking responsibility for *Te Hokioi*. He, like many of his generation, had received an education at a mission school and had taken on a baptismal name transliterated from English. Earlier, he was known as Taieti, and had attended the Pukawa hui as Te Wherowhero's representative.

When the purpose-built iron gunboat *Pioneer* entered the Waikato, *Te Hokioi* publicized the fact. Te Tuhi pointed out that such a presence, in the absence of permission from the tribal owners of the river, was a direct violation of the Treaty. These and other difficult questions demanded a response.

Governor Grey, quick to realize the power of the Fourth Estate, dispatched the Cambridge-educated John Eldon Gorst to Te Awamutu, where he was to establish a rival Māori language newspaper. After nearly half a century of missionary evangelism, Māori literacy levels in Te Reo Māori were high. In order to minimize the impact of Land League and other subversive literature, a pro-Government pamphlet was required. *Te Pihoihoi Mokemoke i Runga i te Tuanui* (named for the sparrow which sits alone on the housetop in Psalm 102: 7) went to print in February 1863 and published four issues. It ceased publication when its editor was expelled from the Waikato on the eve of open warfare. When the war of words, in which Gorst and Te Tuhi were the main protagonists, gave way to active military engagements, *Te Hokioi* also stopped publication; its editor had put down the pen and taken up the sword. In this case, the sword indeed proved to be inferior—a message not lost on later campaigners for Māori unity.

Te Rohe Potae me Te Riri Pākehā

Among the goals of the King movement was an end to the sale of tribal lands, whether such transactions were voluntary or coerced. Since colonization had begun, the amount of land desired by settlers increased steadily. To meet the shortfall, government land-agents became less direct, willing to purchase land even in the face of opposition from within the tribe.[52] This led to disputes between those who would sell, hoko whenua, and those who would not, pupuri whenua—disputes that were at times violent. The Government did little to intercede, except where European lives or property were threatened, and in fact were encouraging individual Māori to lay claim to and dispose of tribal assets. Pupuri whenua groups, known also as Land Leagues, developed to ensure the retention of land, and rangatira assumed mana over the corporate land holdings.

The King provided a focus for iwi who wished to hold on to their lands. The mana whenua of individual rangatira who supported the King was vested in his person. He, as ultimate title-holder, theoretically ensured an end to alienation of land. Through this unity it was hoped that iwi would be better able to resist the pressure to sell lands. He was to act as the titular leader and was charged with the duty to ensure that no further land was alienated.

His own domain, Te Rohe Potae, was surrounded by a closed boundary, known as the aukati. The King Country, as it came to be known after the Waikato War, was bounded in the north for a short space by the Waipa River. The aukati then followed the Puniu River as far as Mount Pirongia, and then the course of the Waikato River through Lake Taupō as far as Mount Ruapehu. From there it went westward out to the coast at Moekau and thence to Aotea Harbour, the landing place of the Aotea canoe. Within this boundary Pākehā and kūpapa alike were forbidden to tread. Several instances which occurred in the region were typified as murders by most European commentators of that day and this, and as late as 1883 a surveyor, C. W. Hurthouse, was arrested and chained up for two days. He was later released when Te Kooti and the Ngāti Maniapoto chief, Wetere Te Rerenga, intervened on his behalf.[53] During the period of Kīngitanga ascendancy many a fugitive from Pākehā law found sanctuary within the aukati of King Tāwhiao, Te Kooti Arikirangi notable among them. It was because of this convivial association that the meeting-house, Te Tokanganui a Noho, was built at Te Kūiti and gifted to the King.

Resistance to the sale of land and the effectiveness of Kīngitanga in promoting the pupuri whenua cause led, eventually, to open warfare.[54] Tension punctuated by increasingly vocal calls for government action, legislative or otherwise, to deal with the Land Leagues, marked the first three years of King Tāwhiao's reign. Fighting commenced in Taranaki on 4 May 1863 following the disputed sale of Tataraimaka, and soon spread to the Waikato. On 12 July 1863, Lieutenant-General Duncan Cameron crossed the Mangatawhiri Stream and invaded the Te Rohe Potae.

The decisive and bloody battle of Rangiriri (20–21 November 1863) and the siege of Orakau (31 March–2 April 1863) were the last major engagements in the Waikato. They cost the defenders of the King Country considerable casualties and caused them to withdraw south of the Puniu River into the southern Waipa Basin. Preparations for protracted aggression continued among the Ngāti Maniapoto warriors of this region, but no major offensive came.

Subsequent to the military reverses inflicted on the Māori, the Government showed its real motive for attacking the Waikato when the New Zealand Settlements Act 1863 was enforced. The legislation authorized the confiscation of 'rebel' lands,[55] but its application was far less specific. Of the 1.2 million acres taken in the Waikato, several thousand acres belonged to Ngāti Whāwhākia, who were loyal to the Crown. Ngāti Apakura, who had taken no part in the hostilities, were also subjected to raupatu.

Major Wiremu Te Morehu Maipapa Te Wheoro a Ngāti Whāwhākia, rangatira who had fought for the British, and others sought to discuss peace terms with Tāwhiao on a number of occasions. King Pōtatau II chose to avoid confrontation with kūpapa officers, and commenced a period of isolation, moving constantly through territory still hostile to the Pākehā. Tamihana Te Waharoa, however, made his peace with the Governor on 27 May 1865, when he surrendered his taiaha to General Carey. Tāwhiao, probably on advice from his senior advisers, remained 'in rebellion' for nearly twenty years. The unjust confiscation of Waikato land, raupatu,[56] no doubt hardened his resolve to hold fast to his residual sovereignty. During this period his reputation as a prophet king emerged and he developed his own spiritualism, founding the Tariao (Morning Star) cult which persists to this day. Millennial in character, the eventual salvation of his descendants from the plight in which he found himself was central to his faith.[57]

Tāwhiao eventually made his peace with the Government at Pirongia, known then as Alexandra. In a ritualized encounter with Major Gilbert Mair on 12 August 1881, he and seventy of his men formally laid down their guns. He then proffered Mair a fantail, imbued with his mana, as a symbol of peace.[58] However, bereft of his former capital, Ngāruawāhia, he continued the itinerant lifestyle he had adopted during his 'exile', and in 1882 made an extensive tour of Te-Ika-a-Māui. He journeyed down the west coast to Ōtaki, then across to the Wairārapa, through Heretaunga and on to Taupō. From there the party travelled to Waiotū and dispersed. During the trip, Tāwhiao was persuaded to lead a delegation to visit the English Queen, and lay before her a petition on land grievances.

Delegation to Queen Victoria

The basis of the King's petition was a letter which he had written to the Aborigines Protection Society before he left Aotearoa. Essentially, it asked the Queen to confirm the Treaty of Waitangi and to consider his proposal to establish a separate Māori parliamentary system. Section 71 of the 1852 Constitution Act made provision for the application of Māori custom and practice in Māori districts, and this could be used to facilitate the King's plan. Under his system, control over land issues would reside with the new parliament, and a Queen appointee would act as a liaison with the colonial parliament.[59]

Accompanied by Major Wiremu Te Wheoro, who had been the Member of the House of Representatives for Western Māori electorate since 1879, Hori Ropiha of Ngāti Parakiore, Topia Turoa of Whanganui, and Parata Te Tuhi, the King's Herald, he embarked for London on 1 April 1884 on board the *Tarawera*. The Orakei rangatira, Paora Tuhaere, was unwell and consequently not able to accompany the party. The delegation was confident that the mana of the King would ensure success—contemporary press commentaries were equally convinced of its impending failure.

Assuming that Queen Victoria, with whom the Treaty of Waitangi had been concluded, would, as Sovereign, pay heed to their grievances, he sought an audience with her. Further, it was seen as appropriate that the two monarchs should meet, face to face, to resolve the difficulties between their peoples. The actuality of British monarchy was soon made clear to them. They were refused an audience with Her Majesty.

An interview with the Secretary of State for Colonies, Lord Derby, was, however, made possible. Arranged by John Gorst, erstwhile Resident Magistrate and Civil Commissioner in the Waikato 1861–63, and now a British MP, the meeting took place on 22 July 1884. Derby apprised the group of the Imperial stance: responsibility for New Zealand affairs rested with the colonial administration operating within the colony, and he was powerless to grant the petition. He did, however, send a dispatch to the New Zealand Government informing them of the petition. His promise of imperial action once the New Zealand Government had answered the complaints was, in light of the transfer of responsibility to the latter, largely empty.

Kauhanganui

Upon the return of King Tāwhiao from England in 1884, the meetings of the King movement came to be held at Whatiwhatihoe, near Pirongia, and Maungākawa, near Morrinsville. Despite his rebuff in Britain, Tāwhiao remained committed to pursuing Māori rights, and in 1886 presented a proposal to John Ballance, the Native Minister, which suggested the formation of a Legislative Council of Chiefs.[60] Validated by section 71 of the 1852 Constitution Act, annual gatherings of rangatira, financed from existing Māori taxation and encompassing existing Māori committees, were proposed. Despite the assertion that this mechanism would enable the Government to honour the Treaty of Waitangi and the Covenant of Kohimārama (discussed in Chapter Five), Ballance declined to act upon it. He deferred, maintaining that the Government was best able to judge what was good for Māori, and that most chiefs preferred the maintenance of the Native Land Court.[61]

The lack of willingness to accommodate the concerns raised by Tāwhiao prompted him in 1891 to establish his own Convention of Chiefs, the Kauhanganui.[62] A House of Assembly was erected at Maungākawa in 1892 to accommodate the Kauhanganui. Established under the premiership of Tana Taingakawa, second son of Wiremu Tamihana,[63] the Kauhanganui was to be as broadly representative as possible. Although an invitation was sent to all tribes of Te-Ika-a-Māui to attend, participation remained confined to the inner circle of Kīngitanga support. A Constitution was promulgated in 1894 that outlined the functions and structure of the King's Parliament (Appendix Seven).

An official newspaper, *Te Paki o te Matariki*, and the machinery for its production, were contained in clause 12, and it was this publication which first advertised the King's Constitution.

A bicameral approach similar to the Westminster model was adopted, consisting of two Kauhanga or Conventions—one for manukura (nobles) and the other for matariki (commoners). They were enjoined to assemble on the 2nd of May in each year to conduct their business, and having made their deliberations they were to place them before the throne of Tāwhiao for ratification. The opening clauses of the Constitution dealt with mechanisms and definitions relating to land and conditions under which it might be leased from Māori, while part eight was concerned with disputed land; provision was made for resolution of such disputes by Māori tribunals.

A judicial system was also contained in the Constitution. Provision for the appointment of magistrates to adjudicate disputes between the King's subjects over property and livestock were included as clause 10. The magistrates were responsible for keeping the peace and upholding the rule of the King's law. Other matters relating to marriage and the settlement of Europeans within the aukati were covered in subsequent clauses of the Constitution.

The Kauhanganui met regularly until the 1920s, and came to be dominated by the Ngāti Hauā chief, Tupu Taingakawa, who had succeeded to the title Kingmaker. Meetings were held at both Parewanui in the Rangitikei and at Waahi.

Te Paki o Matariki (the widespread calm of the Pleiades) is the name given to the King's coat of arms, which was designed by two leading tohunga of the Tainui people and completed during the reign of Tāwhiao. Inscribed at the bottom are the words 'Mana Motuhake' (separate power and authority). These two words encapsulate the fundamental goal of autonomy that the King movement was established to pursue. The movement sought, through diplomacy and with reference to tradition, to initiate and maintain structures by which Māori could develop alongside the European. For Te Hurinui, an important spiritual connotation exists in these words. Accompanied as they are by symbols of considerable significance to initiates of the Io cult, the spiritual dimension of the word 'mana' is emphatic. The Kīngitanga, therefore, is set apart as 'the symbol of the spiritual and cultural life of the Māori'.[64] This coat of arms appeared on each issue of the bulletin.

Kīngitanga Today

The King movement has remained an influential force in Māori society, but most especially among the Tainui tribes. An indication of the esteem in which its current leader, Dame Te Atairangikāhu, is held was evident at the celebrations of the twenty-fifth anniversary of her coronation, held at Ngāruawāhia on 23 May 1991. Along with the senior Māori leaders representing all major tribal and sub-tribal groupings of Aotearoa who gathered for the event were many of the most important mainstream political leaders of the nation. The dignitaries were, however, not only local delegations from across Te Moananui-a-Kiwa—others were also in attendance. They included Malieatoa Tanumafili, Head of State of Western Samoa, Queen Halalevalu Mata'aho of Tonga, Prime Minister Ratu Sir Kamisese Mara and Adi Lady Lala of Fiji, Geoffrey Henry, Prime Minister of the Cook Islands, President Dowiyogo of Nauru, Pa Ariki of Rarotonga, Kekaulike Kawananakoa from Hawaii, and Pomare Ari'i of Tahiti.[65] Such is the high regard and personal esteem that Dame Te Atairangikāhu attracts both nationally and internationally.

The message she enunciated during her address to the gathering that day emphasized the development of individual iwi and unity between and among the tribes of Aotearoa. Her vision for the advancement of not only Māori but of the nation and the Pacific community was premised upon these two

Table 2: Ngā Arikinui o te Kīngitanga

Ruler and Reign	Crowned at:	Crowned by:
Pōtatau Te Wherowhero (2/5/1859–25/6/1860)	Ngāruawāhia	Tamihana Te Waharoa
Pōtatau II, Tāwhiao (27/6/1860–26/8/1894)	Ngāruawāhia	Tamihana Te Waharoa
Mahuta (14/9/1894–9/11/1912)	Maungākawa	Tupu Takingakawa
Te Rata (24/11/1912–1/10/1933)	Waahi	Tupu Takingakawa
Koroki (8/10/1933–18/5/1966)	Waahi	Tarapipipi II
Te Atairangikāhu (23/5/1966–present)	Ngāruawāhia	Te Waharoa Tarapipipi

fundamental goals: unity and the strength unity provides, as well as the development of structures at all levels in the system.

Clearly, the King movement is still a potent force in the domestic and external affairs of Aotearoa.

Pāremata Māori

The final case study illustrating this theme is the Kotahitangi movement of the 1870s and 1880s, which found fruition as the Pāremata Māori established in 1891. This movement must be considered as distinct from the Kauhanganui of King Tāwhiao, which was established at Maungākawa in 1892, as it crystallized earlier and made no direct reference to the King movement. As a result of the hostilities in the early 1860s, the King movement had suffered serious military, political, and spiritual setbacks and had lost the support of some iwi. The Tainui people were the victims of severe retributive policies following the wars of the 1860s, and this reduced the capacity of King Tāwhiao and his adherents to broaden the scope and membership of the movement. The military campaigns of this period had also altered the balance of power. Recourse to armed resistance and the resulting state of flux in inter-tribal relationships had created opportunities for Māori to obtain and use the fire power needed to redress ancient grievances with their neighbours. Apparent loyalty to the Crown may in some instances have masked tribal agendas of utu. Māori leaders continued to meet periodically and to resist the impact of State control.

The establishment of a Māori parliament was a result of the continued erosion of Māori ability to secure a measure of tribal autonomy and a further response to the alienation of land. The Native Representation Act 1867, while at last providing for a Māori voice to be heard in Parliament, even at its inception was an inadequate avenue for constitutional representation. If a similar demographic basis was used to determine the level of representation allocated Māori as was used for Pākehā, then a figure of twenty seats out of the seventy then in existence would have been required to adequately represent Māori. This proportion would more accurately reflect the Māori percentage of the population. Further, the token four seats provided for Māori were determined without reference to tribal leaders, interrelationships, or boundaries, and were imposed by the Crown.

Tribal Rūnanga

The Pāremata Māori, established by ninety-six chiefs at Te Tiriti o Waitangi Marae, Pewhairangi, on 14 April 1892[66] can be seen as a coalescence of 'Land

Figure 6: Gathering of high ranking chiefs of Mataatua and Arawa Tribes (date unknown). *Left to right:* Apirana, Timutimu, Hemi Huata, Tomarau, Mr Laughton, Wharetini Rangi, Nomena Whakamoe-Tamaiti o Takuta, Paerino, Te Pairi, Pakitu, Te Waiunu, Queenie, Takuta, Whatanui, Meta Tapoki, Te Aranga, Tahuri, Pomare, Kohiti, Te Kawa, Te Whenua, Ruatoto. *(Courtesy of the Sister Annie Henry Collection, Alexander Turnbull Library)*

League' movements and of tribal and inter-tribal rūnanga which had been meeting with increasing frequency. The gathering at Manawapou on the Ingahape River in South Taranaki in May 1854, hosted by Ngāti Ruanui to dedicate the wharenui Taiporohenui, is significant among them. Seen as being among the first major hui of tribes, it is also often linked to the formation of the King movement. The house, spacious among its contemporaries, was dedicated to the resolution of internal difficulties which resulted from land sales. One literal translation of the name Taiporohenui is 'a tide to end great wrong'; another less literal is 'the settling of the land problem'.[67]

In the 1870s and 1880s, rūnanga meetings were occurring among the Whanganui peoples, in an effort to establish a regional unity. Among the Te Arawa tribes a 'Great Native Committee' was formed, and the 'Union of Mataatua' was mooted among the hapū of Ngāi Tūhoe.[68]

As mentioned earlier, rangatira, faced with Crown inability to adequately govern Māori or to administer justice to Māori, had during the 1850s begun to meet first in hapū rūnanga, and then to broaden membership of these groups they formed tribal and supra-tribal runanga. Erstwhile Native Secretary and eventual first Chief Judge of the Native Land Court, Francis Dart Fenton, was fulsome in his praise of the tribal rūnanga which formed in the area around Whaingaroa, south of the Waikato heads. Having lost his position of Native Secretary to Donald McLean in 1856, Fenton had been appointed Resident Magistrate at Whaingaroa. Recognizing the King movement and the growing number of rūnanga as a reaction to the exclusion of Māori from the political system, Fenton advocated the legitimizing of rūnanga in order to bring them under Crown control. His insistence that such a policy would not only undermine the mana of rangatira, but would also facilitate the appropriation of tribal lands, led to the passage of three Acts of Parliament in 1858. Introduced by C. W. Richmond, the Acts were the Native Districts Regulation Act, the Native Circuit Courts Act, and the Native Territorial Rights Act. The first two of these were later to prove useful to Sir George Grey when he instituted his system of district rūnanga in 1861.[69]

Repudiation Movement

The Repudiation movement, which had been meeting since 1871, placed particular emphasis on the Treaty of Waitangi as a basis for their claims. The movement developed among the Ngāti Kahungunu of Hawke's Bay, and sought a legal remedy to the dissatisfaction created over the large-scale loss of tribal lands.[70] Incensed at the less than straightforward land acquisition practices adopted by Sir Donald McLean in Heretaunga and Wairārapa under the 1865 Native Land Act, Kahungunu chiefs sought to use European law to obtain redress. Land had been purchased without the full consent of all owners—in some instances fewer than a dozen names were attached to title transactions. Further, traders and liquor sellers had encouraged Māori into debt by offering unlimited credit, only to 'foreclose' and force a land sale. Māori interpreters and some powerful rangatira had been bribed to ensure the processing of land titles.

Henare Matua of Ngāti Kahungunu and Ngāti Te Whatuiapiti was a foremost proponent of the movement. Although he had signed the deed of sale for the Waipukurau Block in the 1850s, he had firmly opposed other land sales in and around Porangahau. Skilled and knowledgeable in Pākehā practice, his business acumen and familiarity with the law won him considerable esteem among Māori and European alike. Appointed an assessor under the Native Circuit Courts Act in 1870, Matua was in a position to advocate the repudiation of land sales. His goal was the investigation of all land transactions in the Hawke's Bay since 1850, and further that this investigation be conducted by Māori. He also advocated that the Māori Land Court ought properly to fall under the jurisdiction of tribal rūnanga. Subsequently, the goals of the Repudiation Party, as it became known, were to include national unity, kotahitanga, especially in relation to dealings with the Crown. Consistently, loyalty to the Crown was emphasized by them, and the suggestion of appointing a man acceptable to Māori and to the Government as an arbitrator was made.

M. P. K. Sorrenson[71] maintains that the movement was in part European inspired, being initiated, or at least strongly supported by two Pākehā politicians. Henry Robert Russell,[72] a squatter from Waipukurau who served in the House of Representatives and on the Legislative Council, and John Sheehan MHR, an Auckland lawyer and later Minister of Native Affairs, agitated long and loud on behalf of the Repudiationists. The vocal denunci-ation of the injustices perpetrated against Māori was something more than mere philanthropy. Both men stood to make political and financial capital over the affair as they were members of the Opposition during the early 1870s. Sheehan's legal fees for 1871–78, received from Russell, were £13,000.[73]

One of the principal land-holders in the Hawke's Bay, the Honourable John Davies Ormond,[74] had on a number of occasions arranged illegal leases with Māori. He was the Minister for Public Works in the Fox Administration in 1871–72 (and again in the 1877 Waterhouse Government), and had acted closely with Sir Donald McLean on defence and Māori-related issues. Ormond, as one of the largest run-holders in the Bay, was a serious rival of both Henry Russell and his brother, T. P. Russell, in entrepreneurial pursuits. Sir Donald McLean, formerly the Chief Land Purchase Commissioner (1853), Native Secretary (1856), and Provincial Superintendent of Hawke's Bay (elected 1863), was also a political adversary of Sheehan and Russell, and a large-scale land-holder in his own right. Predictably, perhaps, Sheehan, when appointed Native Minister under the Grey, did nothing to redress the Ngāti Kahungunu situation he had so convincingly espoused.

The agitation and unrest engendered by the Matua–Russell campaign bore fruit in 1872 when a parliamentary select committee, established to receive petitions on land matters, saw fit to appoint a commission of inquiry.[75] Sinclair is of the opinion that this commission, even though its outcome was not a model of harmony, was a milestone in race relations in New Zealand.

> The attempt, probably the first, to combine, in a Commission, Māori assessors with European magistrates . . . was not a success.[76]

The four commissioners were led by Christopher William Richmond, a Supreme Court judge[77] and the Native Minister at the beginning of the 1860 war. Notoriously unsympathetic toward Māori, especially those such as Te

Rangitake Kingi who chose not to sell their land, Richmond was perhaps more than a little biased. His fellow commissioner, Frederick Edward Maning, was also a judge, but of the Native Land Court, as well as being an author. Major Te Wheoro, who had served as an assessor of the Native Land Court (1865–72), was on the Commission, as was Wiremu Mita Hikairo.

The Commission heard over 300 cases during their three-month period of operation. Even at the outset, Richmond's attitude was negative. He advised litigants that the Commission was an investigatory body, without jurisdiction to alter Native Land Court findings. In his joint report (he and Maning filed a separate report to their Maori colleagues) he found that payments were not only adequate, but that no fraudulent practices were revealed. The report was, however, critical of one aspect of the land transactions, namely the payment of lump sums to interpreters and leading rangatira at the conclusion of a sale. Clearly, interpreters and chiefs in some instances were working for the buyers, and this was undoubtedly detrimental to the interests of Māori sellers.[78]

Ann Parsonson attributes the organization of the Repudiation movement to the Ngāti Kahungunu chief, Karaitiana Takamoana,[79] although initially his enmity with Henare Matua had found him opposed to the movement.[80] A senior rangatira among the Ngāti Te Whatuiapiti, Karaitiana had close links to Rangitāne through his father, Tini-ki-runga.[81] Eventually the two were reconciled sufficiently for Matua to second Karaitiana as candidate for the Eastern Māori electorate during the 1876 elections. Karaitiana was returned and held the seat until his death at Napier on 24 February 1879.

The Repudiation movement was to eventually join with other pan-tribal movements in an effort to further advance their goals. Unimpressed with the existing European political base, they formed the Pāremata Māori together with the Tiriti o Waitangi movement which developed in Te Taitokerau, and the Kotahitanga movement of the East Coast.

Te Tiriti o Waitangi

The rangatira of Ngāpuhi also sought to create a united structure in their region. In 1875 the wharenui, Te Tiriti o Waitangi, was opened at Waitangi in the Bay of Islands, signalling their commitment to ensuring that their rangatiratanga, as guaranteed by the Treaty of Waitangi, would not be forgotten. Indeed, since that time, although remaining loyal to the Crown in deference to the agreement made by their tipuna, the movement has continued to seek ratification of the Treaty. The wharenui was erected as a meeting place to host annual hui on 6 February. At these meetings rangatira discuss the issues facing Māori, among them the advancement of petitions regarding the Treaty.

Early in 1869, a large hui was held in the King Country at Tokangamutu, where Kīngitanga leaders assembled to discuss their postwar policy.[82] Also in attendance were the so-called 'kūpapa' leaders Mātene Te Whiwhi, Tamihana Te Rauparaha, Paora Tuhaere, and Hone Mohi Tawhai. These four men had attended the hui to arrange a reconciliation between the Crown and the King movement; they unfortunately failed. Consequently they circulated a letter among ngā rangatira o Aotearoa advocating a reconvening of the Kohimārama conference, and both Te Rauparaha and Tuhaere petitioned Parliament toward the same end. Among the reasons put forward to justify this course of action was the need to rely upon both the Treaty as signed in 1840 and the subsequent Kawenata that emerged from the Kohimārama conference of 1860 as the basis for Māori participation in governmental activities. Another powerful argument, which also persists to this day, was the need to improve consultative mechanisms between iwi and the State.

Although government sanction was not obtained for such a gathering, Paora Tuhaere hosted what is remembered (in their tradition) as the first Māori Parliament in 1879. Over 300 people, mainly from Ngāpuhi, Ngāti Whātua, and other northern tribes, attended this gathering which was held over nine days. The principal topic of discussion was the Treaty, its meaning, and its effects on Māori. The Tiriti o Waitangi parliaments were again hosted at Orakei, Auckland, in March 1880 and March 1881, where broader issues pertaining to Māori participation in government and changes in Crown policy were also discussed. The Declaration of Independence (1835) was also raised for discussion at these hui, and it was argued that the legislative provisions contained in that document, together with its incorporation into the Treaty of Waitangi, were in fact a constitutional validation of their parliament.[83]

Tiriti movement hui were subsequently held further north in Ngāpuhi territory between 1881 and 1890. A new, larger meeting-house, also called Te Tiriti o Waitangi, was opened in 1881, specifically to host these hui.[84] The movement established links with southern tribes, tribal confederations, and kotahitanga movements, mainly through the good offices of Tamati Hirini Taiwhanga.[85]

By 1888, hui were being held at Waitangi in the north, at Waiomatatini on the East Coast, at Putiki near Whanganui, and at Omāhu in Heretaunga. Encouraged by a renewed relaxation in land legislation whereby a return to individual purchase arrangements was enacted (specifically the Native Lands Act 1888), rangatira Māori strove earnestly towards the ideal of kotahitanga.

The infrastructure and goals of the Te Taitokerau Kotahitanga movement coalesced at a hui at Omanaia between 15–17 May 1890. At that and earlier hui a petition to the Crown to honour the Treaty was circulated. The

Table 3: Resolutions of Te Kotahitanga o Te Tiriti o Waitangi

1.	Get those present to add names to the roll under the mana of: The Declaration of Independence The Treaty of Waitangi Section 71 of the 1852 Constitution Act.
2.	Broaden membership go include the Māori Members of Parliament, as representative of Te Waipounamu, and others in the movement.
3.	Rejection of Māori Land Court and its laws by the movement. Give Māori Committees the power to deal with land issues.
4, 5.	Deal with other court-related matters.
6.	Voting areas were established. Eight districts: two for Muriwhenua, two for the area Auckland to Wellington, two for the area Auckland to Wairārapa, two for the area Whakatu to Oraka. Twelve members for each district—ninety-six in total.
7.	June 1, 1892 was to be the day for the voting. The first hui of Māori Parliament was to fall on June 14, 1892, at Heretaunga in the Hawke's Bay (Hakapei). The issues of 1. The Treaty and 2. Section 71 Constitution Act, 1852: section 71 would be dealt with there. The ritenga for the kotahitanga would also be established at that hui. Direction for the Māori Members of Parliament electorate would also be covered.
8.	This section laid out the electoral boundaries and the number of members in fine detail.

Declaration of Independence and reference to section 71 of the Constitution Act 1852 were also included in what came to be referred to as a roll.

On 14 April 1892, a further meeting was held at Te Tiriti o Waitangi meeting house at Pewhairangi in the Bay of Islands at which a committee of eighteen was established to work through the details of structural organization and the election of representatives for the first sitting of the Māori Parliament. Its members were Meiha Keepa (Chairman), Tunuiarangi Mangakahia, Hoani Nahe, Peni Teuamairangi, Wi Pere, Timoti Whiua, Re Te Tai, Hemi Tupe, Wiki Tewhai, Hare Reweti, Poata Uruamo, Iraia Kuao, Netana Patuawa, Hone Ngapua, Riwi Taikawa, Eramiha Paikea, and Mitai Titore. Table 3 is derived from a translation of the report of their deliberations.[86]

This hui was well attended, with representatives present from nearly all iwi.[87] Over a thousand individuals and more than fifty notable rangatira were involved. The need for a small working party to retire within the whare to conduct its deliberations is obvious. Heta Te Hāra, as 'Timuaki o te Tiriti o Waitangi' welcomed those attending.

As indicated in the above notes, the Pāremata Māori had structural similarities with the colonial system, and the first sitting, Te Nohonga Tuatahi o te Pāremata Māori o Niu Tireni, was held at Waipatu in the

Hawke's Bay on 14 June 1892. The election of members by district had been conducted between the 6th and the 14th of that month. In all, ninety-three names appear in the minutes of the inaugural assembly: twenty-eight from Te Pōti a Ngāpuhi, eighteen from Te Tai Hauauru, thirty-eight from Te Tai Rawhiti (no names are recorded for the Tūhoe delegates), and nine from Te Waipounamu.[88]

The inaugural assembly was impressive, both in its attendance and its adherence to ritual, both spiritual and temporal.[89] Four items, decided upon at the Tiriti o Waitangi hui, were introduced by Hoani Piwaka during his opening karakia and sermon. These were:

1. ko te rūnanga whiriwhiri o te tau 1835
2. ko te Tiriti o Waitangi 1840
3. ko te rarangi 71 o te ture nui mo Nui Tireni o te tau 1852
4. kia kaua e tupu ake he raruraru i waenganui onga iwi o Nui Tireni.[90]

Other agenda items included an election of officers and the establishment of a Rūnanga Ariki[91] that paralleled the Upper House imported from the Westminster model and comprised of forty-four senior rangatira. The officers elected that day appear in Table 4.

Meetings of the Pāremata were held at various venues in the North Island, including Waipatu in Heretaunga, Rotorua Nui a Kāhu, but were eventually centralized at Papawai Marae in the Wairārapa in 1897. During its eleven years of operation, the Pāremata Māori debated many issues which related to the relationship between the Crown and iwi. Indeed, the bulk of its work lay in this area.[92] Matters of land alienation remained a prominent item on the agenda, and the position of Māori electorates was also debated. Opinion ranged from seeking to have Māori Members of Parliament being responsible solely to the Pāremata and thus enabling them to work for the body, to having them removed altogether as they might be seen as providing Māori affirmation of government policy initiatives. A further body of opinion held that their numbers should be increased.

Table 4: Inaugural office holders, Pāremata Māori, 1892

Position	Holder	Iwi/Rohe
Tiamana (Leader)	H.T. Te Whatahoro	Kahungunu/Wairārapa
Pika (Speaker)	Henare Toamoana	Kahungunu/Ahuriri
Pirimia (Premier)	Hamiora Mangakahia	Ngāti Wanaua/Whitianga
Minita (Minister)	Raniera Wharerau	Ngāpuhi/Waima
Minita (Minister)	Mitaititore	Ngāpuhi/Mangakahia
Minita (Minister)	Timoti Te Whiu	Ngāi Tahu/Wairewa

Figure 7: Hone Heke (date unknown) *(Courtesy of Alexander Turnbull Library)*

Responding to and initiating demands for a separate Māori Parliament came to dominate Pāremata agendas. It was felt that a validation from the Crown was necessary, and accordingly a number of petitions and bills were tabled in the Pākehā Parliament to achieve this goal. Hone Heke, grandnephew of the famous northern leader and Member for the Northern Māori electorate, was to table one such bill.

The Native Rights Bill 1894 (see Appendix Five) sought jurisdiction over members of the Māori race and their offspring, to be vested in a duly elected Māori Parliament. The right to investigate and adjudicate upon land grievances was also sought in the bill. It was, however, rejected by the House after European Members of Parliament refused to debate it and walked out of the House, and proceedings were adjourned due to the lack of a quorum.[93]

The Pāremata Māori validated its own position by reference to the Treaty of Waitangi, the Declaration of Independence, and the Constitution Act 1852. It was a wholly Māori body established by Māori to further Māori

Figure 8: Papawai Pa, Greytown (date unknown) *(Courtesy of the S. C. Smith Collection, Alexander Turnbull Library)*

political ambitions, and had a firm iwi base. As such, it represented a coalition of the rangatiratanga of Aotearoa and Te Waipounamu, and could most properly exercise Mana Māori Motuhake for and on behalf of tribes. It did not, however, embrace the other major Māori political movement, the Kīngitanga. While both organizations sought to unite Māori, neither was prepared to accommodate the other in all aspects, and thus chose to remain aloof. Although representatives of the King movement eventually attended Pāremata hui, the Kīngitanga as a body remained apart from it.

It is the contention of this book that, even though absolute unity was not achieved through the Māori Parliament, it was a useful forum through which to harness the diversity of Māori opinion, talent, and authority, and thus influence the Crown. The seeds of its demise were its preoccupation with its own extra-legal status, rather than the conflict with the Kīngitanga. Whilst suggestions based on hindsight are neither subject to validation nor possible to implement, it is asserted that much greater benefit for Māori and for the nation would have accrued if the Pāremata Māori had accepted its own mandate as adequate and concentrated upon concrete issues rather than the abstractions of Pākehā law.

Endnotes

1.   Essentially, this whakatauki speaks of the strength which accrues through the incorporation of many dimensions; it adds an admonition to be charitable, uphold the law, and remain faithful.

2.   Wards, I. M., (1968), *The Shadow of the Land: A Study Of British Policy and Racial Conflict in New Zealand 1832–1852*, Historical Publications Branch, Department of Internal Affairs, Wellington, pp. 2–3.

3.   Adams, P., (1977), *Fatal Necessity: British Intervention in New Zealand 1830–1847*, Auckland University Press/Oxford University Press, Auckland, p. 20, paragraph 2, provides excellent illustrations of this, although the perspective is the European one.

4.   Ibid, pp. 75–7.

5.   P. Tremewan, (1990), *French Akaroa*, parts 1 and 2, University of Canterbury Press, Christchurch.

6.   C. Orange (1987), *The Treaty of Waitangi*, Allen and Unwin/Port Nicholson, Wellington, p. 20. The flag was white with a red St George's Cross and a blue field with a red cross and four eight-pointed white stars in the upper left-hand corner. It measured 16' x 10', flew on ships commissioned in New Zealand, and was the flag of the 'United Tribes'.

7.   Ibid, p. 21.

8.   Self-styled King of Nuku Hiva, de Theirry announced his intention of claiming his New Zealand estate. A body of historical opinion maintains that Busby overdramatized this threat in order to promote his own plans for Aotearoa.

9.   See Orange, *op cit.*, p. 14, and K. Sinclair, (1991), *A History of New Zealand*, 4th edn, Penguin, Auckland, p. 56. General Sir Richard Bourke succeeded Darling as Governor of New South Wales.

10.   J. O. Ross, (1980), 'Busby and the Declaration of Independence', *New Zealand Journal of History*, 14: 85. Much useful discussion on the underlying causes of this document and of its constitutional significance is contained in this essay.

11.   Orange, *op cit.*, p. 21, quotes from *Facsimiles of the Declaration of Independence and the Treaty of Waitangi* (1877, reprint Government Printer, 1976—original in National Archives, Wellington); see Appendix One.

12.   Ross, *op cit.*, p. 84.

13.   Ibid, pp. 86–8.

14.   Not published, but made available to the author through personal contacts. This document makes reference to assertions which ought to be researched by an impartial agent. That history looks different to the parties concerned is without doubt. Similarly, Europeans would favour a view based upon their sources.

15.   Ross, *op cit*, p. 85, 'uncharacteristic haste'.

16.   See Chapter 3.

17.   Sione Latukefu, (1970), 'King George Tupou I of Tonga', in J. W. Davidson and D. Scarr (eds), *Pacific Island Portraits*, A. H. and A. W. Reed, Wellington, pp. 55–6.

18.   See discussion on sovereignty in 'Introduction'.

19.   See M. King, (1977), *Te Puea: A Biography*, Hodder and Stoughton, Auckland, p. 24, footnote §, for a discussion on the accuracy of this date.

20.   See footnote 7 above.

21.   P. Te Hurinui, (1959), *King Potatau: An Account of the Life of Potatau Te Wherowhero the First Māori King*, Polynesian Society/Roydhouse, Carterton, p. 183.

22. Kelly, (1942), p. 430. Te Hurinui, *op cit.*, (1959), p. 183 explains that Piri Kawau (sometimes recorded as Pirikawau) was present during this interview and relayed the idea in a letter to Wi Tako.

23. J. Te H. Grace, (1959), *Tuwharetoa: The History of the Māori People of the Taupo District*, A. H. and A. W. Reed, Auckland, p. 443.

24. Son of the powerful Ngāti Toa leader, Te Rauparaha, and of Akau (Tuhourangi), he was known as Katu until baptized Tamihana on 21 March 1841 by Octavius Hadfield. He left for England in December 1850 and returned in 1852: W. H. Oliver (ed), (1990), *The Dictionary of New Zealand Biography*, Bridget Williams/Department of Internal Affairs, Wellington, T75, pp. 507–8.

25. His mother was Rangi Toperoa (Ngāti Toa and Ngāti Raukawa), a signatory to the Treaty of Waitangi (14 May 1840), and sister to Te Rangihaeata. Their mother, Waitohi, was a sister of Te Rauparaha, Tamihana's father. Matene's father was Rangikapiki (Te Arawa); see *The Dictionary of New Zealand Biography, op cit.*, T89, pp. 528–9 and T103, pp. 546–7.

26. J. A. Mackay, (1949), *Historic Poverty Bay and the East Coast, NI, NZ: A Centennial Memorial*, J. G. Mackay, Gisborne, p. 211.

27. Kelly, (1942), *op cit.*, pp. 431–2, gives a detailed account of his efforts and receptions.

28. P. Te Hurinui Jones, (1968), 'Māori Kings', in Schwimmer, *op cit.*, p. 133; and Kelly, (1942), *op cit.*, p. 431.

29. These two whakapapa experts were close relatives of Moātene Te Whiwhi; Jones, ibid., p. 133.

30. King, (1977), *op cit.*, p. 22.

31. Grace, *op cit.*, p. 445.

32. James Cowan, (1922), *The New Zealand Wars: A History of the Maori Campaigns and the Pioneer Period*, (1983 edn), Government Printer, Wellington, 1: 150.

33. D. M. Stafford, (1967), *Te Arawa: A History of the Arawa People*, Reed, Auckland, p. 347, records that Timoti was the only Te Arawa chief to sign the Treaty.

34. Grace, *op cit.*, pp. 238–9: when refusing to sign Mananui said, 'Hau wahine e hoki i te hau o Tāwhaki', his mana would not be subsumed to that of a woman, however exalted she may be.

35. Hikurangi is not a mountain that moves.

36. I am already a king because of my ancestry.

37. Kelly, (1949), p. 431.

38. Evelyn Stokes, in *The Dictionary of New Zealand Biography, op cit.*, T82: 515–18. Rangianewa was a younger sister to Te Kahurangi, wife of Tuata and mother of Te Rauanganga.

39. L. S. Rickard, (1963), *Tamihana, The Kingmaker*, A. H. and A. W. Reed, Wellington, pp. 70–1.

40. Te Hurinui (1959), *op cit.*, p. 196, which is translated as 'search the land, search the sea'. J. E. Gorst (1864), *The Maori King, or, The Story of Our Quarrel with the Natives of New Zealand* 1975 edn, Capper Press, Christchurch, p. 83, gives 1600 as the attendance figure for this hui. This is the name of the pataka which Te Heuheu Iwikau opened at Pukawa at the time of this hui.

41. This date, November 1856, given by Jones, *op cit.*, p. 133, and by King, (1977), *op cit.*, p. 23, is at variance with those recorded by Gorst, *op cit*, p. 83, Cowan, *op cit.*, p. 151, and Stafford, *op cit.*, pp. 347–8, who give 1857 as the year of this hui.

42. For an account of his individual prowess at arms, see Te Hurinui, *op cit.*, pp. 102–

4. Accounts of his generalship occupy several chapters of this book, especially chapters 4 and 5. Te Rauangaanga is covered in the opening chapters.

43. Jones, *op cit.*, p. 132, provides a rich biographical account.

44. The wife of King Koroki Te Rata Mahuta Tawhiao Potatau was also Te Atairangikahu.

45. Rickard, *op cit.*, p. 74, relates an incident where Tamihana placed two sticks in the ground to symbolize the King and the Governor, with a third stick above representing the Law of God. A circle embracing all three was significant of the mana of Queen Victoria.

46. Te Hurinui, *op cit.*, p. 276. A term of two years would be more accurate if one accepts the 1858 date for the coronation.

47. Ibid, p. 131. Te Ua Haumene established the Pai Marire religion and is seen as a Hauhau prophet. Baptized in the Weslyan Church as Horopapera (Zerubbabel) Tuwhakarao, he took the name Te Ua Haumene in 1864 until his death four years later. The name Tawhiao means, literally, 'encircle the world', and was an exhortation to him to keep the people together. See also *The Dictionary of New Zealand Biography, op cit.*, T79: 511–13.

48. B. Elsmore, (1989), *Mana from Heaven*, Moana Press, Tauranga, p. 191.

49. *The Dictionary of New Zealand Biography*, *op cit.*, T79: 511.

50. Cowan, *op cit.*, 2: 3.

51. *The Dictionary of New Zealand Biography*, *op cit.*, T78: 510–11.

52. Wiremu Kingi Te Rangitake's opposition to the sale of a block of Te Āti Awa land is perhaps the best-known instance.

53. K. Sinclair, (1991), *Kinds of Peace: Maori People After the Wars, 1870–85*, Auckland University Press, Auckland, pp. 40–1.

54. Volumes have been written on these conflicts and the origins of them. This book is not a suitable forum for reviewing those hostilities. See Cowan, *op cit.*, Vol I, Ch. 25–40 and Sinclair, (1957); see also Belich, (1988), *The New Zealand Wars* for a recent re-analysis.

55. A. Ward (1973), *A Show of Justice: Racial Amalgamation in Nineteenth Century New Zealand*, Auckland University Press/Oxford University Press, Auckland, p. 169.

56. Jones, *op cit.*, p. 137: 800,000 acres of land were taken. Some of the tribal territories of Major Te Wheoro's people were included because of their fertility.

57. Elsmore, *op cit.*, p. 270, and also B. Elsmore, (1985), *Like Them That Dream*, Tauranga Moana, Tauranga, pp. 129–31.

58. King, (1977), *op cit.*, p. 28; Jones, *op cit.*, p. 137.

59. Orange, (1989), p. 212.

60. King, (1977), *op cit.*, p. 28.

61. Orange (1989), *op cit.*, p. 218.

62. J. Wilson, (1990), 'The Maori Struggle for Mana Motuhake' *New Zealand Historic Places* 30, p. 27.

63. Rickard, *op cit.*, p. 177.

64. Te Hurinui, *op cit.*, pp. 231–2.

65. *Kia Hiwa Ra*, No. 1 (June 1991), p. 1.

66. R. J. Walker, (1990), *Ka Whawhai Tonou Matou: Struggle Without End*, Penguin, Auckland, p. 165. Wiremu Makura published a booklet on this hui; an attendance list of sixty-six names copied from this booklet is included as Appendix Four. This source gives 1342 as the overall number attending.

67. Grace, *op cit.*, pp. 443–4.

68.   Orange, (1987), *The Treaty of Waitangi*, Allen and Unwin/Port Nicholson Press, Wellington, p. 190.

69.   Grey's rūnanga system is covered in Chapter 3.

70.   M. P. K. Sorrenson, 'The Politics of Land', in J. G. A. Pocock (ed.), (1965), *The Maori and New Zealand Politics: Talks from an NZBC Series with Additional Essays* Blackwood and Janet Paul, Auckland, pp. 40–5: 400,000 acres of land were held by fifty run-holders.

71.   Ibid., p. 41.

72.   His brother, Andrew Hamilton Russell, was at that time Native Minister and Civil Commissioner to the Hawke's Bay, October 1865–August 1866.

73.   Sinclair, (1991), *op cit.*, p. 116.

74.   *The Dictionary of New Zealand Biography*, *op cit.*, 5: 324–5.

75.   The Hawke's Bay Native Lands Alienation Commission resulted from two petitions to Parliament in 1872.

76.   Sinclair, (1991), *op cit.*, p. 117.

77.   Richmond was later elevated to the Court of Appeal and was an original member of that Court; see *The Dictionary of New Zealand Biography*, *op cit.*, R9: 364–5.

78.   Sinclair, (1991), *op cit.*pp. 117–18. Regarding the adequacy of payments, most first buyers resold land with only a small margin—it was subsequent transactions that incurred vast profit.

79.   Ann Parsonson (1981), 'The Pursuit of Mana', in W. H. Oliver, *The Oxford History of New Zealand*, Oxford University Press, Auckland, p. 165.

80.   At a large hui in July 1872 at Pakipaki, both Karaitiana and his half brother Henare Tomoana spoke against the Repudiationists; see *The Dictionary of New Zealand Biography*, *op cit.*T5: 420.

81.   Ibid, T5: 418.

82.   Ward, *op cit.*, p. 272.

83.   Orange, (1987a), *op cit.* pp. 190–1 and p. 195; see also Ward, *op cit.*, p. 283.

84.   Ward, *op cit.*, p. 290.

85.   Taiwhanga became active in the Tiriti movement in the 1870s and is said to be the first to petition the Queen directly by travelling to London in 1882.

86.   Taken from *Ngā Korero o te hui o te Whakakotahitanga i tu ki te Tiriti o Waitangi*, Aperira 14, 1892, printed by Wiremu Makura at Auckland.

87.   An attendance list is included as Appendix 4. The recorded attendance was 1342.

88.   The minutes of this meeting were recorded and published in 1892 as *Te Nohonga Tuatahi o te Paremata Māori o Niu Tireni* by Webbe & Co of Otaki. See pages 4–5 for a list of members.

89.   See Walker, (1990), *op cit.*, pp. 166–8, for a detailed account.

90.   Wīremu Makura (April 1892), p. 7.

91.   See *Te Nohonga 1* (1892), pp. 5–7.

92.   The author was able to locate minutes from only three sittings of the Paremata Māori (one, two, and five) in the Alexander Turnbull Library. They are on microfilm and are available for interloan.

93.   Walker, (1990), *op cit.*, p. 168.

Chapter Five
He Iwi Tahi Tātou

As each of the forty-three rangatira came forward to sign the Treaty of Waitangi on 6 February 1840, Captain William Hobson greeted them with these words: 'He iwi tahi tātou: We are one people',[1] presaging the policies of assimilation and amalgamation that came to dominate race relations in Aotearoa/New Zealand.

Characteristics of Theme Two

The second theme developed to examine Māori unity is 'He Iwi Tahi Tātou'. In this theme the emphasis shifts from iwi initiative to State direction. Consistently, the Crown has sought to impose upon Māori structures which are designed to give a veneer of autonomy yet allow the State to direct and focus activity. These structures were often developed without consultation with tribal rūnanga or individual rangatira, and tended to ignore traditional boundaries, inter-tribal animosities, and Māori aspirations. In addition, the Crown continually ignored efforts on the part of Māori to develop a working relationship between the Treaty of Waitangi partners. Tamihana's appeals to the Governor to establish a Māori Council and to provide for Māori representation in the House of Representatives speak eloquently here.

The goal of unification couched under this rubric was in fact a prescription for assimilation of Māori into the predominant culture. While ostensibly designed to allow Māori a mechanism for input into the governance of the nation, or at least of their own affairs, structural impediments, economic hegemony, and colonialist policies made these new Māori arrangements a tool for the manipulation of political energies to suit State agendas. It will be shown that the acquisition of land or the control of Māori disaffection was the motivating factor which prompted these movements.

Legislation used to establish district rūnanga or Māori councils paid little attention to Māori organizational preferences, and either failed to recognize or deliberately ignored pre-existing Māori structures based not in legislation but upon tribal constructs. It has been shown, however, that in practice administrators often followed the path of least resistance and tried to adapt existing mechanisms to the new regimes. The composition of councils of this type tended to reinforce Crown favouritism. This in turn led to further undermining of traditional leadership and to an alienation of sectors of the Māori community not represented by Crown appointees. Granted, a structure which would not alienate at least one section of a given iwi or one iwi in a given rohe would be very difficult if not impossible to develop. Still, it remains unlikely that such a structure will emerge while the Crown continues to set the parameters for rūnanga, committees, and councils—most especially where this involvement includes the determination of criteria for membership and entitlement to participate.

James E. Ritchie, speaking in one of a series of radio broadcasts in 1962,[2] depicted the Dominion Council structures (Māori Women's Welfare League and New Zealand Māori Council) developed under Acts of Parliament or sponsored by departments of State as being useful primarily as mechanisms for the downward transmission of State policies. His hypothesis was that Māori political thinking and operational reality occurred principally at the grass-roots level, with a particular focus on local, or at best regional, issues. Hapū concerns and relationships with local bodies overshadowed tribal, inter-tribal, and national affairs. That may have been the case three decades ago, but the propensity for legislated national institutions to be of limited value to Māori is a function of their intent, funding, administration, and the paternalistic attitude of the Government rather than an indication of Māori political reality.

A further hallmark of attempts to unify Māori under a State-inspired agenda was the way in which Māori support has been solicited. Leaders who were prepared to cooperate with the State were chosen while those who were less amenable were ignored. To some extent that pattern has persisted: State sponsorship of a selected Māori élite which is then used to reinforce State priorities and directives, although without a wider Māori mandate.

In this theme, the Treaty of Waitangi, if it was referred to at all, became the justification for assimilationist policies. At the expense of the guarantee of tino rangatiratanga in Article II, Articles I and III were emphasized. The right of the State to rule and the equality of individuals under the law were promoted as being in the best interests of Māori. Indeed, the Treaty itself, with its promises of State protection and citizenship, provided both a rationale and a vehicle for State intervention in Māori affairs.

If Māori sovereignty was ever a threat, and there is evidence that it often was, then Crown-inspired Māori Councils were created to undermine that burgeoning sovereignty. Just as the Treaty of Waitangi might be seen as an alternative to the 1835 Declaration of Independence, the 1900 Māori Councils Act was conveniently timed to detract from the operation of the

Pāremata Māori established in 1892[3] and to effectively neutralize it.

The theme 'He Iwi Tahi Tātou' is best illustrated by reference to three structures appearing to reinforce Māori authority, but remaining very much creatures of State initiative and control: rūnanga established in 1861 by Governor Grey; the network of Māori councils provided for by the Māori Councils Act 1900; and the New Zealand Māori Council structure which developed under the Māori Social and Economic Advancement Act 1945 and the Māori Welfare Act 1962.

To preface the discussion of the 1861 rūnanga system, some brief comments on the Government-sponsored inter-tribal conference held at Kohimārama will be made. A limited review of the Young Māori Party (YMP) which emerged just prior to 1900 will provide a context for the first Māori councils legislation, while the significance of the Māori War Effort Organisation that operated during World War II will precede the third case study.

The Kohimārama Conference, 1860

Governor Thomas Gore-Browne (1807–87) arrived in New Zealand to succeed Grey in 1855, but was removed from office in mid-1861. He was charged with increasing settler participation in government, but was reluctant to share control with Māori, despite section 73 of the Constitution Act 1852. He focused instead upon the establishment, structuring, and election of a General Assembly.

His miscalculation of Wiremu Kingi, Te Rangitake, and the Waitara situation led to armed confrontation in Taranaki. His Imperial troops proved unable to deal with the matter efficiently, and to avoid further escalation of hostilities he organized a national conference of rangatira. Had the conflict deepened to include other iwi, the consequences may have been fatal to the colony, so, in an attempt to allay Māori suspicions and to diffuse the growing unrest over land alienation, he invited rangatira from all parts of the island to assemble at Kohimārama on the Waitemata (Auckland) on 6 July 1860.[4] Whilst influenza caused some notable leaders to be absent, representation was nearly universal—the major exceptions being the disaffected leaders of the Waikato and of Taranaki.

The conference, ostensibly convened to discuss the Treaty of Waitangi, was, after a month of deliberation at the Crown's expense, presented (10 August 1860) with seven resolutions for ratification (Appendix Three). These resolutions were strongly supportive of Government policies, and critical of both the Kīngitanga movement and the war in Taranaki. While they did receive the affirmation of the hui, some question regarding the unanimity of understanding among chiefs was raised.[5] It must also be noted that Wīremu Tamihana Te Neke, Te Manihera Matangi, and Epiha Karoro objected to Resolution Three which sought to justify Governor Gore-Browne's action in Taranaki, and went so far as to state that it was Te Rangitake who had initiated the conflict.

The first resolution was an express reaffirmation of the Queen's sovereignty in New Zealand and a pledge to act consistently with that undertaking. The second was a denunciation of the King movement as 'an institution which has brought trouble to the country'. As stated, Resolution Three was critical of the war in Taranaki and apportioned blame for that encounter to Wīremu Kingi Te Rangitake. The fourth statement deprecated the murders of innocent European settlers, while the fifth was an expression of gratitude to the Bishop of New Zealand for hosting the hui. Gratitude to Governor Gore-Browne was expressed in Resolution Six, and Resolution Seven was a recognition of the role played by Sir Donald McLean on behalf of Māori. By and large, the thrust of the resolutions was to establish support for the Crown.

The threat of concerted Māori action, perhaps under the leadership of the new Māori King, Tāwhiao Mātutaera Pōtatatau Te Wherowhero (1825–94), who sought a moratorium on further land sales and who supported the struggles of Wīremu Kingi on the West Coast, provided the catalyst for these talks. Gore-Browne could not hope to contain a general uprising of Māori and so sought to alienate rebellious iwi through a renewed commitment to the Treaty from the other tribes.

As Ranginui Walker points out,[6] Māori leaders failed to obtain a reciprocal undertaking from the Crown to uphold the Treaty, and while rangatira may have increased their understanding of the document and its original intentions, their adoption of it as a Kawenata in no way improved their position. Partnership and the veil of unity were once again employed to diffuse Māori initiatives for the maintenance of Māori sovereignty and for the implementation of the guarantees under Article Two of the Treaty.

One significant outcome of this conference was that tribes who had not signed the Treaty (for example, Te Arawa) were now covered by its mantle.[7] Doubts as to their allegiance could be set aside, and the Governor might now direct his attention to the 'rebels'. Another important outcome, at least for Māori, was the affirmation of Māori support for the Treaty, now recognized as an important agreement between iwi and the Crown: an agreement which could be used to support Māori aspirations for equality. Paora Tuhaere of Ngāti Whātua had during his whaikorero emphasized that the 1840 gathering at Waitangi was regionally unrepresentative. Sir Donald McLean, who presided at Kohimārama, used this to develop the notion of a fuller ratification of the Treaty which was expressed as the first Resolution of the hui.[8]

Figure 9: Paora Tuhaere (date unknown; *Courtesy of the National Museum, Wellington*)

Despite Governor Gore-Browne's intention to convene a further Kohimārama-style meeting of rangatira,[9] his dismissal and replacement by Sir George Grey precluded a further gathering. Grey also stifled the Native

Councils Bill 1860 which proposed a permanent advisory council of rangatira and leading colonists. His view was that these two structures, should they become permanent features of New Zealand's political reality, would diminish Māori preparedness to accept the edicts of central government and lessen Māori loyalty to Parliament. Grey, like Hobson before him, saw an agenda of amalgamation as appropriate and instituted his rūnanga scheme to achieve that goal.

Tamihana Te Rauparaha wrote to both William Fox and Sir Donald McLean on 20 July 1869 urging that a second Kohimārama conference would not only be welcome, but necessary for the national well-being. Paora Tuhaere of Orakei made a similar call in December of the same year. The inadequacy of the four Māori seats to represent iwi views in the House of Representatives was among the reasons put forward for a second conference.

Grey's Rūnanga System

The principal goal early in Governor Sir George Grey's second term as Governor of New Zealand (June 1861–68), indeed the reason for his recall from South Africa, was the pacification of 'rebellious' Māori tribes. The hard line adopted by Governor Gore-Browne in regard to the Tainui peoples of the Waikato was judged to be imprudent and unlikely to lead to either a speedy or an inexpensive resolution to the recent disturbances in New Zealand.[10] The potential for a duplication of the Taranaki affair in the Waikato was sufficient for the Colonial Office to remove Gore-Browne and recall Grey. The earlier harmonious relationship that Grey enjoyed with Māori leaders like Pōtatau Te Wherowhero was sufficient for the then Secretary of State for Colonies, the Duke of Newcastle, to reappoint him as Governor. As well as the need to maintain pax Britannica, the appropriation of Māori land for supply to the steady influx of British settlers was an underlying motive for quelling Māori unrest.

Unlike earlier governors, Grey had taken the time to acquaint himself not only with Māori language and tradition,[11] but also with the customary style of tribal administration. Knowing the propensity for Māori to come together and debate the issues which faced the hapū or the iwi, he devised a mechanism to adapt the Māori structures to serve State-driven purposes. His experience in South Africa, where he had investigated a system of chiefly councils, was valuable in this regard. Grey was reluctant to either action Gore-Browne's intention to convene a second national conference of chiefs based on the Kohimārama model or to take further the notion of an advisory body as prescribed in the Native Council Bill 1860.[12]

Thus, in an effort to control and direct Māori, an elaborate system of local and regional rūnanga was implemented. The 1858 Native District Regulation Act, which allowed for the creation of native districts wherein the Governor could make specific laws with the consent of Māori, provided Grey with a suitable vehicle for this purpose.[13]

At the national level, twenty districts were proposed under the plan devised by Grey, the Premier William Fox, Attorney-General Henry Sewell, and Francis Dart Fenton. Each of the new Māori districts were in areas where Māori predominated. They were to operate under the auspices of European district commissioners and were tasked with rather mundane administrative matters. The local component of the system was embodied in the form of 'Hundreds'.[14] Six Hundreds per district was seen as an optimum number. Each Hundred was to select two representatives, to be known as native magistrates, who as a group would form the district rūnanga.

At the village level, resident magistrates[15] were to convene village rūnanga to administer local affairs.[16] These rūnanga would feed into the Hundreds system in a hierarchical pattern that came to be a hallmark of State attempts to regulate Māori affairs (see Figure 10).

The District Regulation Act was supplemented by the Native Circuit Courts Act 1858 which provided for the appointment of Native Circuit Court judges who were to be advised by Māori assessors and juries and were to enforce by-laws passed by rūnanga on matters of local importance. While in practice assessors and native magistrates were on occasion the same persons, it was intended that a separation of powers would be effected. Those who legislated ought not adjudicate. The Māori officers would have a limited independence with powers to hear cases where the maximum penalty did not exceed £5.[17] The areas of jurisdiction allocated to the assessors, to the resident magistrates, and to the rūnanga, included fencing, stock trespass, sobriety—or rather the lack of it, common nuisance, and, most importantly, title to land.[18] When a land interest, determined by the rūnanga, was confirmed by the allocation of a Crown grant, the land was then available for disposal to Europeans. The rūnanga could authorize this transfer, thus expediting Grey's task of acquiring land for settlement. Alan Ward further clarifies this feature of the new land acquisition scheme, stating that the

> . . . proposal envisaged the preservation of corporate tribal authority over land, during both the determination of title and alienation. It therefore contrasted with the alternative view . . . that Māori title should be individualised as quickly as possible . . .

Figure 10: Flow diagram of the 1861 Rūnanga scheme

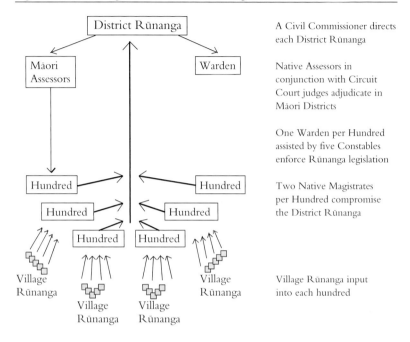

A Civil Commissioner directs each District Rūnanga

Native Assessors in conjunction with Circuit Court judges adjudicate in Māori Districts

One Warden per Hundred assisted by five Constables enforce Rūnanga legislation

Two Native Magistrates per Hundred compromise the District Rūnanga

Village Rūnanga input into each hundred

In all, eight civil commissioners and twenty-two resident magistrates were appointed.[19] A policing system was also contained in the plan. To overcome the inherent difficulties of enforcing law in native districts, each Hundred was to have its own Māori police. Headed by a warden, several constables (called Karere) would be allocated to each Hundred. Uniforms (boots, blue coats, and trousers) and salaries were to be provided from central government. Wardens, whose uniforms included caps with gold braid, were remunerated to the sum of £20 each year while Karere received £10.[20]

Te Taitokerau District Rūnanga

The first district rūnanga was established in Te Taitokerau at Waimate on 25 March 1862.[21] It is significant that this region was chosen for the inaugural district rūnanga, as it was the area of earliest sustained contact and therefore most influence by European colonization. Willingness on the part of Māori to accept the new institutions was crucial to their operation. The relatively calm northern districts were therefore an ideal location for introducing the programme.

Ostensibly at the behest of Tamati Waka Nene, 500 rangatira representing

Figure 11: Tamati Waka Nene (date unknown; *Courtesy of the National Museum*)

the major hapū of the Ngāpuhi confederation were assembled to discuss the new policy. Although approval was sought from the gathering for the membership of the rūnanga, the appointees were selected by the Crown and limited in number. The names of ten appointees were tabled for approval, with a further two to be selected later by the rūnanga. They were provided with a clear set of guidelines for the conduct of the first hui of the rūnanga, which included standing orders and resolutions by which the right to make war was removed and the mana of Crown control was firmly ensconced. Although the conduct of the first day of the meeting was distinctly Māori in format, it was driven by an agenda distinctly colonial in outlook. Indeed, the Governor's consent was sought before a transcript of the proceedings of the hui could be printed. The second and subsequent days of the hui were considerably more European in style, and were minuted and required the formal adoption of motions in the conduct of its business.

The rūnanga was empowered to pass Acts, regulations, and by-laws that would assist the Civil Commissioner and the magistrates of the district, and to appoint officers (wardens and assessors) to ensure adherence to enactments. This seemingly liberal approach to Native Affairs was tempered by powers given to the civil commissioner of each district who was to direct rūnanga activities. Further, the consent of the Governor in Council was necessary for approval of legislation framed by rūnanga. The bulk of its brief was to determine and settle disputes of title to land. A government grant of £100 was made to fund the operation of the rūnanga; further funds were to be raised by that body for the conduct of its affairs.[22]

It was for the rūnanga to decide where and when it would meet and to establish suitable accommodation for itself. These appear to be the only matters left fully to the discretion of Māori—all others were prescribed by the State. The Crown sought to control Māori through their traditional leaders by delegating a semblance of authority while hampering their efforts through fiscal and procedural restraints. That this was to be an effective stratagem is manifest in its recurrence at various stages throughout the course of the nation's history.

The ten rangatira named for the inaugural district rūnanga were Tamati Waka Nene, Maihi Paraone Kawiti, Arama Karaka Pi, Aperehama Taonui, Rangatira Moetara, Wiremu Hau, Hemi Marupo, Hira Mura Te Awa, and Kingi Wīremu Tareha. These men attended the first official hui of the rūnanga, while the tenth member, Hare Hongi Hika, joined them for the second day's debate.

Standing Orders

A set of standing orders was supplied to the rūnanga for the conduct of its business. Similar in form and function to those used by most English-speaking committees of the time, they comprised a set of guidelines by which the President was to direct meetings. He was to resolve issues not covered by the standing orders and to decide upon matters of order. Speakers were required to address issues to him and were allowed only one opportunity to speak on each issue. The reading of the prayer appointed for the rūnanga was to precede the reading and confirmation of minutes. Meeting days (Mondays, Tuesdays, Wednesdays, and Fridays), commencement times (10.00 a.m.), and matters relating to quorum requirements (six) and procedures were all included. A requirement to second motions before debate and the process for putting notices of motion were also stipulated in the orders. Acts, regulations, and by-laws were first to be read and then to be 'considered in detail, in committee of the whole House'. A mechanism for altering the standing orders was also provided.

The operation of this rūnanga, and perhaps of others, was in the initial stages complicated by considerations of individual mana. Native magistrates were ever mindful of their relationship to other rangatira of the rūnanga, and some considerable time was devoted to issues of rank.[23] As the system developed in the north, another difficulty arose. While rangatira were prepared to conclude discussions and produce legislation, it was not always possible to bind them to it once they left the rūnanga hui.[24]

The Effectiveness of the Rūnanga System

Grey's new approach to the management of tribal affairs met with some success amongst the northern tribes. Regular meetings were convened by Civil Commissioner W. B. White at Mangonui and by George Clarke, formerly the Chief Protector of Aborigines, at Waimate. Laws enacted by these rūnanga were gazetted. Hone Wetere, writing in the bilingual newspaper *Te Karere: The Māori Messenger* regarding a hui held at Kāwhia on 14 March 1862 reported unanimous support for both Governor Grey and for the introduction of the rūnanga system. The region was, however, twice embroiled in armed territorial disputes.

The first involved a long-standing animosity between two leading men, and was to draw Arama Karaka Pi, himself a member of the rūnanga, into the conflict. Although his action evoked pronouncements from settlers on the futility of attempting to impose the rule of law upon Māori without military intervention, his position could be justified. His father had twenty years earlier been killed by one of the belligerents and he was bound by tradition and filial loyalty to obtain revenge and honour. The case was ultimately determined by a panel of rangatira in Auckland. The second case, however, might be seen as validating the rūnanga scheme.

An area of land was occupied under arms by two opposing factions in the

Hokianga. The resident magistrate, James Clendon, convinced the principals to submit the case to the district rūnanga for its judgment. The men agreed and subsequently the matter was settled without violence—the successful aggrieved party trusting the system to uphold his claim should any further animosity arise. That incident provided a useful precedent for dispute resolution under the new institutions. Had it been repeated in other areas, it may have provided a model for effective participation by Māori in local affairs despite the inherent limitations of an adversarial dispute-resolution mechanism. It was unfortunately an isolated case.[25]

In other districts matters did not proceed as smoothly. The district boundaries were oriented toward efficient Pākehā administration and tended to ignore tribal territories. Erstwhile antagonists were amalgamated in heterogeneous groupings and, because of the limited membership of each rūnanga, representatives from important iwi were occasionally omitted. At Mangonui, W. B. White overcame the problem to some extent by allowing rangatira who were not appointed to the rūnanga to take part in its activities, but without voting rights.

In the Waikato, where Tamihana had been developing an indigenous rūnanga system for the administration of tribal affairs and where the mana of Tāwhiao dispensed justice, Grey's rūnanga were less than effective. John Eldon Gorst, author of *The Māori King* and publisher of *Te Pihoihoi Mokemoke i Runga i te Tuanui*[26] was appointed civil commissioner and resident magistrate in the Waikato above Taupiri in 1861.[27] (James Armitage held the post in the lower Waikato.) Gorst's attempts to curry favour with the less volatile supporters of the King movement during his term in office were offset by his tendency to aggravate less moderate leaders. Rewi Maniapoto,[28] convinced of the Government's intention to undermine traditional Māori leadership, and displeased with articles printed in *Te Pihoihoi Mokemoke*, led a raid on his office at Otawhao in March 1863. Gorst's expulsion was the end of the Crown's district rūnanga system in the Waikato. Even during the Civil Commissioner's term in office, many Waikato hapū, particularly those affiliated to Ngāti Maniapoto, remained suspicious of the system and, like the Taranaki tribes, refused to cooperate. While some younger, ambitious chiefs who were yet to assume positions of authority may have been willing to accept positions of assessors under Gorst or Armitage, the indigenous rūnanga would not sanction such action.

In Hawke's Bay, the office was held by Colonel Andrew Hamilton Russell, the brother of Henry Robert Russell, who later aided Henare Matua and the Repudiation Party.[29] Distrust of the court system among the Ngāti Kahungunu, and growing concern over land issues in the Bay, created an atmosphere of non-cooperation. Chiefs, led by Te Hapūku, although outwardly compliant, persistently resisted the formation of a district rūnanga.[30]

Edward Shortland, a former Sub-Protector of Aborigines, was appointed civil commissioner to Waihou in Hauraki on 30 December 1862, a position he held until his promotion to Native Secretary on 14 August 1863.[31] Like the other commissioners, he was given the task of improving relations between Māori and the settler government, and of fostering confidence in British rule.

The Taupō position was filled by the Otawhao Mission teacher, G. Law, after a recommendation by a local rangatira, Te Poihipi, who was a political rival of the paramount chief Te Heuheu Iwikau. Consequently, his title and authority meant little outside Te Poihipi's sphere of influence on the northern shores of Lake Taupō.[32]

At the Bay of Plenty, Thomas Henry Smith, who had a long association with the Te Arawa peoples, was appointed civil commissioner.[33] He was at one time (1843–46) an extra interpreter and also a resident magistrate. The situation Smith faced in the Rotorua district was unenviable and an excellent example of the inappropriateness of applying 'convenient' administrative boundaries to Māori districts. He was, not surprisingly, unable to bring together rangatira from Ngāi Te Rangi, Ngāti Awa, and Te Arawa. Generations of internecine warfare and lasting enmity proved an insurmountable obstacle. His reception, however, was not utterly cold: some Te Arawa leaders, wary of developments in the Waikato and weary of war, saw his arrival as potentially beneficial.

Grey's new order was probably most effective at the resident magistrate[34]/ village rūnanga level, especially, as Butterworth says, when the incumbent was supported by local rangatira. In Ōtaki, the resident magistrate, Walter Lawry Buller, a missionary's son and fluent in Māori, met with some success.[35] Able to attain the trust and support of both Tamihana Te Rauparaha and Mātene Te Whiwhi, the rūnanga system operated quite efficiently. (Buller was later to be involved in the purchase from Ngāti Apa of disputed lands in the Rangitikei–Manawatu region, despite strong protest from his Ngāti Raukawa friends.)

John White, who eventually published *The Ancient History of the Māori: His Mythology and Traditions* in six volumes between 1887 and 1890, held the post of resident magistrate in the Whanganui District from 6 October 1862 and 17 April 1865.[36] The local Māori, who had been organized into a church-based rūnanga, volunteered their services in anticipation of salaries. White, like other magistrates, was obliged to explain that only assessors and wardens would be paid, and that earlier activities of their rūnanga would no longer be permitted. He was the only resident magistrate appointed under Grey's scheme actually to settle a boundary dispute. Significantly, in the two cases he heard, his judgment favoured assessors and led to debate among hapū members over the suitability of submitting land disputes to White's adjudication. The practice was discontinued.[37]

The Breakdown of the System

The operation of district rūnanga was disrupted by the outbreak of war in 1863 when General Cameron crossed the Mangatawhiri.[38] Gradually the institutions were abandoned in most areas. Over time the resident magistrates assumed greater significance and although they continued to work closely with Māori officers appointed to implement the rūnanga system, the councils of rangatira ceased to play an important role in district administration. Three hundred and forty-one Māori were still employed by the Native Minister's Department by mid-1865: sixty-nine as wardens, sixty-nine as Karere, forty-two chiefs of rūnanga, and 161 as assessors. They remained vital to the Pākehā administrators.[39]

Fundamental to the collapse of Grey's grand design was an uncertainty over responsibility for Native Affairs. Although Grey had superficially relinquished the portfolio, his autocratic style of leadership meant that a clear mandate was not given to the Legislature regarding responsibility for Native Affairs. Crown Ministers, eager to transfer the costs incurred during the period of unrest, were happy to allow the ambiguity to continue. Thus Government, out of concern for fiscal liquidity, failed to institute adequate mechanisms to govern Māori. An effective central administration office with suitable resources to develop a national communications network and to monitor and advise officials in the districts was sorely needed and sadly lacking. Such an institution, a Ministry of Native Affairs perhaps, may well have enabled Grey's rūnanga to operate effectively. Although Grey sought to undermine the King movement through his policies, this lack of a national infrastructure and the resulting poor performance of the rūnanga system in itself contributed to the strengthening of the movement.

A further cause for the demise of the rūnanga scheme was the financial constraints placed upon it by the prevailing economic conditions. The colony, after some years under arms, was in the midst of a depression. Increasingly, the expenses related to Māori affairs (around £60,000 between 1864 and 1865)[40] were seen as an area for severe reduction. Forced to economize, the then Native Minister, James Edward Fitzgerald[41] reduced civil commissioners' and resident magistrates' salaries and instituted measures for a review of Māori assessors. Other measures he instituted also lapsed and he was replaced by Andrew Hamilton Russell when the Stafford Ministry rose to power in October of 1865. The scheme was officially abandoned under his direction. It was not to be the last State-inspired system that was undermined by a diminishing budget.

During his tenure as civil commissioner in Hawke's Bay, Russell had not been an overwhelming success, and consequently his impression of the system was not favourable. Alan Ward maintains that Russell saw the district rūnanga as an attempt by Grey to curry favour with rangatira and buy allies with political appointments.[42] Further, his perspective on race relations was overtly assimilationist, with a long-term goal of incorporating Māori and Pākehā alike under the same set of laws. Civil commissioners and resident magistrates were accordingly instructed to close down their rūnanga. Of the 450 Māori who were in receipt of Crown salaries, 300 had their annuities suspended or reduced, while the commissioners were variously dismissed, shifted to positions as magistrates or Land Court judges, or merely sidestepped and ignored. The first regime of legislative and administrative participation for Māori was at an end.

Had a representative national body of Māori leadership been developed, perhaps drawn from each Māori district, the scheme may have prospered. Certainly, the political climate among Māori was amenable to the implementation of such a plan, as evidenced by the rise of the King movement. It is possible that a rival national parliamentary structure for Māori in the mould of the Kohimārama Conference would have been supported and could perhaps have diffused momentum for Kīngitanga. This is obviously a largely speculative hypothesis and it would be doubtful if all iwi would have submitted to the authority of such a body. Consultation over membership of the district rūnanga would be a prerequisite, as boundaries and representativeness would surely be issues that would bedevil a structure of this sort. Grey's own assimilationist leanings would have precluded (and probably did) a national body at that time.

The Young Māori Party

Ka pū te rūhā, Ka hao te rangatahi. (Young Māori Party slogan)[43]

The Young Māori Party (YMP) developed from the Te Aute College Students' Association which was formed at a conference held at the College on 29 January 1897. It was not until 1909, however, that the Association, which had by then gained considerable public attention, was officially reconstituted as the YMP. Comprised mostly of Te Aute College graduates who were to enter into professional careers, YMP members were well educated, politically aware, and destined to play key roles in social reform. Both the Association and the YMP sought to reform Māori social structures and to change Māori attitudes toward health. Concurrently, they tried to

Figure 12: Native Affairs Committee (date unknown) *Back row from left:* Sir Peter Buck, ? *Front row from left:* Sir Maui Pomare, Sir Apirana Ngata, ?, Sir James Carroll, ? (*Courtesy of the Alexander Turnbull Library*)

develop mechanisms for Māori economic advancement and to raise Māori achievement in European education. The agenda for reform developed in the earliest days of the Association's existence.

Matters discussed at the inaugural meeting of the Te Aute College Students' Association included temperance, Christianity, the Māori sanitation, improved farming methods, Māori land rights and land affairs, as well as Māori education.[44] These were to become issues that dominated the agenda of the YMP throughout the early part of this century, and formed the basis for the reforms promoted and achieved by these men.

Among the more prominent members of the Party were: Sir Apirana Turupa Ngata, Ngāti Porou; Sir Peter Buck (Te Rangihiroa), Te Āti Awa; Sir Maui Pomare, Te Āti Awa; Dr Tutere Wi Repa, Te Whānau a Apanui, Ngāti Porou, and Ngāti Kahungunu; Reweti Kohere, Ngāti Porou; Dr Edward Pohua Ellison, Ngāi Tahu and Ngāti Mamoe; and the Right Reverend Frederick Augustus Bennett, Te Arawa. Because of the national profile these men attained in their careers, their exploits have come to dominate the history of the Party.[45]

Their philosophy, garnered as it was from the teaching of John Thornton, the College's second headmaster whose involvement with the school spanned thirty-four years from 1878 until 1912,[46] tended towards the emulation of Pākehā structures to strengthen and improve Māori society. Their task was further complicated by a desire not only to regenerate Māori society, but also to maintain the best of Māori cultural heritage and to preserve Māori spirituality. This tripartite mission is perhaps best expressed in the now famous whakataukī coined by Apirana Ngata in 1949:

E tipu, e rea, mo ngā ra o tou ao,
Ko to ringaringa ki ngā rākau o te pākehā, hei oranga mo to tinana,
Ko to ngākau ki nga taonga a o tipuna, hei tikitiki mo to māhunga,
Ko to wairua ki te Atua, Nāna nei ngā mea katoa.[47]

A prerequisite to Pākehā acceptance of Māori as a race was the belief that individual leaders would need to establish standing in Pākehā eyes. European attitudes towards and opinions of Māori, validated to some degree (at least for Pākehā) by a perceivably low socio-economic position, were negative. Even in European fiction Pākehā attitudes reflected the low esteem in which they held Māori.[48] Before Māori could be accepted as an ethnic group worthy of European respect, some Māori would need to enter into the Pākehā realm and make a powerful and positive impact. This impact would necessarily be couched in Pākehā terms and would be validated by standards laid down by Pākehā. Māori aspirations would be translated into European goals, in what they considered the only viable path to securing Māori advancement. The concentration by the YMP upon social reform rather than emphasizing past grievances made them more acceptable to European observers and commentators of the period, and they attracted favourable attention from the press.[49]

One of their earliest attempts to direct the course of Māori society was a tour of the Māori settlements in the Hawke's Bay, undertaken in 1887 by Maui Pomare, Reweti Kohere, and Timutimu Tawhai—then a trio of very youthful enthusiasts. Their lectures on the need for sobriety and improved sanitation were not well accepted on many marae. It was not that the messages themselves were unpalatable, but the messengers and their delivery mitigated against them. Elders took exception to these young men who presumed not only to speak on the marae (a privilege reserved in most tribes to senior men) but also to preach a Pākehā lesson.[50] The necessity for more than education and initiative based upon the European models was emerging. In company with Reweti Kohere and his brother, Ngata also embarked upon a walking tour of marae in 1881. They encountered not only resentment and disapproval but, perhaps worse, indifference. Their dream of galvanizing Māori and equipping them for the new world would, it seemed, take longer than the summer holidays they had available to them.

To attain their goals, it was soon realized that political participation was essential. The development of autonomous Māori legislative bodies, however, was seen by them as an inappropriate mechanism in the light of Pākehā reluctance to relinquish control over Māori and their lands. The withdrawal from mainstream European systems advocated by Paora Tuhaere and other Kotahitanga leaders of the late nineteenth century (discussed in Chapter Four) held no allure for the Young Māori Party. Consequently, when they embarked upon their mission of reform, some of them chose political careers.

Although some members of the YMP entered the House of Representatives their organization was not a traditional political party. Typified by Condliffe as 'a movement, rather than a party',[51] the YMP was ambitious in an arena wider than the purely political one of Parliament. Counted among their numbers were lawyers, doctors, warriors, and priests. Mere political action was insufficient to bring their goals to fruition. Those who achieved success inside the legislature affiliated themselves with major political parties, including the Liberal Party, who governed from 1891 until 1911 under the leadership of John Ballance, and the Reform Party of William Massey. Prominent amongst them were Apirana Ngata, Maui Pomare, and Peter Buck.[52]

These men, building on the work of earlier Māori parliamentarians like Sir James Carroll[53] and Hone Heke,[54] fulfilled the function of articulating Māori needs to Pākehā audiences. Through their work, Pākehā learned that Māori problems ought to be addressed by Māori and resolved through Māori customs and beliefs, albeit with significant modification to meet new times.

Apart from achieving positions of eminence in European terms, the leaders who formed the Young Māori Party were obliged, in order to achieve their aims, to develop positions of authority and respect among their own people. This latter task was perhaps initially the more difficult. Māori deference to age, to experience, and to scholars of mātauranga Māori (Māori knowledge) required younger men to take a subordinate position in tribal affairs. Advocates of the Young Māori Party soon found that it required more than mere Western education to influence their people.

With the possible exception of Apirana Ngata they did not supplant traditional leaders. Ngata, a central figure in the movement and certainly among the best-known leaders to emerge from this group, did eventually win the respect and support of his own Ngāti Porou people and also that of tribes throughout the nation. The key to his success was threefold: mastery of the traditional wisdom of the Māori, observance of customary protocols and prerogatives in dealings with Māori, and thirdly, a sound background in European education.[55]

Māori remained demographically rural until after the Second World War, and were conservatively tribal in their outlook.[56] Opposition to Māori parliamentarians, whose role it was to provide an interface between Pākehā and tribes, was not uncommon when they sought to address Māori issues. Traditional leaders still wielded much influence in tribal affairs and reserved unto themselves the rangatiratanga of their people. While cognizant to act in matters distinctly political in the parliamentary arena, elected officials such as the men of the Young Māori Party were not empowered, in Māori eyes, to act as spokesmen on Māori matters. Traditional leaders did form relationships of mutual support with Māori in Parliament—links which they developed to channel resources into their home areas.[57]

The Effect of the Young Māori Party

Central to the Young Māori Party's campaign to improve the situation of Māori, indeed to secure their racial survival,[58] was the positive promotion of healthy living. Under the guidance of Apirana Ngata, their public health reforms were broader than the mere policing of sanitary regulations performed by Māori Councils in the early 1900s. Physical living conditions (housing and drainage) were addressed, but, importantly, education in hygiene and inoculation from disease were provided for Māori children. Later this was supplemented by initiatives to revive some traditional arts, both performing and visual, community development and building programmes, as well as education.[59]

John A. Williams maintains that it was largely as a result of Ngata's advocacy that Māori came to accept the parliamentary system as a viable mechanism for the resolution of their social ills. In his thesis he sees the demise of the Kotahitanga Parliament following the implementation of the Māori Councils Act 1900 as an indication that Māori had developed faith in the General House of Assembly.[60] More accurately perhaps, the 1900 legislation should be seen for what it was: a deliberate attempt to diffuse Māori initiative.

Sir James Carroll, the Native Minister in the Seddon Administration elected in 1899, was given the task of coming to grips with the Kotahitanga movement, ably represented in Parliament by Hone Heke (Rankin) of Ngāpuhi.[61] To answer the repeated and persistent calls for legislative recognition of the Pāremata Māori, Carroll devised the 1900 Act which gave funding as well as limited legislative and administrative power to Māori Councils—just as Grey's district rūnanga had done four decades earlier. Similarly, and importantly, contracting budgetary considerations can be seen as instrumental in the demise of the 1900 District Councils.

Figure 13: Sir James Caroll on board the *Tutanekai* from Gisborne to Waiomatatini, July 1897, for the funeral of Ropata. Photo: W Crawford. (*Courtesy of the Sheila Williams Collection, Alexander Turnbull Library*)

For all that, the role of the Young Māori Party in the promotion of Māori participation in central government cannot be denied. The influence wielded by Ngata and Pomare from within the Party, and also from Carroll and Heke, was to be an example to T. W. Rātana, Sir Eruera Tirikatene, Matiu Rata, and Koro Wetere.

The so-called Māori renaissance which the Young Māori Party led early this century may in fact be an overstatement of the situation. Māori had continued to maintain tribal integrity within their respective rohe, and had not abdicated their social, political, spiritual, or economic responsibilities. What had occurred was a withdrawal from Pākehā structures. In adopting an assimilationist stance to Pākehā, the Young Māori Party merely recalled Māori to Pākehā awareness.

The Māori Councils of 1900

The general election of December 1899 saw the return of the Liberal Party for a further term as government. James Carroll, who had supported Richard

Figure 14: Native Lands Committee *Back row from left:* ?, Henry James Greenslade, Robert Heaton Rhodes, ?. *Middle row from left:* Sir Peter Buck, Thomas Edward Youd Seddon, Bradshaw Dive, William Donald Stuart McDonald. *Front row from left:* W. H. Herries, Sir James Carroll, William Thomas Jennings, Sir Apirana Turupa Ngata, Tame Parata (date unknown; *Courtesy of Alexander Turnbull Library*)

John Seddon at various hui held prior to the election,[62] was made Minister of Native Affairs.[63] Under his guidance, and with the support of Ngata and Heke, two Acts of Parliament were passed:[64] The Māori Councils Act 1900 and the Māori Lands Administration Act 1900. The former established nineteen elected Māori councils that had powers considerably less than those exercised by local authorities. The latter provided for the establishment of Māori-dominated Land Councils to control the leasing of Māori land. Both of these council structures were responses to Māori issues: the first to concern generated by a declining Māori population; the other to demands for involvement in land administration.

The Māori Councils Act 1900 was developed to attain improved sanitation in Māori villages, an issue that provided Carroll with sufficient support within the Seddon administration to secure the passage of the Act. The principal tasks of the councils were the enactment and enforcement of sanitary regulations affecting dwellings, water supplies, and meeting-houses.

Other duties included the control of liquor sales to minors and the suppression of customs deemed to be pernicious, such as tohungatanga.[65]

While providing Māori with a degree of autonomy and a level of input into local affairs, they fell short of the demands which were being voiced by adherents to both major Kotahitanga movements of the period, the Kauhanganui and the Pāremata Māori. The hierarchical structure of 1861 was replicated in provision for the election of village committees. These committees had the power to exercise delegated council authority as specified by the Act. The councils recognized the communal nature of Māori organization and used these structures to supervise Māori affairs. The Act was innovative in one respect: it allowed for annual national conventions of Māori council representatives to be held. This important difference to the earlier model was perhaps central to Māori acceptance of the system and the decline of the independent Māori Parliament.

The legislation was gradually implemented under Carroll's leadership. Late in 1900, a conference with the Young Māori Party and Kotahitanga leaders was held in Whanganui. From this hui, a set of by-laws for the Māori councils emerged. During 1901 the election of the councils was undertaken. The overall administration of the councils was delegated to a superintendency of the Māori councils whose officers included Gilbert Mair, as Superintendent, and Apirana Ngata, as Organizing Inspector. The Native Health Officer, Maui Pomare, worked closely with these two for the promotion of initiatives to improve Māori health.

Under the Lands Administration Act 1900 remaining Māori land was reserved for the use and benefit of Māori, with the aim of allowing Māori to reap the benefit of their lands without further alienation. For a while these councils impeded the acquisition of Māori land in line with Carroll's 'Taihoa' policy. The European, however, still sought to gain control of native land and the councils were consequently transformed into Land Boards in 1905. These new Boards were composed predominantly of Pākehā and acted as conduits for the leasing of Māori land to Europeans. The demands for a Federated Māori Assembly with a series of district committees[66] to administer Māori lands were thus captured and nullified.

Carroll's councils gave Māori limited legislative authority but constrained activities through financial controls enforced by the State and a narrow focus for activities. While it cannot be denied that the health, sanitation, and temperance issues dealt with by the councils were of considerable necessity for the maintenance and improvement of Māori society, it is important to note that the fundamental area of Māori concern—land—was soon removed from Māori jurisdiction. The only activity undertaken during Carroll's ministry that was subject to public outcry was the leasing of Māori land which had been controlled by the Māori-dominated Land Councils. The extent of this public indignation was sufficient for the enactment of the Māori Land Settlement Act 1905. This legislation altered the composition of the administrative bodies established to supervise leasing arrangements. Māori, deprived of authority, were no longer to reap benefits from their resources— this was to become another Pākehā privilege.

The Liberal Party, to whom Ngata and Carroll both gave allegiance, succeeded in distracting Māori from the Kotahitanga movement, as exemplified by the Paremata Māori. The activities of the Councils formed under this legislation fell into decline a scant decade after their establishment. A gradual strangulation of activities effected by a diminution in Crown funding was responsible.

Figure 15: First meeting of the Takitimu Maori Council, in front of the second Poho-o-Rawiri Meeting-house, 10 June 1902. *Seated:* Mr Brooking, Otene Pitau. *Front row from left (standing):* Takina, Charles Ferris, Hetekia Te Kane Pere, Paratene Tatae, Hemi Tutapu, Matenga Taihuka Te Kooti, (far right). *Back row from left (standing):* Hapi Hinaki, Paora Kohu, Pewhairangi, Rangi, ?, Arani Kunaiti (*Courtesy of the Gordon Collection, Alexander Turnbull Library*)

By the close of the century, Māori tribal and political unity based on Māori structures and aspirations had been all but supplanted by the might of the State. Ironically, the greatest challenge had come from other Māori who saw Māori futures, rightly or wrongly, as an integral part of the mainstream. While it would be oversimplistic to regard either the Young Māori Party or Carroll as antagonistic to Kotahitanga and its vision of Mana Māori Motuhake, the strength of their close affiliation to major political parties certainly contributed to the demise of the Pāremata Māori. The search for Kotahitanga, however, has remained.

The Māori War Effort Organisation

The outbreak of hostilities in 1939 galvanized the nation and provided Māori with an opportunity for input into national affairs. The first objective of Māori leaders—Apirana Ngata principle among them—was the formation of a Māori battalion. Ngata had advocated a Māori military unit modelled on the Māori Pioneer Battalion of 1914–18[67] months before the invasion of Poland by the Wermacht which had precipitated global warfare on 3 September 1939.[68]

Eruera Tirikatene and Paraire Paikea, the respective Rātana/Labour political alliance Members of Parliament for the Southern and Northern Māori electorates, made a similar public demand for Māori representation in the war effort. The Māori proposal was that the battalion would be comprised of Māori officers, non-commissioned officers, and other ranks. Although it was not intended to preclude Māori from participation in other national military units, direct European involvement in the battalion was considered both inappropriate and unnecessary.[69]

The 28th Māori Battalion

On 4 October 1939 the Government, after a period of reservation, announced that a Māori battalion would indeed be formed. Despite strenuous Māori protest, however, the force was to be led by a European commander. Māori were prepared to concede the necessity for an inaugural European commanding officer who would eventually be replaced by a Māori, but thought it totally unacceptable that company commanders and non-commissioned officers should also be European.

The objection was not in itself anti-Pākehā, but rather it was pro-Māori. Military expertise existed among Māori in the shape of World War I veterans and territorial soldiers, while college and university graduates could provide

Figure 16: Prime Minister Peter Fraser with the Hon Paraire Kakara Paikea at the opening of the Savage Memorial, 1942 (*Courtesy of the Pascoe Collection, Alexander Turnbull Library*)

additional leadership after suitable military training. Among Māori, only one generation had been born who could not speak of war from first-hand experience. Iwi had offered to form tribal contingents and participate in the Sudan (1884), South Africa (1896), and Samoa (1899),[70] and could anticipate no reason for Pākehā middle-echelon involvement in the Battalion.

The first Battalion commander, nevertheless, was European—Major (later Brigadier-General) George Dittmer, who took the unit overseas on 2 May 1940.[71] His second-in-command was Major G. F. Bertrand, a part-Māori veteran of the First World War. As the conflict deepened and the Battalion distinguished itself in the North African and Italian campaigns, leadership of the Battalion became subject to the fortunes of war. In all, ten commanding officers led the Battalion, six of whom were Māori (see Table 5).

Table 5: Commanders of the 28th Māori Battalion

Lt-Col. Edward Te Whiti Love, MID, Te Āti Awa
Lt-Col. Frederick Baker, DSO, ED, MID, Ngāpuhi
Lt-Col. Charles Mohi Bennett, Lt-Col. CM, DSO, Te Arawa
Lt-Col. Kingi Areta Keiha, Lt-Col. KA, MC, MID, Rongowhakaata
Lt-Col. Arapeta Awatere, Lt-Col A, DSO, MC, Ngāti Porou
Lt-Col. James Clendon Henare, DSO, MID, Ngāti Hine (later Sir James)

The internal organization of the 28th Māori Battalion, although determined regionally, was based upon tribal divisions. Four companies were formed, imaginatively designated 'A', 'B', 'C', and 'D'. 'A' company took in the tribes of the far north, 'B' company those occupying the central regions of Te-Ika-a-Māui (Te Arawa, Tainui, and Tuwharetoa), 'C' company included the tribes of the East Coast (Ngāti Porou, Rongowhakaata, and Te Whanau a Apanui), while 'D' company included the remainder of the North Island and the whole of the South Island and the Chatham Islands.

The Home Front

The rigours of global conflict also had an effect on the domestic affairs of Aotearoa. Apart from the absence of men who were engaged in combat, the efficient development of resources to sustain the military was required. By 1941 the War Cabinet, formed from members of both major political parties, realizing the importance of Māori input, charged Northern Māori MP, Paraire Paikea, with stimulating Māori involvement in the war effort. He was elevated to the Executive Council[72] and given considerable autonomy in the conduct of his assigned tasks.

His first objective was to boost Māori recruitment into the armed forces. With Ngata, he embarked upon a publicity campaign which achieved a considerable degree of success. The only regions where response was initially unenthusiastic were Taranaki, Waikato, and parts of the Bay of Plenty where the raupatu of the last century and the imprisonments of the last war were still causing ill feeling.[73]

His next task was prompted by a practice which had developed since the inception of the four Māori electorates whereby voter registration was not required for Māori seats. Unable to obtain an accurate list of Māori eligible for domestic and overseas duties from either the Department of Native Affairs or any other source, the War Ministry turned to Paikea. Realizing that an opportunity to develop a structure independent of the Native Department had presented itself, Paikea took up the challenge, and in May of 1942 submitted his plan to Prime Minister Fraser.[74]

His proposal, developed with the support of Eruera Tirikatene, suggested the establishment of a Māori parliamentary committee that would coordinate, through a military-style chain of command, a network of tribal committees. Apart from their principal recruitment function, the committees would engage in civilian manpower deployment and oversee primary industrial activities such as food production. The parliamentary committee comprised the four Māori Members of Parliament together with Rangi Mawhete of the Legislative Council.[75]

The structure which they developed was, like others discussed in this book, hierarchical. Twenty-one districts termed 'zones', probably in deference to the military, were established with paid Māori recruitment officers appointed to each of them. These officers were given the rank of Second Lieutenant and

Figure 17: 'Maoris of three generations, mostly women, complete their day's work on the Otaki vegetable farm while their menfolk fight on the North African front.' (*Courtesy of the J. D. Pascoe Collection, Alexander Turnbull Library*)

remunerated from the war expenses account. A total of 315 tribal committees were formed and each was permitted a maximum of two representatives on one of forty-one regional executive committees. The breadth of Paikea's structure allowed input from all iwi and provided an example of Māori capacity to organize effectively at a national level.[76] The proposal received Cabinet approval on 3 June 1942 and the scheme was given a six-month probationary period in which to develop.

As the work of the Māori War Effort Organisation expanded from military recruitment for both the Home Guard and service abroad to encompass domestic labour needs, it also became involved in matters of social welfare. Initiated by concern for young Māori women relocated to urban centres for industrial work, the parliamentary committee prevailed upon the National Service Department to appoint 'lady welfare officers' in the larger centres.[77] Although this proved a timely and worthwhile initiative and secured an extension of the Organisation's mandate, it was viewed by Native Minister Rex Mason and his Department as an encroachment into their domain. Further, Māori were displaying a marked preference for dealing with the War Effort Organisation and were bypassing departmental officials. The administrative and jurisdictional overlaps between the two structures heightened the power struggle which was emerging between the entrenched bureaucracy and the Māori Members of Parliament. Despite this opposition and treasury calls for its disbandment, the organization was maintained throughout the war years.[78]

The New Zealand Māori Council

Departmental Opposition

Following the cessation of hostilities in 1945, the Māori representatives in the House sought the enactment of a legislative framework that would allow the structures established during the war to continue to be of benefit to Māori. Their vision was to form a national organization that stood apart from the Department of Native Affairs and was directly responsible to Members representing Māori electorates. This redefinition of administrative responsibility would, it was hoped, provide greater independence for Māori and remove Māori affairs from the control of Ministers appointed by the majority government. Theoretically at least, Māori would have a real say in who would establish and implement Māori policy.

The iwi-based network constructed for the war effort had not only fulfilled required administrative functions but had also come to embody the aspirations of Māori leaders, and could conceivably facilitate Mana Māori Motuhake. Tribes not only had an avenue for direct, bilateral communication with the Māori Members of Parliament, and through them with the legislature, but they were also able to make meaningful contributions in the area of service delivery to iwi. The Māori War Effort Organisation had also proved acceptable in another regard: its staff were predominantly Māori.

Conversely, the Native Department had consistently failed to encompass Māori aspirations, and did not deliver to Māori the services they required in a manner which they deemed appropriate. The disinclination of successive permanent heads to develop adequate welfare systems and to continue the rather narrow focus on land development did not in Māori eyes measure up to the example of the War Effort Organisation.

Sir Eruera Tirikatene and Rangi Mawhete were prominent in promoting to Cabinet the inception of a new Department of State.[79] The Ministry they proposed would coordinate and expand the activities of tribal committees and act as a liaison centre for other government departments involved in interaction with iwi. This would allow the development of a coherent and comprehensive approach to Māori social, economic, cultural, and educational issues, while concurrently retaining autonomous tribal representation.[80]

The existing department, however, was not easily displaced, and despite increasingly vocal lobbying by Māori Members of Parliament it was retained. Rex Mason, the Native Minister, had as early as mid 1943 canvassed the idea of reconstituting a Māori committee structure based upon the 1900 model.[81] He also initiated some reforms within the Department and appointed a number of 'Placement Officers' to coordinate departmental welfare programmes. This albeit belated demonstration of the Department's willingness to adapt to meet Māori demands was influential in its retention.

The matter was eventually resolved by Premier Fraser, who had assumed the post of Minister in Charge of the Māori War Effort in 1943, when Paraire Paikea passed away. This close involvement with the Organisation gave him a clear perception of its value. He was simultaneously reluctant to disband the existing Department, and consequently determined to absorb the Māori War Effort Organisation into the Native Department. Despite his intentions, the compromise he suggested eventually emerged heavily biased towards the Department, and it neither adequately reflected Māori aspirations nor advanced Māori autonomy. The drafting of the bill was undertaken by R. Blane, a law clerk in the Native Department. He was directly responsible to Rex Mason, the Native Minister whose opposition to the bill submitted by Tirikatene and Mawhete was well-known.[82]

Tribal Commitees: The 1900 Act Revisited

The result of this determination was the establishment of a multi-tiered structure of Māori committees (originally called tribal committees), district councils, and the National Māori Council (Dominion Council). Their legislative validity derives from the Māori Social and Economic Advancement Act 1945 which was later modified by the Māori Welfare Act 1962. The initial intent of the former Act was to grant statutory recognition to the tribal committees that had proved so effective during the Second World War.

The tribal committees described in the 1945 Act required triennial elections to be held on an appointed day and in a defined manner. Any Māori domiciled within the clearly delineated and gazetted boundaries of a tribal committee was entitled to participate in a ballot to elect up to seven (subsequently eleven) representatives for that committee. This feature of the legislation created two important conflicts for many traditional Māori leaders.

The first involved the appropriateness of determining rangatiratanga through mechanisms derived from the kāwanatanga tradition and highlighted a fundamental divergence between the prescribed leadership of the committees and the ascribed control inherent in tikanga Māori. The view expounded by Joan Metge is, in part, accurate:

> In the early days, many rangatira and kaumatua opposed the committees as a threat to their authority, refusing to 'belittle' their mana by submitting to a vote . . .[83]

Rangatira were, under the Act, effectively made equivalent in stature to any other Māori who happened to live in the same area. Persons of less exalted status, or perhaps from another tribe (i.e., not tangata whenua), might potentially poll as well or even higher than traditional rangatira, and come to hold an inappropriate level of power in local political affairs. While traditional mechanisms for social control were in fact premised upon popular support, the electoral system had within it the potential to seriously undermine existing tribal dynamics by defining the parameters of Māori political power. Requiring traditional leaders to submit to the machinations and vagaries of an election is unconscionable in traditional terms. It is this conflict between kāwanatanga and tino rangatiratanga that contributes most to the limitations of State-inspired movements as adequate vehicles for the assertion of Mana Māori Motuhake or for a united Māori voice.

Further, the legislative basis of the committees has on occasion been used to validate the claims of elected leaders that they in fact represent the tino rangatiratanga of their iwi. The interaction of these two diametrically opposed philosophical bases is perhaps the greatest drawback of this structure.

Figure 18: Tribal Committee in session, North Taranaki, September 1962
(*Courtesy of the National Publicity Studios Collection, Alexander Turnbull Library*)

The second conflict was a matter of representativeness. All adult Māori were eligible to stand for office and to vote in a committee election. In rural districts, committee areas often accorded to hapū rohe, and closely paralleled marae catchment areas. Consequently, rangatira and kaumātua were often returned as committee members. The situation in larger cities, however, was very different. Māori settlement patterns were changing in the postwar era, and often several hundred people of Māori but not necessarily tangata whenua descent were included in a given committee area. European concepts of majoritarianism, reinforced by arbitrary geographical considerations, could, and often did lead to a marginalization of tangata whenua in their home areas.

The Māori Social and Economic Advancement Act 1945[84] also had provision for executive committees modelled on those used to administer tribal committees during the war. Tirikatene's proposed district councils, which would have provided an upper level of Māori control in the structure were, however, omitted. The executive committees were incorporated into the Department's structure and provided an administrative overseeing of

Table 6:   NZMC Districts (and members attending the meeting of
20/9/91)

Region	Representative
Taitokerau	Sir Graham Latimer
Auckland	Pita Rikys
Waikato	Monty Retemeyer
Maniapoto	Pare Joseph
Tauranga Moana	Tiopi Faulkiner
Hauraki	Jim Nicholls
Waiariki	Mānu Paul
Tairawhiti	Lou Tangaere
Takitimu	Eru Smith
Raukawa	Peter Richardson
Wellington	Boy Christie
Te Wai Pounamu	Monty Daniels
	Anne Thompson

tribal committee activities. The need to deal with departmental officers in the exercise of committee functions effectively curtailed the autonomy sought by leading Māori politicians of that time.

The Māori Welfare Act 1962, however, incorporated two further tiers into the structure: a series of district Māori councils based upon the seven Land Court areas, and a national body comprised of delegates from each district council.[85] The districts corresponded to those contained in the Māori Land Act 1909 as modified by Hon. Sir William H. Herries in 1913,[86] and comprised Te Taitokerau, Waikato-Maniapoto, Waiariki, Tairawhiti, Aotea, Ikaroa, and Te Waipounamu. Since that time, further council districts have been added at the instigation of existing councils. The disparities in size and composition of the constituent base of each district has led to a further rationalization of the districts.[87] Currently, twelve district councils send delegates to New Zealand Māori Council hui as shown in Table 6.[88]

The New Zealand Māori Council, outwardly an organization based firmly upon elected localized committees that feed into a national body, is a potentially useful structure. Two factors emerge as significant regarding its effectiveness, however: an inadequate pool of resources and insufficient funding, and its perceived abstraction from mundane social reality.

Māori committees are resourced from their own efforts. The first committees were required to raise their own monies and were eligible for a one-for-one subsidy from the Government for money spent on welfare activities. Latterly, some committees have come to rely upon various welfare-inspired funding structures developed to service a wide range of socially active groups.[89] The necessity to compete with other bodies, both Māori and non-Māori, for a share of the communal wealth, has the potential to distract committees from essential business. This competition is not wholly appropriate and can also di-vert funding from other worthwhile projects. Certainly the reverse is also true.

The district bodies draw upon their member committees for their resources, both human and fiscal. They in turn provide representatives for the national structure, and are levied to fund that body. Until 1971, this money was subsidized by the Government, but ultimately a direct annual grant was established because that system proved inadequate. Recent New Zealand Māori Council judicial activities —such as the State-owned Enterprises case, the fisheries dispute, and the broadcasting case—have placed a severe strain on the organization. If successful, legal fees are recoverable—if not, the burden of carrying Māori civil cases may inevitably contribute to the demise of the Council. Further, as most of these actions are directed at the State on behalf of Māori, the likelihood of increased or even continued funding is diminishing.

The progressive steps inherent within the New Zealand Māori Council, however, create considerable distance between the national and the local levels. Often perceived as a Government-planned organization that operates largely independently of grass-roots institutions and individuals, many Māori remain outside its ambit. Urban-based Māori committee elections, even after deliberate steps are taken to inform constituents, are seldom well attended. Committee members are often unknown to many of those who reside within their catchment area.

Many urban Māori are unaware of how the structure operates and are ignorant of the processes that are involved in the election of Māori committees. Most have heard of the New Zealand Māori Council and may even know who its president is. That district Māori councils exist is also known in the community—whether or not there is an awareness of the link between them is, however, open to speculation. The third tier, Māori committees, while providing an opportunity for input into the upper levels, is not widely perceived by the majority of urban Māori as an option for the expression of their views.

Indeed, both Schwimmer[90] and Ritchie, when commenting upon the realities of Māori political life in the 1960s, assert that the Council's structure was most useful as a mechanism for downward communication of government policy. In their view, the concrete issues of hapū existence dominated in Māori political awareness, and the activities of bodies outside their daily lives were of little or no particular significance. This book, however, contends that the observed reality upon which they commented arises from a combination of structural unsuitability and a desire for Mana

Māori Motuhake, rather than from any disinclination to participate.

At least since 1987, when the New Zealand Māori Council brought the State-Owned Enterprises case before the Courts, the Council has demonstrated effectiveness at a national level and has strongly influenced legislation and government policy. Perhaps the price for their effective action at a national/central level has been a weakening of ties at regional and local levels. Additionally, the successes in recent years have come at a time when Māori have deplored continued dependence on State-inspired structures, even when a record of achievement can be demonstrated.

But the distinction between kāwanatanga and tino rangatiratanga is more than a subtlety: it is crucial to the understanding of Māori political unity. The New Zealand Māori Council has not been able to shrug off its links with the State and with mainstream political intrigue. Because of that, its appeal as a rallying point for all Māori has suffered.

Endnotes

1.   Dr Pat Hohepa—(1978), 'Maori and Pakeha: The One People Myth', in M. King (ed.), *Tihe Mauri Ora: Aspects of Māoritanga*, Methuen, Auckland, p. 98—questions the accuracy of this commonly accepted historical 'fact', his thesis being that it may merely be a homily used to justify Pākehā domination.

2.   Later published as J. E. Ritchie, (1965), 'The Grass Roots of Māori Politics', in J. G. A. Pocock (ed.), *The Māori and New Zealand Politics: Talks from an NZBC Series with Additional Essays*, Blackwood and Janet Paul, Auckland, p. 85.

3.   Discussed by H. M. Durie in 'Partnership and the Advancement of Māori Health', read before the International Convention of Health Administrators (December 1990), pp. 6–7.

4.   See *Great Britain Parliamentary Papers*, Vol. 29, which contains a dispatch from the Governor to the Duke of Newcastle and a copy of his address to the gathering.

5.   See *Great Britain Parliamentary Papers*, Vol. 12, pp. 130–1: a letter to this effect to the editor of the *Southern Cross* from Rev. R. Burrows.

6.   R. J. Walker, (1990), *Ka Whawhai Tonu Matou: Struggle Without End*, Penguin, Auckland, pp. 114–15.

7.   As mentioned in Chapter Four, D. M. Stafford—(1967), *Te Arawa: A History of the Arawa People*, Reed, Auckland p. 347—comments upon Te Arawa involvement with the Treaty.

8.   C. Orange, (1987a), *The Treaty of Waitangi*, Allen and Unwin/Port Nicholson, Wellington, p. 148.

9.   He had intended that the Kohimarama conference would eventuate into an annual gathering; see A. Ward, (1973), *A Show of Justice: Racial Amalgamation in Nineteenth Century New Zealand*, Auckland University Press/Oxford University Press, Auckland, p. 176.

10.   Specifically the war in Taranaki.

11.   Te Rangikaheke of Te Arawa is said to have taught Grey to speak Māori; see W. H. Oliver (ed.), *The Dictionary of New Zealand Biography*, Bridget Williams/

Department of Internal Affairs, Wellington, G21: 161.

12. See G. Butterworth and H. Young, (1990), *Māori Affairs: A Department and the People Who Made It*, Department of Māori Affairs, Wellington, p. 35; *The Dictionary of New Zealand Biography*, *op cit.*, B39: 47; and Ward, *op cit.*, pp. 176–7.

13. The origin of these Acts and the role played by F. D. Fenton in their development is discussed in Chapter Three.

14. A traditional English subdivision of a shire or district, similar to a riding but having its own court.

15. This term seems to imply that the magistrates were resident in the district rather than the village. They were Pākehā.

16. Alan Ward gives a comprehensive coverage of this area in *A Show of Justice*, *op cit.*, pp. 125–7, while pp. 125–46 deal with the whole rūnanga plan in some detail.

17. Ward, *op cit.*, p. 125.

18. Butterworth and Young, *op cit.*, p. 35.

19. Ibid, p. 37.

20. Ward, *op cit.*, p. 132.

21. The minutes of this first meeting were published in Vol. II, No. 10 of the *Te Karere Māori* or *Maori Messenger*, 26 May 1862.

22. Ward, *op cit.*, p. 126; £49,000 were allocated nationally for the scheme in 1861, and £43,000 per annum for subsequent years.

23. Ward, *op cit.*, p. 137.

24. Ibid, pp. 137–8.

25. Ibid, pp. 139–40.

26. A periodical published in response to the Kingite pamphlet *Te Hokio*; see preceding chapter for details.

27. J. E. Gorst (1864), *The Maori King, or, The Story of Our Quarrel with the Natives of New Zealand*, (1975 edn), Capper, Christchurch, p. 9.

28. *The Dictionary of New Zealand Biography*, *op cit.*, M19: 264. Details of this encounter are related in Chapter 4.

29. H. R. Russell and his involvement with Matua and the Repudiation Movement are covered in Chapter 4.

30. Ward, *op cit.*, p. 131.

31. *The Dictionary of New Zealand Biography*, *op cit.*, S12: 396. Shortland contributed two books to the early literature on Māori society: *Traditions and Superstitions of the Māori* and *The Southern Districts of New Zealand*.

32. Ward, *op cit.*, p. 133.

33. D. M. Stafford—*op cit.* pp. 359–60—gives details of early hui to implement the scheme and names of rūnanga members.

34. *The Dictionary of New Zealand Biography*, *op cit.*, B46: 53–4.

35. Butterworth and Young, *op cit.*, p. 36.

36. *The Dictionary of New Zealand Biography*, *op cit.*, W18: 587–9.

37. Ward, *op cit.*, pp. 138–9.

38. As mentioned in Chapter 4, this occurred on 13 July 1863.

39. Butterworth and Young, *op cit.*, p. 37.

40. Ward, *op cit.*, p. 197.

41. Fitzgerald held this post for the last two months of the Weld Administration, August–October 1865; see *The Dictionary of New Zealand Biography*, *op cit.*, F9, 125–6.

42. Ward, *op cit.*, p. 195.

43. A whakatauki which speaks of continuity in a changing order; youth eventually

replacing age. M. P. K. Sorrenson, (1986), 'A History of Maori Representation in Parliament', in *Report of the Royal Commission on the Electoral System: Towards a Better Democracy*, State Services Commission, Wellington, Appendix B, p. B-41.
44.   D. Sigley, (1974), 'The YMP', in Mark Te Aranga Hakiwai (ed.), *Te Aranga o Te Aute: Ta te Rangatira Tana Kai he Korero ta te Ware he Muhukai*, Pukehou, p. 24.
45.   Most accounts of the Young Māori Party are couched in biographical terms and concern key players in the movement.
46.   Sigley, *op cit.*, pp. 22–365.
47.   Written 'Ki a Rangi . . . at Potaka, 10-11-1949' in Sir John Bennett's daughter's autograph book, 'Pounamu: A. T. Ngata, 1874–1950' which aired on 24 June 1990 on TV One. See E. Stirling and A. Salmon (1980), *Eruera: Teachings of a Māori Elder*, Oxford University Press, Auckland, p. 205 for a translation. Essentially, this whakatauki reminds youth that success in the modern world requires a blending of modern western skills and technologies and traditional Māori cultural values within a spiritual context.
48.   W. H. Pearson, (1958), 'Attitudes to Maori in some Pakeha Fiction', *JPS*, 67 (3): 213.
49.   J. A. Williams, (1969), *The Politics of the New Zealand Māori*.
50.   Sorrenson, (?? date), *Māori and European Since 1870*.
51.   J. B. Condliffe, (1971), *Te Rangihiroa: The Life of Sir Peter Buck*, Whitcombe and Tombs, Christchurch, pp. 102–3.
52.   Pomare: MHR, Western Māori, 1911–1914 (Independent), 1914–1931 (Reform); Ngata: MHR, Eastern 1905–1928 (Liberal), 1928–1931 (United), 1931–1935 (Coalition), 1935–1943 (National); Buck: MHR, Northern, 1911–1914 (Liberal).
53.   Carroll was MHR for Eastern Māori, 1887–1893; for Waiapu, 1893–1908; and for Gisborne, 1908–1919. He was the Member of the Executive Council Representing the Native Race, 1892–1899 and Minister of Native Affairs, 1899–1912; see D. Hamer (1988), *The New Zealand Liberal Party*, p. 362.
54.   Heke held Northern Māori from 1893 until his death at forty years of age on 9 February 1911. He was succeeded by Te Rangihiroa, who had been invited to stand by Heke's mother. See Condliffe, *op cit.*, p. 111.
55.   Condliffe, *op cit.*, p. 102.
56.   M. King, (1981), 'Between Two Worlds', in W. H. Oliver (ed.), *The Oxford History of New Zealand*, Oxford University Press, Auckland, pp. 290–1. See also the section on demography contained in Chapter Six of this book.
57.   Te Puea Herangi at times cultivated both Pomare and Ngata to achieve her goals.
58.   King—(1981), *op cit.*, pp. 280–1—explores the basis for the widely held European belief that Māori were doomed to extinction. Ian Pool—(1977)(1991), *Te Iwi Maori: A New Zealand Population Past, Present and Projected*, Auckland University Press, Auckland—refutes this notion, providing evidence that the rate of population decline began to diminish as far back as 1874.
59.   Condliffe, *op cit.*, p. 85.
60.   J. A. Williams (1969), *Politics of the New Zealand Māori: Protest and Cooperation*, University of Auckland/Oxford University Press, Auckland.
61.   The grandnephew and namesake of the illustrious Ngāpuhi rangatira, Hone Heke, who was the first to sign the Treaty of Waitangi.
62.   Carroll's involvement in Seddon's rise to power is covered in D. Hamer (1988), *The New Zealand Liberal Party: The Years of Power, 1891–1912*, Auckland University

Press, Auckland, pp. 104–6.

63. Carroll was the first Māori to head the Ministry, a post he held from 1899 to 1912; see M. King, (1981), *New Zealanders at War*, Heinemann, Auckland, p. 285.

64. Ibid, p. 289.

65. Butterworth and Young, *op cit.*, p. 58.

66. J. A. Williams, (1969), *op cit.*, p. 108 discusses a bill drafted by the more moderate Kotahitanga leaders which suggested the abolition of the Native Land Court and its replacement with six District Land Boards and an Appeal Board.

67. During World War I, 2227 Māori served overseas: 336 were killed or died of wounds or illness and 734 were wounded; see Lt Richard J. Taylor, (1988), *Special Exhibition, 28th Māori Battalion*, p. 1.

68. J. F. Cody, (1956), *28 (Māori) Battalion: Official History of New Zealand in the Second World War 1935–45*, Department of Internal Affairs, Wellington, p. 1.

69. C. Orange, (1987b), 'An Exercise in Māori Autonomy: The Rise of the Māori War Effort Organisation', *NZJH*, 21: 157.

70. M. King, (1983), *Māori: A Photographic and Social History*, Heinemann, Auckland, p. 217.

71. The Battalion sailed on the *Aquitania* as part of the Second Echelon.

72. Butterworth and Young, *op cit.*, pp. 83–4. Paikea was Minister Representing the Native Race from January 1941 until he took up the post of Minister in Charge of the Māori War Effort in June 1942.

73. See M. King, (1977), *Te Puea*, Hodder and Stoughton, Auckland pp. 206–7 for examples of Waikato reluctance to take up arms.

74. Fraser took the Premiership after M. J. Savage died in March 1940.

75. Rangi Mawhete was appointed to the Legislative Council on 9 March 1936 and served until 8 March 1950; J. O. Wilson, *New Zealand Parliamentary Records, 1840–1984*.

76. Orange (1987b), *op cit.*, p. 159. Much of her data, as she explains, was drawn from Love R. Ngatata, (1977), 'The Politics of Frustration: The Growth of Māori Politics', PhD thesis, Victoria University of Wellington.

77. Butterworth and Young, *op cit.*, pp. 84–5.

78. Orange, (1987b), *op cit.*, p. 163.

79. Butterworth and Young, *op cit.*, p. 85, to be called either the Ministry of Māori Welfare or perhaps the Ministry of Māori Administration.

80. Details of the Māori Social and Economic Reconstruction Bill, prepared by a committee convened by Tirikatene and presented to Fraser, appear in Orange, (1987b), *op cit.*, p. 166.

81. This was strenuously opposed by Tirikatene and eventually abandoned; see Orange, ibid, p. 164.

82. Mason instead resurrected his earlier bill to revive the 1900 Māori Council system; see Orange, ibid, p. 167.

83. J. Metge, (1976), *The Maoris of New Zealand: Ruatahi*, 2nd edn, Routledge, Kegan and Paul, London, p. 208.

84. The full title of this Act is 'An Act to make Provision for the Social and Economic Advancement and the Promotion and Maintenance of the Health and Social Well-Being of the Māori Community'.

85. Another important alteration was that the tribal committees became Māori committees as the appellation was more suitable—some committee areas did not correspond to tribal rohe.

86.   Butterworth and Young, *op cit.*, pp. 68–70.

87.   Metge, *op cit.*, p. 209.

88.   Table 6 is based on the minutes of the New Zealand Māori Council Executive meeting of 20 September 1991 held at the Quality Inn, Willis Street, Wellington.

89.   The COGS programme is one example of a contemporary funding source utilized by some Māori committees.

90.   E. Schwimmer, (1968b), 'The Māori and Government', in E. Schwimmer (ed.), *The Māori People in the 1960s*, Longman Paul, Auckland, p. 330; and J. Ritchie, (1965), 'The Grass Roots of Maori Politics', in J. G. A. Pocock (ed.), *The Maori and New Zealand Politics: Talks from an NZBC Series with Additional Essays*, Blackwood and Janet Paul, Auckland, pp. 80–6.

Chapter Six
He Paihere Tangata

Paiherea; kahore i whati, pēnā ano i ngā rākau e whitu.[1]

Characteristics of Theme Three

The third theme explored in this book is 'He Paihere Tangata', under which heading are grouped national Māori bodies that seek to unite Māori people on a basis of common ethnicity. This section, therefore, emphasizes pan-tribal movements that focus on particular sectoral interests.

The structures developed by each movement do not as a group conform to a specific pattern. Some are distinctly Māori, while others echo a European approach; often a combination of the two provides a framework to give effect to the interests of a given organization. The tendency has been to aggregate the most effective methodologies from each cultural strand into an effective system for the group. The decision to consider these bodies as a group is not based upon the mechanisms by which goals are attained, but rather upon the common desire of each body to pursue a defined goal.

A reaction to a perceived inequity has often been the catalyst for groups of this kind. The major difference in impetus of these Kotahitanga movements is that the theme of political autonomy is given a lower priority than the particular socio-cultural motives which each group seeks to address.

Māori prophetic cults and so-called millennial movements conform to this pattern. The Rātana movement covered in this section was selected as an example because of all the religious movements through which Māori have sought to address perceived ills it has been the most effective at a national level. Further, traditional tribal affiliations are accorded little regard in the movement's philosophies, and a pan-tribal approach is advocated.

The Māori Women's Welfare League is another case study analysed as a national movement seeking to address a particular set of social disadvantages. Established to address issues facing Māori women whom, by almost all recognized socio-economic indicators exhibit lower standards of well-being, the League has come to exert some considerable political influence. This is not inconsistent with the principle tenets of the League, and is in fact essential to the realization of many of the goals of the group. The early paternalistic attitude toward Māori, and especially to Māori women, may have led initially to a focusing on issues such as basic hygiene, parenting skills, and cooking. Latterly, however, the ambit of League concerns has broadened markedly. Currently the League is seen as a powerful proactive voice in both Māori and national affairs.

The development of pan-Māori organizations that focus upon common ethnicity and specific non-tribal goals is a comparatively recent phenomenon. The movements addressed thus far in this book have been in the main built upon a framework of tribal integrity and autonomy. With the demographic shift away from rural areas and the resultant diminution of traditional affiliations to ancestral territories, a distinct ethnic perception has developed among Māori. In an urban environment where contact not only with Europeans but also with Pacific Islanders, Asians, and other tribal groups is regular and unavoidable, and where continuous contact with direct kinsmen is perhaps lessened, Māori find common cause with other Māori comforting. A clear link, then, between pan-tribal Māori kotahitanga and increased urbanization among Māori can be hypothesized. It was that link which encouraged the Mana Motuhake political party.

Contemporary Demographic Trends

Studies of Māori society undertaken during the 1960s and 1970s[2] point to a dilution of traditional structures. Whānau groupings have become more dispersed, partially because of an increased participation in the monetary economy of New Zealand which has led to relocation to urban centres. A further contributing factor to the dispersal of whānau groupings and to the urbanization of Māori is diminished land holdings and an increase in State-induced individualization of land title. Māori agricultural and horticultural pursuits have become family-based (whāmere—Hohepa: 93–100) and dwelling patterns have diminished the geographic propinquity between group members.

Another consequence of the postwar urban drift has been a wider distribution of Māori throughout the country. While Māori predominantly live in the North Island, and particularly in the upper half of the North Island, a noticeable southern movement is apparent in the demographic make-up of the population. One can assume, therefore, that increasingly Māori are no longer occupying traditional tribal regions. Affiliation to and participation in tribal politics, society, and culture are therefore less readily maintained. This, too, has coloured the nature of tribalism in the 1990s.

An interesting feature of Māori population movement has been a

Figure 19: Māori urbanization (percentage)

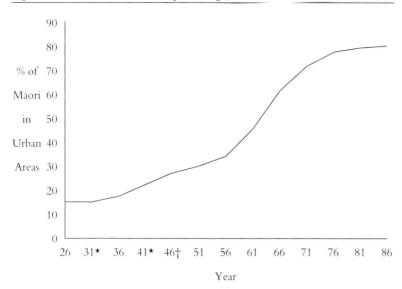

★ The figures for 1931 and 1941 are estimates based on observable trends
† This figure is that recorded in the 1945 census

discernible but numerically small move back to rural areas among older urban Māori. Again this trend can be tied to the monetarist economy. Upon retirement, the need to reside in the cities is lessened, allowing the cultural pull of the rural marae to dominate. By 1986, the number of Māori migrating to rural areas was almost equal to the number relocating to the cities.[3] This trend may equally reflect a reduction in movement to urban areas as it shows an increase in rural migration.

The Rātana Movement

Kei te pai! Whakakotahi ki te Matua i te tuatahi ana Tātou ki te whakakotahi ki te whenua. (Tahupotiki Wīremu Rātana to Tupu Taingakawa at Rātana, November 1920)

As discussed in Chapter Two of this book,[4] Māori political power is closely aligned to the exercise of ritual authority. As the traditional bases, both temporal and spiritual, were eroded by the incursion of European practices and culture, the vacuum was filled, in part, by Christianity. Māori experience with the realities of colonization, however, led to a disillusionment with European structures—religious, political, and otherwise. This disillusionment, based in part upon an observed divergence between religious rhetoric and temporal practice,[5] was eventually reflected in the emergence of alternative Māori churches under the leadership of charismatic prophets.[6] Commonly, Māori religious independence from mainstream Christian churches has been analysed in terms of protest against perceived social disadvantage and political impotence. This indeed is the perspective adopted in this book, but it is tempered by Elsmore's recent observation that Māori society now and in the past has always had a firm religious undertone.[7] It is to be expected, therefore, that any protest might well assume a spiritual format, and that the millenarian[8] cults of the Māori are an assertion of spiritual autonomy.

Commenting on the spirituality of Māori, Te Pākaka Tāwhai[9] provides some useful perspectives on the alignment between it and temporal activities. In his view, Māori are concerned by issues such as

> the effectiveness of the relationship between a person and a superhuman controlling power in magnifying that person's capacity to work his will: or the constraints and obligations upon that person in order to sustain the relationship.

Herein can be observed a consistent Māori perception of the relationship between political power and ritual authority. A capacity to understand, interpret, and observe the edicts of Atua (Mana Atua) ascribes considerable influence (Mana Tangata) to the bearer. When considering the eventual political power which attached to the Rātana movement it will be important to remember this facet of Māori philosophy.

The Prophetic Tradition

It is a well-rehearsed anthropological theory that Messianic movements emerge when a particular sector of a society, often an ethnic division, becomes acutely aware of its own disadvantaged position.[10] In such a climate, religious solutions to social ills may be expressed in terms of salvation from the hands of the oppressor and the ultimate ascendancy of the oppressed. The socio-political environment of Judea and Palestine during the Imperium of Rome and the subsequent emergence of Christianity provide the conceptual framework for these theories. Some of the indigenous tribes of that region, who oriented themselves according to various legendary apical ancestors, and whose political, religious, and cultural life was dominated by an imported and unwelcome doctrine, were willing to believe in the promises of hope and salvation delivered by Jesus Christ.[11] Of course, there were among them many entrenched power brokers who would profit little from change and accordingly resisted it.

The leaders of these cults, as they are often termed, are usually cast as prophets, whose teachings, when observed, will facilitate the eventual supremacy of their followers, just as the first Messiah would restore to his disciples the Kingdom of God. The origins of religious doctrines propounded by these prophets is often a visitation from a supernatural messenger: variously a manifestation of the principal deity, or one of the central figures associated with the God. In Christian and Judaic theology, these may be the Holy Ghost, the Virgin Mary, or perhaps one of the Parthenon of Angels.

The plight of the Jews, some of whom found comfort in the teachings of the Lamb of God, was not dissimilar to the situation in which Māori found themselves enmeshed once the full impact of colonization was felt. Indeed, Te Atua Wera adopted the term Hūrai (a transliteration of the Hebrew 'Jew') to refer to the Māori.[12] The faith he developed has strong Christian overtones but his reference to Māori as Jews is seen as an identification with the chosen people of God rather than as the forebears of Christianity. The introduction of Christian symbolism had modified Māori spiritual thinking, and many of the religious movements which emerged over time can be seen as an amalgam of the Messianic message of Christ couched in terms familiar to Māori. Bronwyn Elsmore, after a comprehensive analysis of the multitude of Māori responses to this new spiritual paradigm, states that the nature of the response is shaped by the depth of contact with the Scriptures which Māori had obtained.

The cult inspired by Te Ua Haumene referred to in Chapter Four, is one movement which grew from the animosities in Aotearoa in the 1860s. While superficially little like the familiar European interpretation of the biblical message, Te Ua's teachings have been shown to contain many references to the philosophical and spiritual teachings he received as a Wesleyan catechist.[13] The impetus for Te Ua to assume his prophetic role came primarily from an encounter with the Archangel, Gabriel, who guided him through a series of commands, some of which seem fairly extreme. On one occasion he was ordered to kill his son, truly a test of conviction. It was, however, followed by a miraculous healing which not only convinced Te Ua of the validity of his encounters with Gabriel, but also demonstrated something of his power to those who witnessed the event.[14] Thus the Māori concern with an effective relationship with a superhuman facilitator is given substance.

The Emergence of the Prophet

Tahupotiki Wiremu Rātana also received the inspiration for his mission from a divine visitation.[15] While camping with his wife, Urumanao, and two of their sons, Arepa and Omeka[16] (Alpha and Omega) at Te Takutai Moana o Whangaehu, Rātana received a sign of his calling. Two whales were cast upon the beach, one dying immediately and the other struggling fruitlessly for a period. He knew the oil and meat would be needed at a later period, and was proved correct as several hundred guests were to descend upon him in the next twelve months. This incident was portentous in another regard. The two whales came to symbolize the dual facets of Rātana's mission: the first, Ture Wairua, spiritual works; the second, Ture Tangata, material works.

On 8 November 1918, the Holy Ghost appeared to Rātana in the form of a small cloud. The cloud rose over the Tasman Sea and moved toward him as he sat relaxing on his veranda after his day's work. Rapidly it approached and engulfed him, and spoke to him, telling him that after a considerable period of searching, Aotearoa and its indigenous people had been chosen by God to be the vehicle for the redemption of mankind. He was to cleanse himself and his family and, as the Mouthpiece of God, Māngai, unite the tribes of New Zealand under Ihoa o Ngā Mano, Jehovah of the Multitudes. Convinced by this and other supernormal occurrences, which are amply recorded elsewhere,[17] the prophet from that moment on forswore alcohol and gambling and embarked upon his appointed task.

During the months which followed his accepting the mantle of Māngai, foretold by the renowned Ngāti Apa seer, Mere Rikiriki six years earlier, Rātana immersed himself in the Scriptures and in Pope's *Health for the Māori* (1884).[18] His kinsmen, hearing of the dramatic change and mysterious events which had precipitated it, gathered themselves in makeshift accommodation on his family farm at Orakei-nui.[19] Periodically, the prophet would speak to them of their beliefs, of Jehovah, and of Mana Māori Motuhake. Thus was formed a powerful religious movement which would eventually unite many Māori, not as members of individual tribes, but as Mōrehu, the remnants of the tribes of Aotearoa.

An important aspect of Rātana's ministry was healing—healing not only the physical afflictions which beset the faithful, but also the social and political ills which they faced. When conducting the miraculous faith-healing acts for which he became renowned throughout the country and beyond, Rātana converted his patients to his ever-growing congregation. Having been healed of their ailments, his patients renounced their earlier beliefs and pledged themselves to the Holy Trinity. More importantly, perhaps, they became members of Te Iwi Morehu, and distanced themselves from their tribal identity.

This feature of the movement—the denial of tribalism—is central to the teachings of the Church, and allowed erstwhile belligerents to forget past wrongs promulgated in the furtherance of tribal mana, and unite under the mantle of Jehovah. It is in this respect that the Rātana movement differs most from other Kotahitanga movements discussed in this book. In an increasingly urbanized population, the concept of being a member of a race of people,

Figure 20: Tempara o Te Hāhi Rātana, Rātana (date: unknown; *courtesy of the Gober Collection, Alexander Turnbull Library*)

Māori, as opposed to being a part of a kinship network, iwi or hapū, also became increasingly useful. To identify with a fellow Māori regardless of tribal origin was oft times more applicable than tribal membership.

The denial of tribalism can be linked to a rejection of traditional religious beliefs, such as tohungatanga, and other social constructs including tapu and mana. There was a denial of hereditary chiefly prestige and, although this appealed to many Māori, it did alienate other notable leaders. The later animosity toward the movement from the powerful Waikato leader, Te Puea Herangi, could be attributed in part to the modernist attitudes that were fundamental to the Rātana doctrine.

An important attribute of the Rātana movement, kotahitanga, was the humble origin of its leader. While some of the cult leaders who arose before

Figure 21: Princess Te Puea (date unknown)

him were not drawn from the traditional hierarchy, many who assumed national prominence were. The leaders of other unifying organizations such as Pāremata Māori and the Kīngitanga were uniformly drawn from the senior families of their iwi. Participants in the district rūnanga and Māori councils were also drawn, in the main, from rangatira families. Tahupotiki Wiremu Rātana, known to his peers as Bill, was, however, by his own admission, 'a common man'. At forty-five, although he had a strong grounding in the lore and spirituality of his iwi, he was otherwise not a member of the academic élite, as were other kotahitanga leaders such as the members of the Young

Māori Party. Two aspects of Rātana's appeal to those who followed him were that his mantle was thrust upon him by God, and he was a member of the working class. This affiliation was couched in the following words borrowed from King Tāwhiao:[20]

> Ne oku hoa, ko te hūmeka, te parākimete, te wātimeka, ngā kāmura, ngā pani, ngā pouwaru.

Rātana affinity for 'the common man' led inexorably to a firm identification with the Labour movement which also emerged early in the twentieth century. As discussed below, the continued failure to influence entrenched political power structures and the leaders who directed them continued to frustrate Rātana in his mission to address the ill-being which beset Māori. The Labour Party, committed as it was to social reform and to the well-being of workers, had common cause with the Rātana movement.

In the two years preceding Christmas 1920, Māori flocked to the Rangitikei to behold the prophet. Literally thousands came and went, and during the Yuletide festivities 3000 people had joined him at his farm. Earlier that year, members of the Ringatu faith, which was based upon the teachings of Te Kooti Arikirangi, came to hear his message and to find a way in which the two movements might be made compatible. It was, however, not to be. Tupu Taingakawa, Tumuaki of the Kauhanganui, also came to Rātana. Taingakawa (in company with Rewiti Te Whena)[21] asked the Māngai not to heal him physically, but to minister to the suffering of the land. Rātana's reply (which prefaces this section) was that unity under the Father was to be a prerequisite for unity in the land.[22]

The gathering at Rātana (the family homestead was by now the centre of a developing village)[23] for Christmas 1920 was an occasion marked by the opening of the Church, Piki Te Ora. Members of both Protestant and Catholic clergy participated in the dedication of the building. At this time, Rātana was concerned with bringing Māori to Christianity and, although he preached hygiene, the rejection of superstition, and faith in the Holy Trinity, he had not formulated his own religious doctrine.[24] Indeed, many adherents were concurrently involved in the more orthodox Christian churches, and services were conducted by many ministers of diverse backgrounds. The faithful brought with them their own dogma and, while this situation was initially sanctioned by the Māngai, controversy eventually developed.

As Rātana developed his theological standpoint, areas of contention between his followers and the conventional ministries increased. On 31 May 1925, Rātana declared the existence of a separate Church, Te Hāhi Rātana, which was formally registered two months later (21 July 1925). The reaction of the Anglican Synod was uncompromising. Although the Venerable Archdeacon H. W. Williams of Waiapu had earlier found no fault with his work, the Church declared Rātana a schismatic and stated that some of his teachings were contradictory to Christian beliefs. The Methodists were more conciliatory and maintained a relationship with the new Church, hoping to be able to influence it in some way.[25]

Once established, the administration and control of the spiritual aspects of Te Hāhi Rātana were undertaken by the Church Committee, which was at the apex of the synod structure. Below it were Branch Committees that functioned at a regional level. The next step in the hierarchy was unpaid ministers, Apotoro. These were also graduated as follows:

Apotoro Rehita	Registered Apostle	purple stole
Apotoro Wairua	Spiritual Apostle	red stole
Akonga	Assistant Curates	gold stole
Awhina	Sisters	purple stole[26]

Now that the Ture Wairua was in place, Rātana turned to the other half of his mission, Te Ture Tangata.

Rātana and The Treaty

Kei tetahi o āku ringa ko te Paipera Tapu; kei tetahi ko te Tiriti o Waitangi. Ki te oti te taha wairua he mea mama noa iho te taha kikokiko.[27]

Like Tāwhiao, Rātana determined to place directly before the Crown his people's grievances over land and the Treaty of Waitangi. In April of 1924 he travelled to London with a delegation of thirty-nine Mōrehu, Tupu Taingakawa among them, to lay his case before King George V and Edward, Prince of Wales. Although he could legitimately claim the support of 30,000 adherents, the New Zealand High Commissioner, Sir James Allen, under instructions from the New Zealand Government, blocked his way. No audience was granted with the King nor with the British Prime Minister. His deputation, like those of Tāwhiao and Taiwhanga[28] before him, was sent home unsatisfied. The prophet was undeterred, however, and continued his campaign for recognition of the Treaty of Waitangi. He channelled his energies into submissions to successive prime ministers, and was each time rebuffed.[29] Joseph Gordon Coates, Joseph George Ward, and George William Forbes all dismissed his claims made under the Treaty of Waitangi.[30]

He set in motion a petition seeking statutory recognition for the Treaty. A hui, convened at Rātana Pā during the Christmas of 1929, launched what was to be the largest Māori petition to Parliament. By Easter of 1930, 26,407 signatures had been appended to it.[31] It was formally presented in 1932 by Eruera Tirikatene (later Sir Eruera)[32] who had taken the Southern Māori seat in a by-election that year. By then, 30,128 names were attached to the petition.[33]

Legislation to give effect to the petition did not eventuate. Indeed, it seems that the only action taken, and this thirteen years later, was the publication and distribution of copies of the Treaty of Waitangi to be displayed in schools.[34] It was not until the Rātana/Labour political alliance MP for Northern Māori, the Hon. Matiu Rata, piloted the Treaty of Waitangi Act 1975 through the House that this dream of the prophet reached fruition.[35]

Political representation in parliamentary politics featured in the Rātana movement as early as 1922. Hāmi Tokouru Rātana, the eldest son of the Māngai, contested the Western Māori seat in the general election of that year. The seat was held by the Liberal candidate, Dr Maui Pomare (later Sir Maui)[36] who was supported by King Te Rata. Although Pomare had advocated conscription in the Waikato during World War I, thus alienating Te Rata's chief adviser, Te Puea Herangi, the King remained loyal to him because he had been chosen as the Kīngitanga candidate by King Mahuta. Pomare had also promised to convene a commission of inquiry into the Waikato raupatu—a promise he kept in 1925.[37]

The election outcome was closer than either Herangi or Pomare had expected—a mere 798 votes separating the two candidates.[38] Māori dissatisfaction with successive Liberal and Reform administrations contributed to the rise of the Rātana movement as a political force in the Dominion.[39] The Western Māori seat included Hawera, the home of Tokouru's mother, as well as Whanganui and Rangitikei, where Rātana's support was strongest. Tokouru continued to meet with success in Western Māori, consistently polling around 3000 votes and eventually taking the seat in 1935. However, he did not stand in 1925, due to the controversy invoked by the establishment of Te Hāhi Rātana.

By 1928, the Rātana movement was firmly committed to parliamentary politics when the Māngai established his Four Quarters, Ngā Koata e Whā. His vow was to take the four Māori electorates and to use them to promote his Treaty of Waitangi goals, to address the grievances of the past, and to ameliorate, where possible, the plight of Māori. Four men who had been close to him over the years were selected to contest the election—each of them signing a covenant pledging them not to rest until they were in the House.[40]

The four chosen in 1928 to stand in the general election (the 'first cut') were: Eruera Tihema Tirikatene, Southern; Hāmi Tokouru Rātana, Western; Paraire Karaka Paikea,[41] Northern; and Pita Moko, Eastern. Although none of them was successful that year, Tirikatene only failed to

Figure 22: Rātana leaders. *Back row from left*: Tiaka Ormond, Tapihana Paraire Paikea. *Front row from left*: Haami Tokouru Ratana, Tahupotiki Wiremu Ratana, Sir Eruera Tirikatene (date: unknown, circa 1943; *courtesy of the National Museum*)

upset the sitting member, Tuiti Makitanara,[42] by a single vote. In the 1931 general election a mere fifteen-vote margin was recorded against Tirikatene. He finally took the seat the following year when the incumbent's death forced a by-election. Returned with a 247-vote majority, Southern Māori became the first of the four quarters to be held by Rātana.

Having consistently polled well against Sir Maui Pomare in 1922 and 1928, Tokouru Rātana unsuccessfully challenged Taite Te Tomo for the Western Māori seat in 1931. He finally joined Tirikatene in the House of Representatives in 1935. P. K. Paikea was the next Rātana MP, taking Northern Māori from Tau Henare[43] in the 1938 general election.

It was in the Eastern Māori electorate where the growth of support for the Rātana/Labour alliance was slowest. Held by Sir Apirana Turupa Ngata since his election as the Liberal Party candidate in 1905, the mana of this great Ngāti Porou leader was almost insurmountable. It was not until 1943 that Tiaki Omana took the seat. Eruera Stirling relates in his autobiography that

Some of the Rātana people at Waipiro Bay, Tupāroa, and Te Araroa turned against him and they voted for Jack Ormond, and Ngata was beaten by 246 votes![44]

In the election of 1938, the last to be won by Ngata, the Rātana candidate, Tiaki Omana, polled third to the Labour representative, Reweti Tuhorouta Kohere[45]—combined, their votes exceeded Ngata's by 1062.[46] In 1943, however, Omana stood as a Labour representative. It is apparent that this sponsorship, combined with his own support, won him the seat.

Rātana political power had come of age. Based upon the support of Mōrehu, the landless remnants of Māori, the fruition of Rātana's dream marked the beginning of a new alignment in Māori parliamentary politics. The leaders of the early twentieth century, Carroll and Ngata, who had come to represent the traditionally powerful, conservative members of Māori society, had been displaced as the spokespersons in the House. The majority of Māori, who had been relegated to the lower rungs of New Zealand's social hierarchy, had registered a commitment based upon class. This new alignment eventually developed into an affiliation with the nation's other champions of the poor in the form of an alliance with Labour.

The Rātana/Labour Political Alliance

The New Zealand Labour Party, formed in 1916, was a coalition of the various disparate Labour movements which had arisen since the turn of the

Table 7: Ngā Koāta e Wha, a summary of the Rātana hold in Māori electorates (the three Members in italics were not of the Rātana faith)

Southern	Western	Northern	Eastern
Hon. Eruera T. Tirikatene, 1932–1967(d).	H. Tokouru Rātana, 1935–1944, (d).	Hon. Paraire K. Paikea, 1938–1943, (d).	Tiaki Omana, 1943–63, (d).
Hon. T. Whetu M. Tirikatene-Sullivan, 1967–present	Matiu Rātana, 1945	T. P. Paikea, 1943–63, (d).	*Steve Wātene*, 1963–67, (d), (m)
	Mrs Iriaka Rātana, 1949–68, (r)	Hon. Matiu Rata, 1963–1980, (res)	Paroane (Brownie) Reweti 1967–81, (d)
	Hon. Koro Wetere, 1969–present	*Bruce Gregory*, 1980–present, (a)	*Hon. Peter W. Tapsell*, 1981–present, (a)

(d) = died in office (r) = resigned from seat (m) = Mormon (a) = Anglican century. The United Labour Party (ULP), formed in 1912, had represented, in the main, the moderate members of the trade union movement. The more militant New Zealand Federation of Labour and its parliamentary subsidiary, the New Zealand Socialist Party, joined with them to form the Labour Party at a conference in Wellington in June 1916. They perceived the conflict in Europe as part of the class struggle prophesied by Marx and Engels, and, seeing World War I as presaging the collapse of Western capitalism, moved to consolidate their interest with those of the ULP.

Going into the 1922 general election under the leadership of Henry Esmond (Harry) Holland,[47] the Labour Party held eight seats in Parliament. After the election they had acquired a further nine. By 1931 they had, with twenty-four seats, established themselves as the Opposition to the coalition of the United and Reform parties, and were eventually to take power in a crushing landslide victory in 1935, securing fifty-five of the available seats.

Labour's philosophy was based on the advocacy of worker rights, and the Party also represented a break with traditional power structures. This held considerable appeal to Rātana and his adherents as they, in promoting the interests of Mōrehu, the landless, and the unemployed were of similar mould. The Depression of the 1930s had added to the numbers of Māori unemployed and consequently was increasing the movement's political sway. Rātana had been successively foiled in his attempts to influence Prime Ministers Coates, Ward, and Forbes over the Treaty of Waitangi, but was to find an ally in Harry Holland, and struck an informal alliance with him in 1931. This agreement, whereby Labour would not contest the four Māori electorates in return for Rātana support in the House, resulted in part from the influence of Rangi Mawhete, a firm Labour man and a former candidate for Western Māori. Mawhete, a cousin of Rātana,[48] saw that the Labour Party required a political partnership with the Māngai if it was to have any influence in the Māori electorates.[49] Accordingly, he convinced Walter Nash, Peter Fraser, and Harry Holland[50] to court Rātana support, and they attended meetings at Rātana Pā and elsewhere to hear discussion of Rātana policies on Māori issues.

When Labour swept into power in 1935, this informal association was placed on a more secure footing. On 4 February 1936, Rātana travelled to Wellington to meet with Prime Minister Michael Joseph Savage[51] at the House of Representatives. He brought with him four talismans—symbols of the plight of Mōrehu and the mechanisms required to restore them to their birthright. These he gave to Savage, who in return promised to address issues relating to Māori welfare.[52]

The final success of the Rātana movement in its quest to hold the Four Quarters can therefore be attributed to the alliance formed with the Labour Party in April of 1936. Had Labour and Rātana formally endorsed all of each other's candidates for the 1938 general election, the Māngai's dream may have been fulfilled in his lifetime.

He had, nonetheless, convincingly demonstrated the power of oppression as a motive for unity. The Kotahitanga movement of Rātana had all the ingredients of a solidarity based on dispossession, belief in God, cultural uniformity, and political determination. Missing was the tribal base, traditional leadership, and confidence in conservative Māori hierarchies.

Te Rōpu Wahine Māori Toko i Te Ora

The Māori Women's Welfare League held its first General Conference in Wellington during September of 1951, at which delegates from 187 branches formally adopted a prepared constitution. The proceedings were conducted in an atmosphere of '. . . goodwill, cooperation and assistance . . .'[53] (just as the Taitokerau District Rūnanga had accepted the model developed by the State bureaucracy in 1862). Delegates at the conference were drawn from women's welfare committees established by Rangi Royal after World War II by Māori Welfare Officers operating under the Māori Welfare Act 1945.[54]

At the inaugural General Conference, Awhina Cooper, now Dame Whina, was elected as the first president of the Dominion Council of the Māori Women's Welfare League, while Miraka Petricevich, now Szaszy, was elected secretary. Whina Cooper was quick to realize that the Dominion Council was the only national Māori organization extant at that time. Accordingly, having first toured the country establishing branches and district councils, she commenced to vigorously lobby Government to ensure League issues received the attention due them.[55] The New Zealand Māori Council did not emerge until the passage of the 1962 Māori Welfare Act, and so during the intervening years the annual conferences of the League became the principal platform for the discussion by Māori of national issues. Housing, health, education, welfare, equal opportunities in employment and accommodation, and crime were all debated, and suitable submissions presented to Parliament.[56]

The League was established as an incorporated society with government patronage, and as such was structured along the lines of the now familiar hierarchical blueprint. This relationship with the State, and in particular with the Department of Māori Affairs, has meant that since the early years of its existence secretarial and other services were provided by the Department and funded from its budget.[57] The League, although operationally autonomous, is still dependent on government grants for its existence and, while much of the funding for branch operations is generated locally, the national structure still

Figure 23: First General Conference Māori Women's Welfare League, Wellington, September 1951. *From left*: Roda Ropiha, Mr Corbett (Minister of Māori Affairs), Mr Holland (Prime Minister), Rumatiki Wright (Chairperson of Conference) (*Courtesy of the National Publicity Studios Collection, Alexander Turnbull Library*)

relies heavily on State finance. The number of full-time staff employed at National Headquarters in Wellington has increased from one in 1976 to three in 1989. According to the 1989 financial report, the Māori Women's Welfare League held over $350,000 worth of cash and assets.[58]

The Secretary of Māori Affairs at that time (1951) was Tipi Ropiha. Together with his Minister, Ernest Corbett, and the Controller of Māori Welfare, Rangi Royal,[59] Ropiha played a formative role in the establishment of the League and in drawing up its Constitution.[60] The League, according to its Constitution, is to be neither sectarian nor aligned to any political party, and its aims are to:

- provide an organization to enable effective participation by members in cultural, social, and economic development in their communities
- render humane service whenever and wherever possible
- preserve, revive, and maintain Māori language, arts, and culture and to perpetuate Māori ethics

- promote understanding between women of all races through improved and mutual understanding
- promote health
- promote parenting skills
- promote prisoner welfare and rehabilitation
- promote education in hygiene, homecraft, mothercraft, handcraft, and horticulture
- work closely with governmental, New Zealand Māori Council, and other welfare organizations.

While all of these goals are pursued actively by members of the League, it remains the prerogative of local organizations to determine the areas of activity upon which they concentrate. Some prefer to develop a range of cultural activities whereas others emphasize mothercraft, and yet others see direct political action as a priority. All are within the ambit of the League, and this range and diversity of issues makes it an organization attractive to Māori women across a broad spectrum of social, political, cultural, and economic interest areas.

Here indeed is a true strength of the Māori Women's Welfare League. It enables membership to be drawn from the broadest possible base among Māori women. This breadth facilitates active involvement by Māori women in affairs that concern them immediately and through the Dominion Council at a national level.

Despite the obvious government involvement in the formation of the League, it was not purely a Crown initiative. On the contrary, the movement grew from a desire among Māori women to establish a forum through which they might express their views and compliment the role of the tribal committees. It is this feature, where Māori women actively sought an avenue for political participation at a national level, that has contributed to the ongoing success of the organization. While the hierarchy of committees format may have effectively been imposed, it was not only welcomed, but has grown into an effective and adaptable structure that has withstood the test of time.

The Structure of the League

Today, Dame Te Atairangikāhu is the patron of Te Rōpu Wāhine Māori Toko i te Ora, and the current president is Aroha Rereti-Crofts. The hierarchy that they head has at its base local organizations known as branches, described variously as independent branches, junior branches, or branches. The recent Manatū Māori publication *Te Aka Kumara*[61] records a total of 204 organizational elements as affiliates to the Māori Women's Welfare League: one is the National Society, four are regional or district councils, while of the remaining 199, nine are junior branches. The distinction between independent and other branches is determined by whether or not the branch affiliates directly to the Dominion Council or via their district or regional body. For convenience, the Māori Women's Welfare League districts are modelled on the same Land Court districts used by the New Zealand Māori Council (see Figure 24).

The branch structure is a real strength in the case of the Māori Women's Welfare League. Local issues can be discussed at branch level or aired nationally if required. Conversely, national policies can feed back from the Dominion Council directly into the homes of Māori, and thus have an affect upon the fundamental building block of Māori social organization, the whānau.

Nationally the Māori Women's Welfare League has a strong relationship with the New Zealand Māori Council, and through its patron has a good relationship with the Kīngitanga movement. It is represented on the Māori Education Foundation and is affiliated to the National Council of Women. In the international arena it has links to other indigenous women's groups and is affiliated to the Pan Pacific Association, as well as having a few branches in Australia.

Forerunners to the League

Some Māori women in 'traditional times' wielded considerable political and social influence within their whānau, hapū, iwi, and waka groupings, but external politics and defence tended to remain a male preserve. According to Vapi Kupenga et al., 'It cannot be said . . . that prior to the coming of the Pākehā that Māori women suffered from oppression'.[62] In their paper, Vapi Kupenga et al. produce convincing historical and linguistic evidence to show

Table 8: League Presidents

	Term
Dame Whina Cooper, MBE, CBE, DBE	1951–57
Mrs Miria Logan	1957–60
Mrs Māta Hirini	1960–64
Mrs Ruiha Sage	1964–68
Mrs Miria Karauria	1968–71
Mrs Hine Potaka, OBE	1971–73
Dame Miraka Szaszy, OBE, CBE, DBE	1973–77
Mrs Elizabeth Murchie	1977–80
Mrs Violet Te Pou	1980–83
Mrs Maraea Te Kawa	May–Sept. 1983
Mrs Georgina Kirby	Sept. 1983–87
Mrs June Mariu	1987–90
Mrs Aroha H Rereti-Crofts, QSM	1991–present

Figure 24: MWWL regional council areas

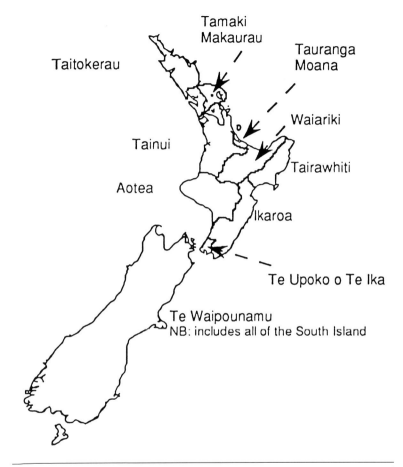

Tamaki
Makaurau

Tauranga
Moana

Taitokerau

Waiariki

Tainui

Tairawhiti

Aotea

Ikaroa

Te Upoko o Te Ika

Te Waipounamu
NB: includes all of the South Island

This map is not to scale, nor is it precise. It is intended to only give a general impression.

---

that Māori women have always possessed and exercised power and authority within Māori society: mana wāhine. That this mana was and is different to that accorded their male counterparts is obvious and is emphasized in their article.

Mana wāhine, however, is perceived and demonstrated to be complementary to male authority rather than inferior to it. The clearly defined operational spheres occupied by the two genders are shown as the basis upon which tribal, hapū, and whānau affairs were conducted both effectively and harmoniously. By 1951, however, much had changed. The world had only just emerged from a conflict which had surpassed all others in the extent and degree of violence and destruction exhibited. While the cataclysm remained away from these shores, its effects were felt, and Māori women adapted to meet them. These acute alterations are themselves insignificant when compared to the gradual violence of one hundred years of colonialism.

Although Ngahuia Te Awekotuku[63] is a little more reserved in her assessment of the gender relationships prior to the colonial period, she too highlights the loss or deprivation of economic, social, political, and spiritual power among Māori women. In her paper she maintains that introduced perceptions of the economic value of women's roles, which came to be couched in monetary terms, tended to minimize these roles and, by inference, Māori women. Māori men increasingly undertook paid employment, often outside the traditional sphere of economic activity, and were introduced to European attitudes towards women, and in some respects adopted them. Urbanization has also contributed to the evolution of how Māori women perceive themselves, and how they are perceived by society. The role of women has been considerably altered by an increasing wage-earning capacity and by changes to family structures. The aggregate effect of these influences has been an erosion in status of Māori in general, and of Māori women in particular.

By 1951, Māori society was not only ready for women to emerge as a collective political entity, it was also in need of such an emergence. At a Ngāti Porou wānanga held at Kokiri Marae in the Hutt Valley in May 1990, Tilley Reedy spoke on the role of women in her youth during Te Pakanganui, World War II. With the male leaders of her iwi embroiled in a foreign war, the women of the rural district where she was raised undertook new roles. Later, when the fighting was over, the disparity in number between genders led to a situation in which women were not only used to performing tasks formerly the domain of men, but were perhaps the only ones available and capable of doing so.

In her autobiography, Amiria Stirling provides some insight into the development of the League in her area, Raukokore.[64] During World War II, as a part of the Māori War Effort Organisation, a Young People's Club was established at Raukokore to raise money and gather food and resources for the men overseas. Later this structure was bifurcated and eventually emerged as a tribal committee and a Māori Women's Welfare League branch; Amiria's husband, Eruera Stirling, led the tribal committee, and Amiria became the first president of the local League branch.

At that time Māori women were not widely encouraged to participate in the tribal committees established under the Māori Social and Economic

Advancement Act 1945. Of course, many capable Māori women did and still do contribute at this level, but the philosophy and structure of the tribal committee limited the involvement of many Māori women. Social mores and traditional political roles also mitigated against them in this regard.

The League then developed to coordinate the many welfare activities undertaken by Māori women and drew upon the experience of the Māori Health League (Te Rōpu O Te Ora, 1931),[65] which still operates in some areas, and Māori committees of the Country Women's Institute.[66]

In its operations at all levels the Māori Women's Welfare League utilizes two procedural traditions. It follows both the committee procedures evolved in tikanga Pākehā as well as adhering to marae protocols. While transacting its business, consensual passage of motions is preferred to formal voting, just as with other Māori committees.

The League provides a mechanism for the coordination of Māori opinion from a broad base, and an avenue for its expression at a national level. At annual conferences attended by delegates from all parts of the nation, remits

Figure 25: First Meeting of the Māori Education Foundation, December 1961. *Back row from left:* J. K. Hunn, Sir Eruera Tirikatene, Miraka Szaszy, A. E. Campbell, J. S. Joliff, A. E. Webb, R. L. Bradley. *Front row from left:* Hanon, D. G. Ball, Tennent (*Courtesy of the* Evening Post *Collection, Alexander Turnbull Library*)

are discussed and either adopted or allowed to lapse. When they express their members' opinions on matters of policy and legislation they are forwarded to Government. Similarly, more prosaic issues are implemented locally by branches as appropriate. During its history, the League has made a number of important contributions to the development of housing, health, and education policies, has expressed opinions on issues related to justice and the law, and has provided social assistance to impoverished households through donations of food and clothing. Cultural successes include participation in the development, operation, and maintenance of Kōhanga Reo and Kura Kaupapa Māori as well as stimulating interest in traditional craft activities.

The limitation of the League as a vehicle for national Māori unity, if it has one, is the potential for developing an overtly feminist overtone which may alienate Māori men. It would be simplistic to describe Māori society in terms of gender divisions, and to seek national unity premised upon two distinct but cooperative structures would ultimately be divisive. Unity premised on gender will introduce an incompatibility with the broader goal of national Māori unity. In this regard, the Māori Women's Welfare League is unlikely to emerge by itself as the major vehicle for kotahitanga.

The Mana Motuhake Political Party

Formed in the late 1970s under the leadership of Amster Reedy,[67] and Matiu Rata,[68] the Mana Motuhake Party evolved out of disenchantment with the two-party system. Rata had held the Northern Māori seat for seventeen years (since 1963) as the Rātana/Labour representative, and was well versed in the parliamentary system. He assumed the portfolio of Māori Affairs[69] following the landslide Labour victory at the polls in 1972. During his nine years in Opposition, he had been a vigorous critic of National Party policies on Māori Affairs, and as Minister he attempted to restructure the Department and to increase its budget allocation. His career as Minister is also noteworthy because of the legislation he introduced into the House.[70] Stifled by an occasionally less than enthusiastic Party line, many of the advances he sponsored were gained only through dogged persistence. In hindsight, his achievements as Minister are recognized as having had considerable impact at a national level. His contemporaries, however, were slow to accord him his due, the media preferring to portray him as an ill-educated man incapable of finishing a sentence.

After resigning from the Labour Party in November 1979 and from the Northern Māori seat in April of the next year, he contested the resulting by-election as an independent candidate. He polled a close second to Dr Bruce Gregory, significantly Anglican, who represented the Labour Party. Rata captured 38 per cent of the vote to Gregory's 53 per cent[71] in the 7 June 1980 by-election and came within 1000 votes of wresting the seat from the Rātana/Labour alliance—by far the closest outcome in forty years.

Encouraged by the level of community support, the Mana Motuhake Party continued to actively pursue Māori issues within the existing political system, and has contested every subsequent election. Although as yet unsuccessful at the polls, the Party has made considerable inroads into the Labour majority and, in light of the proposed referendum on electoral reform, may yet obtain a presence in the House. Should a system of proportional representation be implemented, it would, on current performances, guarantee Mana Motuhake a seat.

Another issue related to the promised referendum is the status of the four Māori seats. Even at their inception, the seats in no way provided an adequate avenue for the expression of Māori opinion, nor were they an effective vehicle for Māori development. Not only were they temporary and subject to possible manipulation by the Crown, they did not and do not accurately reflect, in proportional terms, an equitable representation of iwi.[72] While the Mana Motuhake Party is at least in the short term prepared to operate within the bounds of the present system, the Māori electorates do not enable the emergence of a meaningful sharing of power between the Treaty of Waitangi partners. Therefore, Mana Motuhake in its 1984 election manifesto advocated an immediate increase in the number of Māori seats and, further, that representation ought to be decided on a tribal basis.

In line with its name, the Mana Motuhake Party (which might be translated as 'distinct and discrete power')[73] is dedicated to a philosophy of Māori autonomy: political, social, and economic. It seeks to diminish dependence upon the State and to increase Māori self-reliance. Among the other aims of the Party have been:

- the official recognition of Te Reo Māori and the implementation of strategies to ensure a progressive increase in its use
- legislative recognition of the relationship between Māori and land and an increase in Māori land ownership
- the development and implementation of strategies to ensure increased Māori participation in the paid work-force
- a nuclear-free Aotearoa and a withdrawal from the ANZUS military alliance
- the establishment of a Ministry for the Environment with a Māori secretariat to ensure Māori cultural and spiritual values are considered in the utilization of national resources.

Matiu Rata's main support is located in the far north and rests upon his personal charisma and kinship networks. Similarly, others who have stood for election as Mana Motuhake candidates have had limited general support. While the Party is committed to autonomy for Māori, it continues to operate within the existing political structure, and as such cannot truly be thought of as standing apart from the State. Although some of their policies have been used by successive governments as the basis for a degree of reform, the Party has been less than influential nationally.

Endnotes

1. Strength in unity.
2. See: J. Metge, (1976), *The Maoris of New Zealand: Ruatahi*, 2nd edn, Routledge, Kegan and Paul, London; P. W. Hohepa, (1964), *A Māori Community in Northland*, Department of Anthropology, Auckland University, pp. 56–93; and E. Schwimmer, (1968a), *The Māori People in the Nineteen Sixties*, Longman Paul, Auckland, pp. 28–30.
3. See Manatū Māori, (1991), *Nga Take i Neke ae te Māori*, Manatū Māori, Wellington, p. 23.
4. Ibid, pp. 11–12.
5. Te Pākaka Tawhai, (1991), 'Aotearoa's Spiritual Heritage', in Peter Donovan (ed.), *Religions of New Zealanders*, Dunmore, Palmerston North, p. 11.
6. Bronwyn Elsmore—(1985), *Like Them That Dream*, Tauranga Moana, Tauranga, pp. 94–5—estimates that over sixty such religions have been referred to in written records since the early 1830s.
7. B. Elsmore, (1989), *Mana From Heaven: A Century of Maori Prophets in New Zealand*, Moana, Tauranga, p. 10.
8. Refers to Christ's prophesized reign of 1000 years (a millenium).
9. Tawhai, *op cit.*, pp. 11–12.
10. Peter Webster, (1979), in *Rua and the Māori Millenium*, Ch. 2, pp. 43–73, provides a useful overview of some of these theories.
11. Elsmore—(1985), *op cit.*, pp. 75–92—details similarities, contrived or otherwise, between Māori and Jews.
12. Known also as Papahurihia, the first accounts of his activities appear in the early 1830s; see W. H. Oliver (ed), *The Dictionary of New Zealand Biography, vol. 1*, Bridget Williams/Department of Internal Affairs, P4: 329–31. He was the first post-contact millennial prophet and was among the first wardens appointed under Grey's rūnanga scheme of 1861.
13. A. Ward, (1973), *A Show of Justice: Racial Amalgamation in Nineteenth Century New Zealand*, Auckland University Press/Oxford University Press, Auckland, pp. 167–9.
14. This incident bears some resemblance to the biblical tale wherein Abraham is ordered to kill his son, Isaac.
15. The following account is paraphrased from J. McLeod Henderson, (1963), *Rātana: The Origins and the Story of the Movement*, Polynesian Society, Wellington, pp. 24–5.

16. These twin sons also symbolized the dual mission Rātana undertook, and their names appear on Te Temepara; see Figure 15, built 1926–27.

17. See especially Henderson, (1963), *op cit.*, pp. 23–9.

18. James Pope was appointed Inspector for Native Schools in 1880. Fifty-seven such schools were in existence in 1879, giving Pope ample access to tribal communities.

19. Moana Raureti, (1978), 'The Origins of the Rātana Movement', in M. King, *Tihe Mauri Ora: Aspects of Maoritanga*, Methuen, Auckland, p. 43. Twelve miles east of Whanganui, the 800-acre farm developed into Rātana Pā.

20. Often quoted. See: Raureti, ibid, p. 57; Henderson (1963), *op cit.*, p. 57. Rātana used this whakatauki to underline his close links with those traditionally not perceived to weild political power, and attributed his power to those links.

21. Raureti, *op cit.*, p. 54.

22. M. King, (1977), *Te Puea*, Hodder and Stoughton, Auckland, 97: 103, mentions Taingakawa's association with the Rātana movement.

23. Raureti, *op cit.*, p. 44. By 1921 a tent village had developed at Rātana Pā housing 400 people.

24. H. W. Williams, (1921), 'Rātana and his Work', in H. W. Williams, *The Ministry of Healing and Rātana and his Work*, Poverty Bay Herald, Gisborne, p. 11.

25. Elsmore, (1989), *op cit.*, p. 380.

26. See Henderson, (1963), *op cit.*, p. 117, Appendix I for a schematic overview of the organization.

27. In this whakatauki, Rātana links temporal well-being with spiritual health. Ibid, p. 55, for a translation.

28. Held to be the instigator of petitions to London, this Ngāpuhi leader had visited England in 1882 to protest Government action over Te Whiti O Rongomai at Parihaka; see Ward, *op cit.*, p. 292.

29. R. Walker, (1990), *Ka Whawhai Tonou Matou: Struggle Without End*, Penguin, Auckland, p. 184.

30. Coates (Reform) was Prime Minister 1925–1928; Ward (United), December 1928–May 1930; Forbes (United), 1930–1935.

31. Henderson, (1963), *op cit.*, pp. 87–9.

32. Eruera Tihema Tirikatene was created Knight Commander of the Most Distinguished Order of St Michael and St George in June 1960, and was the fifth Māori to be knighted; ibid, p. 92.

33. J. M. Henderson, (1965), 'The Rātana Movement', in J. G. A. Pocock (ed.), *The Maori and New Zealand Politics: Talks from an NZBC Series with Additional Essays*, Blackwood and Janet Paul, Auckland, p. 71.

34. Henderson, (1963), *op cit.*, pp. 87–9.

35. W. Renwick, (1990), *The Treaty Now*, GP Books, Wellington, pp. 11–12. The bill passed unopposed by National as the Tribunal would be recommendatory only. Māori leaders, although welcoming the Act, were disappointed over its jurisdiction: the Tribunal could hear claims from 1975 only.

36. Pomare was conferred the honour KCBE in the Queen's Birthday honours list, 2 June 1922.

37. King, (1977), *op cit.*, footnote 97. The Commission reported in 1928 that the confiscations were unfair and that £3000 per annum ought to be paid to Waikato. They declined this settlement; ibid, footnote 135.

38. Rātana received 3037 votes to Pomare's 3835; see Henderson, (1963), *op cit.*, p. 85.

39. J. C. Beaglehole, (1944), in *New Zealand and the Statute of Westminster*, p. 58: '. . . autonomous communities within the . . . Empire, equal in status, in no way subordinate . . . in any aspect of their domestic affairs . . .'. New Zealand became a Dominion in 1901.

40. J. M. Henderson, (1965) 'The Rātana Movement', in Pocock (ed.), *op cit.*, p. 71.

41. Paikea of Ngāti Whātua had been Rātana's private secretary since 1925; see Butterworth and Young, (1990), *Māori Affairs: A Department and the People Who Made It*, Department of Māori Affairs, Wellington, p. 83.

42. Henderson, (1963), *op cit.*, p. 92. The casting vote of the electoral officer prevented Tirikatene from taking the seat.

43. Father of the late Sir James Henare, Tau held Northern Māori for the Reform Party from 1914 until 1938; B. Gustafson, (1986a), *The First Fifty Years: A History of the National Party*, Reed Methuen, Auckland, pp. 241, 245, and 320.

44. E. Stirling and A. Salmond, (1980), *Eruera: The Teachings of a Maori Elder*, Oxford University Press, Auckland, p. 173.

45. Kohere had stood as an independent in 1935, but had had no real impact in that election.

46. To be fair, it must be mentioned that the independent candidacies of Harry Dansey and M. Rangi may well have detracted from Ngata's portion of the vote. They polled 343 and 334 votes respectively.

47. Holland was elected the leader of the parliamentary Labour Party in 1919—a post he held until his death in October 1933.

48. Mawhete was a grandson of Peeti Te Aweawe, a senior rangatira of Rangitāne and a Te Aute College Old Boy.

49. M. King, (1981), *New Zealanders at War*, Heinemann, Auckland, p. 293–4.

50. Holland died climbing Maunga Taupiri at the tangihanga of King Te Rata.

51. Savage entered the House in 1919 and was made deputy to Holland in 1923. He assumed leadership of the parliamentary wing following Holland's death in 1933.

52. B. Gustafson, (1986b), *From the Cradle to the Grave: A Biography of Michael Joseph Savage*, Reed Methuen, Auckland, p. 189.

53. From a paper by June Mariu, (1988), former National President, 'Māori Women's Welfare League Healthy Lifestyles Programme', *Proceedings of the Nutrition Society of New Zealand*, 13: 95–8.

54. Metge, (1976), *op cit.*, p. 180–1.

55. Butterworth and Young, (1990), *op cit.*, pp. 98–9.

56. Walker, (1990), *op cit.*, p. 202.

57. Butterworth and Young, (1990), *op cit.*, pp. 98–9.

58. Māori Women's Welfare League, *Minutes of the 37th Annual Conference held in Rotorua, 7–11 May, 1989*, p. 3.

59. Ropiha was Acting Secretary 1948 to September 1953 and Secretary 1953 to October 1957. Rangi Royal, a veteran of the 28 Māori Battalion, was made Chief Welfare Officer in 1944 and promoted to Controller in 1946; Butterworth and Young, (1990), *op cit.*, pp. 92 and 124.

60. Last revised at the 26th Annual General Meeting, Turanganui-A-Kiwa, 10 May 1978.

61. Released in three volumes during September 1991, *Te Aka Kumara* is a consultation directory. Māori Women's Welfare League appears in Vol. 1.

62. V. Kupenga, R. Rata, and T. Nepe, (1990), 'Whaia Te Iti Kahurangi: Māori

Women Reclaiming Autonomy', in *Puna Wairere: Essays by Maori*, Wellington, pp. 8–12.

63. N. Te Awekotuku, (1990), *Mana Wahine Māori*, New Women's Press, Auckland, p. 10.

64. A. Stirling and A. Salmond, (1976), *Amiria: The Life Story of a Māori Woman*, A. H. and A. W. Reed, Wellington, p. 109.

65. See Merania White, (1988), *The Unfolding Years 1937–1987: Women's Health League*, and Irihapeti, (undated), *The Binding of Te Arawa*.

66. Walker, (1990), *op cit.*, p. 202.

67. Te H. H. Hakaraia (1986), 'Mana Motuhake: The Nature of its Business', *Tu Tangata*, 32, p. 52. Reedy is a member of Ngāti Porou.

68. Born at Te Hapua in 1934, Rata is of the Te Aupouri iwi.

69. Rata was the third Māori appointed as Minister (December 1972–December 1975). Carroll and Ngata both served as Minister of Native Affairs.

70. The Treaty of Waitangi Act 1975 was arguably his greatest achievement. While some disparaged the Act as being half-hearted, he had succeeded in introducing legislative recognition for the Treaty where others had failed.

71. Walker, (1990), *op cit.*, p. 228.

72. M. P. K. Sorrenson—(1986), 'A History of Maori Representation in Parliament', in *Report of the Royal Commission on the Electoral System: Towards a Better Democracy*, State Services Commission, Wellington, p. B-21—gives these figures: 50,00 Māori—4 seats; 250,000 European—72.

73. Hakaraia, *op cit.*, p. 52.

Chapter Seven
Te Whakakotahitanga o Ngā Iwi o Aotearoa

Ko taku korero e pēnei ana. Ko tēnei kaupapa ehara i te kaupapa awhina i te kawananatanga, engari e awhina i a tātou.[1] (Sir Hepi Te Heuheu, 12 August 1989, Hui Whakakotahi, Rātana Pā)

The National Māori Congress, founded at Turangawaewae Marae on 14 July 1990, is the most recent Kotahitanga movement. Delegates representing thirty-seven iwi (or composite iwi groupings),[2] after debating issues outlined by the Whakakotahi Taskforce (whose inception is discussed later in this chapter), proceeded to formally constitute the Congress. Although the recommendations outlined in the Taskforce *Discussion Paper No. 7* were viewed by the authors as being 'neither complete answers nor long term solutions', the Taskforce had determined that the establishment of a national Māori body demanded urgency.[3]

The Taskforce was a compact working party formed as a result of the Hui Whakakotahi held at Rātana on 11–12 August 1989. It operated under the mandate of the iwi who had gathered that day, and was representative at a regional or waka level.[4] The membership of the Taskforce was, however, limited and input from a broader, iwi-based forum was considered essential to cement in place the goals of the Congress, its membership, and its constitution.

During the preliminary planning phase it was important to have a small working party that could determine the parameters within which Congress would operate. Although the Taskforce implemented a system of regular and comprehensive correspondence with iwi delegates, the opportunity for direct participation in the development of Congress was not great. Accordingly, it was recommended that an interim arrangement be adopted whereby an Executive drawn from participating iwi would meet more frequently to take up Congress business and develop it further.

The Need for Urgency

As early as February 1990 the Whakakotahi Taskforce was aware that two critical factors were likely to colour iwi views on the formation and role of a Congress.

The first was the general election, scheduled for October 1990. While neither of the two main political parties had given a comprehensive outline of their medium- and long-term policy on Māori affairs, it was likely that, no matter who won the election, Māori policy would be determined on the basis of mainstream philosophies. Further, the performance of both National and Labour regarding the Treaty of Waitangi indicated that a restrictive approach would be adopted. Claims before the Waitangi Tribunal and also the implementation of Treaty-driven policies were unlikely to be high on the priority list of either party. The concepts of 'partnership' and 'reasonableness' would be interpreted from within the cultural constructs of Pākehā, and would reflect their political agenda, rather than Māori priorities.[5] Consultation was likely to continue along *ad hoc* lines with little genuine opportunity for Māori to drive Māori policies. Certainly in the past government consultation processes had seldom sought Māori input during the developmental phases and tended to be restricted to minor details once the party line had been firmly ensconced in the form of a bill.

Regardless of the election outcome, a degree of uncertainty was anticipated among iwi. Whoever triumphed, the position of Māori *vis-à-vis* key policy decisions was vulnerable and there was every indication that a 'divide and rule' approach would set iwi against each other. The establishment of a nationally representative Māori organization to provide cohesive and comprehensive restatement of iwi concerns was therefore deemed essential. Rather than awaiting the result of the upcoming ballot and the possible distraction of iwi from forming such a body, the Taskforce urged deliberate and immediate action.

The second concern that influenced the activities and planning of the Whakakotahi Taskforce was the proposed Rūnanga Iwi legislation,[6] and the likely impact that it would have not only at the iwi level, but also nationally. Iwi would be required to conform to Crown-instituted structures to enable funding to flow. The level of funding and also the requirements needed to receive it would be in the hands of the State, and remote from direct iwi influence. As recipients of State monies, rūnanga would be required to conform to State agendas, and would in effect act as State agencies delivering a limited range of services at a local level, and consulting with local authorities.

Under the initial terms of the bill, incorporated rūnanga would become, at least in the State's perception, the primary political units of Māori society. Central and local government consultation would be with rūnanga who would be required to respond on behalf of iwi and to represent them in all dealings with the Crown. While the legislation would considerably simplify the interaction with Māori from Government's perspective, it would leave rūnanga in the invidious position of dual allegiance. Accountable to the State for funds and services, while concurrently expected to promote iwi interests—which may not be in accord with State programmes—there was considerable potential for conflict. To avoid or at least mitigate any ill-effects on tribes, a representative national structure with the mandate and skills to develop policy was sorely needed.

Another possible scenario would see iwi forced to compete with other iwi for a finite pool of resources. The impact upon kotahitanga of inter-tribal competition for access to resources might be great indeed. Unity and cooperation were unlikely to emerge in a climate of heightened economic rivalry between iwi. Indeed, within the tribal boundaries of some iwi, various leaders and structures were already beginning to compete.

Competition and division within iwi was also a distinct threat. The section of the Rūnanga Iwi Bill,[7] which empowered the registration of 'Authorized Voices of Iwi', created an atmosphere of internal unrest among some tribes. The authorized voice could be an incorporated rūnanga established under the Rūnanga Iwi Act, or any other corporate body chosen by the iwi and registered under the Act. This registration would require the Crown, local authorities, and public authorities to consult with the authorized iwi voice when required regarding legislative or policy development and implementation.[8] Other existing Māori structures—Māori committees or tribal trust boards, for example—could be disadvantaged or even bypassed in favour of a rūnanga that might conceivably be less than representative. In some regions, kin groups that had formerly been perceived, at least by related groups, as hapū were, rightly or wrongly, using the legislation to assume iwi status and speak with their own 'authorized voice'.

Realizing that this competitive environment was damaging to Māori as a whole, and mindful that such occurrences were likely to increase rather than be resolved, the foremost proponents of the new Kotahitanga determined to accelerate the formal inauguration of Congress. The establishment of an iwi-based and iwi-driven forum such as a Congress would be required to strengthen the Māori position, particularly in its relationship with the State. Where iwi voices spoke individually they might have little impact; collectively, however, considerable political influence could accrue.

Origin

The impetus to establish the National Māori Congress came from Sir Hepi Te Heuheu of Tuwharetoa, Dame Te Atairangikāhu of Tainui, and the late

Mrs Te Reo Hura, Tumuaki of the Rātana Church. These three leaders, whose whakapapa link them to the most prominent Kotahitanga movements, were perhaps the most appropriate rangatira to emerge at the forefront of Māori national unity in the 1990s. On their behalf, and in response to calls from other Māori leaders, Sir Hepi convened a Hui of National Māori Leadership at Turangi in June 1989.

Figure 26: Hui Rangatira, 23 June 1989. *Seated from left*: (Late) Sir Kingi Ihaka, Morgan Kanawa, Te Whatumoana, (Late) Mrs Te Reo Hura, Dame Te Atairangikāhu, Sir Hepi Te Heuheu, Archie Taiaroa, Stephen Asher, Biship Mariu. *Standing*: Huri Maniapoto *(Personal source)*

At the same time, or even earlier, the New Zealand Māori Council was also exploring options for the creation of a new national structure for Māori. Dr Whatarangi Winiata, a Raukawa District Māori Council delegate to the New Zealand Māori Council, had in March of 1989 developed a proposal to restructure the Council.[9] Concerned over the operational overlaps and the interrelationships between current Māori organizations, he suggested the formation of a new, more inclusive national Māori body: Te Rūnanganui o Aotearoa. He envisaged the inclusion of statutory bodies (New Zealand Māori Council, The Māori Trustee, The Māori Education Foundation, Māori Trust Boards and the like), non-statutory Māori organizations (for example, Te Kohanga Reo Trust, Te Runanga Whakawhanaunga i Nga Hāhi, Māori Women's Welfare League), as well as representatives from tribal rūnanga.

Figure 27: Sir Hepi Te Heuheu, Hui Rangatira, 23 June 1989 (*Personal source*)

In January 1989 a planning unit was given the task of preparing for the establishment of the Iwi Transition Agency (ITA). Headed by Kara Puketapu,[10] the unit laid the groundwork for the second phase in the Hon. Koro Wetere's plan to restructure Māori Affairs.[11] Puketapu also realized the advantages which might accrue through the formation of a national Māori structure based upon iwi. In a letter to the Minister dated 12 June 1990, he sought support to proceed with plans he had discussed with Sir Hepi Te Heuheu, Dame Te Atairangikāhu, and others to form a National Forum, Executive, and Secretariat. Under this proposal, an estimated $1.6 million would be channelled into the development. It appears that he had in mind the Congress as a vehicle for the implementation of Iwi Transition Agency policy.

Hui-a-Iwi

The National Māori Leadership Hui called by Sir Hepi Te Heuheu at Turangi on 23 June 1989 to discuss a National Congress of Māori Leadership was well attended. Like his ancestor, Te Heuheu Iwikau (Te Heuheu Tukino III), his eminent position among tribal leaders and the need for concerted Māori action at a national level both precipitated and facilitated his role in the new Kotahitanga.[12]

The Māori Queen, Dame Te Atairangikāhu, is listed among the eighty-one participants in the official record of the Hui Rangatira, as it came to be known.[13] Her input, however, both prior to this initial hui and subsequently, was of immense significance, and one of the key factors in the movement's eventual emergence as a powerful political force. Three of the four current

Figure 28: B. Couch and K. Wetere, Hui Rangatira, 23 June 1989. *Nearest stage*: Bishop Mariu (partially obscured), Bishop Bennett, and Sir Monita Delamere (*Personal source*)

Māori Members of Parliament (Dr Peter Tapsell was overseas and sent his apologies), two Māori Bishops (the Right Reverend Bishop Manuhuia Bennett (Anglican) and the Right Reverend Bishop Takuira Mariu (Catholic)), and the leaders of the Ringatu (Monita Delamere) and Rātana (the late Mrs Te Reo Hura) Churches were present. Six Māori Knights and Dames and four past or present Ministers of Māori Affairs also attended the meeting.[14] Representatives from the Māori Women's Welfare League (Georgina Kirby) and the New Zealand Māori Council (Sir Graham Latimer) were present, as were leading Māori academics. The names of rangatira from throughout the length and breadth of both islands (as well as the Chatham Islands) are also recorded on the list of participants contained in the official record. Thus both the spiritual and secular leadership of Māori were represented and provided input into the establishment of Congress.[15]

The conference opened with a karakia and an address by the Right Reverend Bishop Takuira Mariu,[16] who emphasized the need for unity. He stressed that concerted Māori action was essential for the spiritual and physical well-being of Māori and of the nation, and that competing against tauiwi ought to be seen as a secondary goal. A further important message contained in his powerful speech was that 'unity does not mean sameness'. For Mariu, unity encompassed the opportunity to consult with others and to achieve mutual understanding and to utilize the available spiritual, physical, human, and natural resources for corporate advantage. Independence from Government and the absence of personal and tribal biases were vital ingredients in the unity that he envisaged. To enable the proposed council of leaders to be 'the custodians of tino rangatiratanga, and to defend the Mauri, the Mana and the Wairua of Māori', he saw 'the principles of Justice, Aroha and Tika' as those which must guide them.[17]

In his whaikorero, Sir Hepi Te Heuheu, having greeted the assembled leaders, reminded the group that the task at hand was by no means a new undertaking. Rather, it was a continuation of the endeavours of earlier leaders. He made special reference to the aspirations of the late Sir James Henare and his recognition of the need for unity.[18] He told the gathering that following the tangi for Sir James he had consulted with Dame Te Atairangikāhu, and together they had approached Mrs Te Reo Hura. These discussions and the resultant mutual perception of the urgency required to establish a national forum for Māori had prompted this hui. His vision was to form a body which would unite and strengthen Māori, rather than a group which would merely respond to Government initiatives. An independent, self-constituted Congress with its own agenda could develop initiatives that were pro-Māori, as opposed to being anti-Government.[19]

Throughout the course of the hui, rangatira rose and expressed support for the proposal and offered historical and political insights into the Kotahitanga movement. Monty Daniels of Ngāi Tahu reminded the gathering that consultation and communication within each tribal group would be required: 'We need to take the kaupapa back to the people'. Claude Edwards of Whakatohea later emphasized this point and stressed the requirement to strengthen the home base.[20]

Jim Elkington, speaking on behalf of the Ngāti Koata people of D'Urville Island, raised another pragmatic issue when he enquired into the 'nuts and bolts' of the proposal. His sentiments were echoed by subsequent speakers including Professor Hirini Moko Mead, Ngāti Awa: 'What was needed now was to put flesh on and give it substance'. Professor Mason Durie, Ngāti Raukawa, enunciated the following principles which might serve to focus and guide the Congress. The Council should

- be for the advancement of Māori people and not a creature of government
- build upon what already exists
- be representative of all sections of Māoridom, women and rangatahi included
- extend Māori interests and not limit them.

Dianne Ratahi, Taranaki, in endorsing the concept of kotahitanga, listed tino rangatiratanga, survival, cultural change in attitudes, and the notion of a mandate behind which efforts could be placed as significant to the body mooted at the hui. Nick Pirikahu recalled the 1984 Hui Taumata[21] which provided an excellent example of the potential for Māori which might result from the deliberations of representative Māori leadership. Aside from the Kawenata containing innovative solutions to Māori development issues which emerged from that conference, a realization developed within governmental bureaucracy that greater emphasis on traditional Māori social structures would be required to give effect to a partnership between the Crown and iwi. The consultation documents *He Tirohanga Rangapū* and *Te Urupare Rangapū*,[22] and the devolution policies which resulted from them can be traced back to the Hui Taumata.

Some concern over the distinction between spiritual and temporal roles in leadership was voiced by Mānu Paul. He also raised the issue of the mana of iwi and whether it would be subjugated to the mana of Congress. Would Congress hear individual iwi proposals and act upon them? John Tahuparae (Te Ati Haunui a Paparangi) added a further cautionary note to the proceedings and suggested that any Congress which may be established should:

- have no power over tribal resources
- have no power to negotiate with Government over tribal matters
- have power to provide tribes with information
- have power to provide secretarial services to tribes
- act as a catalyst to pull tribes together
- have the power to extract resources for trades, skills, and the like.[23]

Tom Gemmell of Ngāti Kahungunu saw the Congress as an opportunity for iwi to come together and, through a sharing of resources, the strong supporting the weak, achieve the goal of Māori development. Steve O'Regan, Ngāi Tahu, spoke of the need for a 'new central expression for Māori political opinion'. The New Zealand Māori Council had been preoccupied with running the State-Owned Enterprises case[24] through the Waitangi Tribunal and duplicating that process in the High Court. They had consequently been unable to adequately represent Māori opinion regarding devolution and the resource management legislation review. The need for a collective legal personality was therefore quite clear. Both Congress and the Taskforce which preceded it had been active in providing Māori with a collective voice and had held forums to debate issues and develop submissions on recent legislation. The Rūnanga Iwi Bill and the Resource Management Bill were two examples for which special hui were convened to enable iwi to canvass issues and prepare a joint response.[25]

In drawing the meeting to a close, Sir Hepi Te Heuheu reiterated the need to consult with kinsmen in the home areas, and suggested that a further hui ought to be held. Tribal representatives were therefore invited to Rātana Pā on 12 August to finalize details. Bishop Bennett closed the meeting with a karakia.

It had been a remarkable if brief meeting. Only one substantial issue had been debated: was there a need for a new nationally representative Māori body? The overwhelming response had been enthusiastic, but, in a typically Māori way, delegates withheld total support, pending further discussion with their own people.

Obviously, the follow-up hui at Rātana Pā could be crucial.

Rātana Pā, 14 August 1989

The then Tumuaki of the Rātana Church, the late Mrs Te Reo Hura, hosted the follow-up conference of Rangatira Māori at Rātana on 11–12 August 1989. While, as is customary, koha were laid down on the marae, it was felt appropriate that the hui be self-funding, and accordingly a registration fee of $30 was requested from each iwi delegate to cover secretarial and other expenses. This notion, that Congress activities ought to funded by Congress, has developed over time into a firm principle of autonomy from the Crown and its purse strings. By 14 July 1990, the principle of financial independence had developed to the extent that constituent iwi were willing to pledge $5000 per annum per iwi to maintain Congress.

The Rātana meeting was convened jointly by Sir Hepi Te Heuheu, Mrs Te Reo Hura, and Dame Te Atairangikāhu, and was attended by 432 registered delegates, and over 1500 observers. In a press statement issued at the conclusion of the day's events, it was stated that fifty iwi were represented. Most registrants included a tribal or a rūnanga name on their form enabling a comprehensive list of representation to be compiled (see Appendix Eleven). The huge response from individuals, iwi representatives, iwi authorities, Taura Here groups, government agencies responsible for Māori policy development and implementation, and other Māori organizations was indicative of the high level of interest generated by the possibility of forming a national Māori Congress. There was, of course, concern and debate about how the Congress might be structured and its membership determined.[26]

Regional Workshops
Participants assembled before the whare, Manuao, to take part in the deliberations, which commenced at 9.00 a.m. with a karakia by Apotoro

Figure 29: Informal discussion, Rātana Pā, August 1989

Takiwa Te Rino Tirikatene. Following the formal exchange of greetings, the programme for the day was outlined by Stephen Asher, the Secretary of the Tuwharetoa Māori Trust Board. Ten workshop groups were formed, based upon either waka affiliations or regional groupings, and at 10.00 a.m., iwi assembled in these working parties to consider an order paper prepared prior to the hui. These workshops were: Taitokerau, Tainui, Aotea/Kurahaupo/ Tokomaru, Mataatua, Horouta, Tākitimu, Te Upoko o te Ika, Te Waipounamu, Wharekauri, and Te Arawa.

Having gathered in workshop groups, iwi delegates elected a chairperson and a recorder for each group, and worked through the set agenda.

The first task for each group was to consider the principles that would guide Congress, and the aims and objectives Congress would pursue. Tino rangatiratanga and whakakotahitanga were two principles that had emerged from the earlier Turangi hui. While these were endorsed by all, some workshop groups augmented the principle of tino rangatiratanga by emphasizing the need to respect iwi mana and identity. Any structure that was subsequently developed would need to recognize the rangatiratanga of

Table 9: Workshops at the Ratana Hui Rangatira, 11–12 August 1989

Waka	Chairperson	Secretary Recorder	Spokesperson	Taskforce Nominee
Takitimu	Hon. Ben Couch	Te Oriroa Taylor	Hon. Ben Couch	Tom Gemmell
Mataatua	Mac Temara	Wira Gardiner	Maanu Paul	Henare Pryor
Tainui	Hare Puke	Ina Te Uira	Hare Puke	
Te Upoko o Te Ika	Mason Durie	Queenie Hyland and Te Waari Carkeek	Mason Durie	Mason Durie
Aotea/Tokomaru /Kurahaupo	Nick Tangaroa	Ruth Harris and Dianne Le Ceeve	Nick Tangaroa	
Horouta	Hunaara Tangaere	Tutekawa Wyllie	Hunaara Tangaere	Apirana Mahuika
Wharekauri	Jack Daymond		Jack Daymond	Jack Daymond
Taitokerau			Richard Dargaville	Richard Dargaville
Te Waipounamu	Tipene O'Reagan	James Russell	Tipene O'Reagan	Tipene O'Reagan
Te Arawa	Manu Bennett and Takuira Mariu	Louise Waaka and Tumu Te Heuheu	Louise Waaka and Tumu Te Heuheu	George Asher

iwi as paramount, and ensure that it remained uncompromised by efforts towards unity.

The need to retain autonomy from the Crown was also emphasized. Many iwi felt that tino rangatiratanga must be paramount. At this early stage, the protection of tribal integrity overshadowed the urge to unite. While iwi actively sought the solidarity and strength which would flow from kotahitanga, no diminution of tribal mana would be considered. Congress would derive its mana from iwi, and not the reverse.

One addition to the primary principles was an almost universal desire to incorporate the Treaty of Waitangi or principles derived from it into the Congress agenda. The Treaty, foundation of the partnership between the Crown and iwi, was considered central to the aspirations of iwi. Many perceived the Treaty as the only possible basis for redressing injustices perpetrated by the Crown in the pursuit of colonization, and as such saw it as a cornerstone of any pan-tribal movement.

The call from the Mataatua working party to acknowledge and retain 'the functions and strengths of other Māori groups'[27] is in itself relevant. While many rangatira were urging that the new structure must stand apart from Government and must be seen to be an independent entity, others were reluctant to abandon earlier structures which had latterly been the vehicle for Māori political unity. Mānu Paul, an active member of the New Zealand Māori Council and the spokesperson for the Mataatua working party, later delivered a paper to the Whakakotahi Taskforce suggesting a possible structure for the Congress which would incorporate existing bodies.

There was general agreement concerning the other issues raised in the briefing paper circulated to each workshop. The Te Waipounamu and Te Taitokerau groups both returned to the afternoon plenary session with a clear position on funding. The proposed Congress must stand upon its own resources. State funding ought to be avoided, and iwi should contribute the resources necessary to sustain the national body. A strong focus upon iwi was also present as the workshop reports were tabled, as was the aversion to affiliation to any particular political party, religion, or to the Crown and its agents.

The hui ended on a note of optimism and commitment. Kotahitanga was endorsed in principle although matters of detail were left in abeyance. To enable iwi to discuss issues raised and then to subscribe to further deliberations, a task force was commissioned to coordinate iwi input and to consider possible strategies and mechanisms to advance the Congress concept. Accordingly, representatives from each workshop were appointed to form the Whakakotahi Taskforce (see Figure 26 above).

Figure 30: Mason Durie, July 1988 (*Personal source*)

The Whakakotahi Taskforce

The Taskforce, comprised of delegates drawn from the waka and regional groups who had participated in the Hui Whakakotahi held at Rātana, first met at the Tokānu THC Hotel on 13 January 1990.

Table 10: Whakakotahi Taskforce meetings

Date	Venue
13.1.90	THC Hotel, Tokānu
25.2.90	Tuwharetoa Māori Trust Board Office, Turangi
10.3.90	Tongariro High School, Turangi[a]
25.3.90	Bridge Lodge, Turangi
29.4.90	Bridge Lodge, Turangi
19.5.90	Wharerata, Massey University, Palmerston North[b]
20.5.90	Manu Flights,Palmerston North
17.6.90	Bridge Lodge, Turangi

[a] Denotes hui-a-iwi to discuss the Runanga Iwi Bill
[b] Denotes Taskforce hui to discuss the Runanga Iwi Bill

At this meeting, Mr Apirana Mahuika was nominated for the position of Chairman by Sir Hepi Te Heuheu, and seconded by Henry Pryor. No other nominations were received, and Mr Mahuika took the Chair. Professor Mason Durie was elected to the position of Secretary for the Whakakotahi Taskforce, and Mr Derek Fox was given responsibility for media/press communications and liaison.[28] Having established an executive body, the group commenced to discuss the goals and objectives which they were to address.

Goals of the Taskforce

The Taskforce was established to plan and shape the Congress on behalf of iwi. Initially a three-year timetable was envisaged, but, as explained earlier, this was reduced to six months to ensure that the Congress was in place before the general election. During the early meetings of the Taskforce the possibility of establishing an executive body, with adequate administrative resources and a mandate from iwi, was canvassed. The executive mooted at that time was to be compact (of similar composition to the Taskforce) and was to incorporate a paid secretariat. The initial proposition involved seeking funding for its operation from the ITA, which was, it was believed, amenable to such a proposal. This option was in part abandoned when the likelihood of ITA funding became not only less viable but also less desirable.

Funding

Throughout the preliminary Hui Rangatira and during the period of the Taskforce, much debate and deliberation surrounded the financing of the operation and administration of the Congress. During the earliest meetings of the Taskforce, serious consideration was given to the establishment of a Taskforce secretariat comprising an executive officer and suitable support staff. Following the second meeting of the Taskforce on 25 February 1990, the Secretary, Dr M. H. Durie, was asked to correspond with the General Manager of the ITA, Mr Wira Gardiner, to ascertain the general feeling on this matter. A letter, which referred to the principle of equity and outlined the purposes to which any assistance might be applied, was subsequently dispatched. The Taskforce Chairman, Mr Apirana Mahuika, also had informal discussion with the ITA Chief Executive on the possibility of ITA support for Congress.

Gardiner's initial, informal attitude towards negotiating an assistance package with the officers of the Taskforce was positive. Indeed, some of the early operating costs had already been met by the Agency. The early view was that the formation of a Congress would assist iwi to develop suitable internal mechanisms which would ultimately prepare them to receive State funding. The goal of a Congress, then, was seen as being compatible with the overall direction and aims of the ITA (i.e., devolution) and as such was deemed worthy of support. This amenable attitude was somewhat modified, however, after the collective response to the Rūnanga Iwi Bill developed at Turangi on 10 March 1990 was made public.

The resolution issued at that meeting, which rejected the bill as it was, led to a revision of the official ITA position. Not only had the Congress been seen to disagree with the official agency position, it had resolved to present its view to Prime Minister Palmer, to Koro Wetere, the Minister of Māori Affairs, as well as to the Leader of the Opposition, Mr Jim Bolger and his spokesman on Māori Affairs, Winston Peters. This was too much for the ITA, and Gardiner was forced to distance himself and his staff from the Congress movement. Any prospect of financial support from the Agency evaporated, and in fact an internal departmental memorandum was issued instructing ITA staff that, in the official view, the duties of a State servant and participation in Congress activities were incompatible. This apparent conflict of interest eventually led to calls for ITA staff to either resign their positions or to desist from Taskforce involvement.

That incident brought to prominence the inherent difficulties that would arise if Congress were to be funded from the public purse. Subject to the vagaries of political fortune, the State would be a difficult bedfellow. The Congress would be open to manipulation, not only from elected officials, but also from permanent heads of departments. The tino rangatiratanga of iwi, emphasized at both of the foregoing hui-a-iwi as being a vital ingredient of any proposed national forum, would be subjugated by kāwanatanga.

In his annual report to iwi, delivered at Turangawaewae on 14 July 1990, Api Mahuika enunciated the view of the Whakakotahi Taskforce on the matter. Referring to offers of resignation from Taskforce members prompted by the ITA directive, he noted that the Taskforce had been established by iwi, and did not itself have the power to accept resignations. Iwi had determined the membership of the Taskforce, and it was for iwi alone to determine who may or may not resign.

The Shaping of Congress

The Taskforce had an unenviable job. Entrusted with shaping Congress, yet always mindful of its limited mandate, it adopted the practice of raising issues for discussion by iwi. Subsequently, a number of discussion papers were circulated through a mailing list of in excess of 400 names which was developed from registration forms received at Turangi and Rātana. The strategy was only partially successful; responses from iwi were few, and feedback tended to be limited to the impressions of Taskforce members.

In presenting its views to iwi, the Taskforce was mindful that it ought to emphasize points of common agreement while simultaneously minimizing areas of difference. Its plan would need to lead on to a process of practical implementation. Much time and effort would be expended to no particular purpose if the proposals made by the Taskforce were likely to be rejected. To ensure maximum support, the new body would need to be perceived as compatible with existing Māori organizations, and if possible incorporate mechanisms through which cooperation with them might be developed. The object of Congress was to unite, not divide.

Similarly, the body which it was shaping needed to have a clear kaupapa. Unity by itself was not sufficient—to what end was unity being promoted? The Congress would not wish to duplicate existing programmes or, even worse, assume to take charge of functions more properly undertaken by iwi.

A danger of which the Taskforce remained aware was the possibility that Congress activities could distract iwi from other issues. At that time the Labour Government was committed to a policy of devolution. Iwi, faced with the need to develop their own internal structures through which they might action Crown initiatives, were preoccupied and often overburdened. Moreover, there was reason to fear that iwi might be asked to commit their own scarce resources to the new body.

Increasingly, the need to solicit informed opinion from iwi shaped the operation of the Taskforce. As an adjunct to the regular posting of minutes to the more than 400 persons on the mailing list, three editions of a newsletter were also distributed.

Among the documents prepared for iwi by the Taskforce were a series of seven discussion papers. Initially written to provide a view that the Taskforce members could consider and use to focus their own discussions, they were uniformly revised for distribution to iwi delegates. The facility for wider canvassing of opinion that these papers provided enabled dialogue with iwi, keeping them informed of progress and allowing input into the development of Congress. Based upon principles derived from both the Rātana and Turangi Hui Rangatira and on issues which arose at Taskforce hui, the discussion papers were, with the exception of the first, produced by the Taskforce Secretary, Professor M. H. Durie.[29]

Turangawaewae, 14 July 1990

At the beginning of the Hui Whakakotahi held at Turangawaewae Marae, Ngāruawāhia, on 14–15 July 1990, a series of recommendations were presented by the Whakakotahi Taskforce as the basis for workshop discussions.

Membership

Perhaps the most significant issue with which the Taskforce grappled was that of membership. Who should be able to join the Congress and how should their affiliation be determined? All preceding discussion at Turangi and at Rātana had emphasized rangatiratanga and the need to empower iwi. The submissions received by the Taskforce had further reiterated the desire among many tribes for a firm iwi basis for the Congress and the need to protect and enhance rangatiratanga.

Simultaneously, the notion was being advanced that existing structures and experience would be crucial to the representativeness and validity of the Congress. The Mataatua Workshop had emphasized this point at Rātana. The New Zealand Māori Council, the Māori Women's Welfare League, and the Rātana Movement, all well-established and highly respected Māori institutions, ought to have a proper role to play in the new national body. The need to accommodate these potentially incompatible opinions did cause some consternation among Taskforce membership.

An additional disadvantage of a realignment based solely upon traditional tribal groupings was also to emerge. Māori who, for whatever reasons, operated outside recognized iwi structures could be marginalized if membership of Congress was defined on exclusively tribal lines. This issue was particularly problematic for the Taskforce. The 'iwi-only' lobby would not countenance the inclusion of any organization which functioned totally outside of iwi control. While various solutions were suggested to include the New Zealand Māori Council and the Māori Women's Welfare League, whose memberships were defined primarily on tribal affiliation, extra-iwi bodies were an anathema to some tribal stalwarts. The recommendations in *Discussion Paper No. 7* accordingly made no provision for the inclusion of such bodies but, importantly, neither did they seek to define the parameters of iwi.

Objectives and Principles

The urgency to establish Congress as perceived by the Whakakotahi Taskforce (discussed above) was conveyed to delegates. It was suggested that an interim arrangement be adopted for the first twelve months and during that time, in lieu of a constitution, a set of guiding principles and objectives would govern Congress activities.[30] These recommendations were the culmination of deliberations at Taskforce hui, and were based upon the concerns raised both at Turangi (24 June 1989) and at Rātana (11 August 1989).

Table 11: Taskforce Recommendations 4 (a) and (b)

(a) Objectives	(b) Principles
The Congress objectives shall be:	In meeting these objectives, the Congress shall be guided by:
1) The advancement of all Māori people	1) The *philosophy of whakakotahi* based on the shared traditions and aspirations of all Māori people
2) The exercise, by each iwi, of tino rangatiratanga	2) The principle of *Māori Mana Motuhake* which recognizes the right of Māori people to decide their own destiny
3) The provision of a national forum for iwi representatives to address economic, social, cultural, and political issues within Tikanga Māori	3) The principle of *tino rangatiratanga* in which is embodied the mana and autonomy of each iwi in respect of their own affairs
4) The promotion of constitutional and legislative arrangements that enable Māori people to control their own right to development and self determination	4) The principle of *paihere tangata* acknowledging the strengths that accrue when people are joined together in the pursuit of common goals
	5) The articles of the Treaty of Waitangi

The objectives suggested in *Discussion Paper No. 7* epitomize the path iwi proposed to undertake when gathered as a Congress. The first—'to advance all Māori'—underlines the need to, on occasion, look outside the confines of traditional iwi-based structures, and to institute programmes and policies that will be of benefit to Māori as a whole. This objective incorporates and includes the notions of cooperative effort by tribal groups to not only support and advance each other but also to enter into dialogue and partnership with other Māori organizations.[31] Those organizations might include long-established bodies such as the New Zealand Māori Council, the Māori Women's Welfare League,[32] and Te Rūnanga Whakawhanaunga o Ngā Hāhi,[33] more recent structures such as the Federation of Māori Authorities (FOMA),[34] or developing bodies such as Tino Rangatiratanga, a collective of Māori educationalists formed in 1989.[35]

The second objective emphasizes the independent and autonomous nature of iwi. Most of the responses from the Rātana workshops had identified the interface between whakakotahitanga and tino rangatiratanga as an area of tension. The proposed Congress, therefore, was to be established to facilitate, inform, and promote iwi initiatives, rather than to direct or impose them. The safeguarding of iwi prerogatives has been foremost among the concerns of both the Taskforce and the Congress. Should an iwi or group of iwi choose to adopt a position at variance with the majority of Congress, it shall remain the responsibility of Congress to support them.[36]

The third objective is a straightforward enunciation of Congress's vision to establish an institution that will allow and foster debate on issues affecting the advancement of Māori. It also contains a prescription for conducting this discourse 'within Tikanga Māori': the protocols and practices that have evolved from those passed down from ngā tipuna Māori.

The final objective, 'The promotion of constitutional and legislative arrangements . . .', echoes in part the attempts by Hone Heke and other Kotahitanga leaders to achieve the passage of a bill to empower Pāremata Māori. The Congress, however, while perhaps seeking constitutional reform in the longer term, recognizes the mandate of iwi as sufficient empowerment.

The Initial Structure

The recommendations in *Discussion Paper No. 7* included an organizational chart (see Figure 31).

Under this plan the National Māori Congress would comprise five delegates from each participating iwi. The Whakakotahi Taskforce, when suggesting five delegates as a suitable number, was mindful of the need to create a broadly representative body. While the Taskforce sought to avoid dictating terms to iwi, it was felt that interest groups within iwi as well as sections of iwi could be allowed a voice if each iwi had five delegates. Conceivably, rangatahi, wāhine, kaumātua, and pakeke might all be represented. If iwi felt so inclined, their delegates might also be members of existing bodies (Māori Women's Welfare League, New Zealand Māori Council, etc.), which would facilitate the incorporation of persons already familiar with and experienced in national Māori politics.

To facilitate the operation of the Congress, an executive body was suggested. The executive would have delegated authority to make decisions on behalf of the National Māori Congress. Full Congress, comprised as it is of five delegates from each iwi or composite iwi grouping, would be logistically cumbersome—conceivably 250 or more persons would be involved. Apart from the sheer cost of hosting such a large body, opportunity for incisive and meaningful discussion would be diminished. Accordingly, an executive body was established that would meet on five or six occasions each year.

The full Congress would remain the supreme source of authority for all Congress transactions, policies, and dealings with the Crown (Cabinet, departments, ministries, agencies), other national and international bodies or

Figure 31: Proposed structure to establish Congress (derived from *Discussion Paper No. 7*)

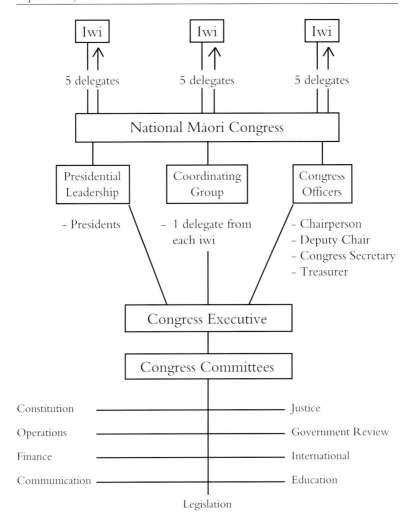

agencies, other Māori organizations, and also with iwi.

When required, it could also be the final arbiter in disputes falling within its perceived jurisdiction. In line with the philosophy that Congress Executive should be both large enough to encompass the range of Congress issues and opinion, while remaining small enough to enable decisive action, the Executive was initially comprised of:

- three Presidents
- Congress officers (Chairperson, Deputy Chairperson, Secretary, and Treasurer)
- members of the coordinating group (i.e., one delegate from each constituent iwi or iwi grouping).

Proposed Leadership Structure

Behind the recommendation to include a presidential level of leadership[37] was the realization that, at times, Congress would assume a high profile in national and possibly international affairs. The President(s) (three were eventually selected by iwi) would of necessity be sufficiently qualified in Māori terms to relate to iwi, to Government, and the Courts, as well as to the international community. It was further realized that, to ensure the support of a wide iwi base, Congress would be the only appropriate body to appoint them.

The second tier of congressional leadership, Congress officers, was suggested to allow the distinction between the respect and authority vested in the Presidents, and the need for a day-to-day executive capacity to be realized. It was deemed inappropriate to burden the Presidents with administrative and managerial duties which could be readily undertaken by other capable leaders. The Chairperson would convene and chair Congress and Congress Executive meetings, whereas the Deputy Chairperson would support the Chair and undertake the Chair's offices when delegated to do so. The Secretary would be responsible for maintaining Congress and Executive records and minuting meetings, dealing with correspondence, and undertaking other duties to ensure the efficient administration of Congress activities. The Treasurer would have overall responsibility for Congress finances.[38]

In order to facilitate a two-way communication link between iwi and Congress, a coordinating group of one delegate per iwi was suggested. The establishment of such a group would concurrently enable iwi concerns to be raised at Congress while allowing a flow of information back to iwi. Delegates, however, were reluctant to adopt this initiative, and the group was not established. Instead, the Executive itself, through delegates, provided this link with iwi.

The final component proposed for the Congress Executive was a number of standing committees that would deal with delegated executive matters and provide a much-needed planning and research component for the Congress. The Committees were selected by and responsible to the Congress Executive. Recommendation 10, *Discussion Paper No. 7*, suggested that eight committees be established: four to advance the developmental aspects of the Congress, and a further four to address particular areas of Congress activities.

Table 12: NMC Executive Committees proposed on 14 July 1990 at Turangawaewae

Committee	Functions	Convenor (appointed Wairoa, 11.8.90)
Constitution	To develop a constitution and report back in twelve months	Tamati Reedy
Operations	To plan an administrative base for Congress including a Secretariat and accommodation To plan for Congress meetings	Te Atawhai (Archie) Taiaroa
Finance	To prepare a Congress budget To explore avenues for funding	Whatarangi Winiata
Communications	To inform Congress participants and others about issues confronting Congress, actions undertaken, and any decisions pending	Derek Fox
Legislation	To initiate and draft new legislation To review and monitor proposed legislation and the implications for Māori people	No appointment
Government review	To scrutinize policies and practices of Government Departments To suggest responses and initiatives that Congress should consider	Jaqui Te Kani
Justice	To explore the implications of judicial interpretations of the law To explore the delivery of effective justice to Māori people To recommend Congress responses and initiatives	Donna Durie-Hall
International	To establish links and alliances with other nations and international bodies	Ropata Te Kotahi Mahuta

It had been the experience of the Whakakotahi Taskforce that pressing issues (for example, the Rūnanga Iwi Bill debate) can quite quickly dominate proceedings and distract from equally important but less urgent activities. Accordingly, it was recommended that at the first meeting of the Congress Executive a convenor and four members be appointed to each of the committees outlined in Table 12.

On Saturday 14 July, the Congress itself was established. That event happened on the marae Ātea in front of the whare Turongo following the

Figure 32: Dame Te Atairangikāhu (reproduced with her kind permission)

reporting back from the waka/regional-based workshops. Morgan Kawana had earlier proposed that Ta Hepi Te Heuheu of Tuwharetoa, Te Ariki Nui, Dame Te Atairangikāhu, and Tumuaki Te Reo Hura be appointed as the inaugural Presidents of the Congress. This proposal, along with other recommendations from the Taskforce, was unanimously accepted.

The following day, the inaugural meeting of the Congress was held. A financial forecast had been developed by a small working party, which consisted of Whatarangi Winiata, John Dyall, and Bob Mahuta, and was presented. Its statement was premised on the need to establish an effective and efficient administrative network, and contained options for the establishment of a secretariat and the appointment of a chief executive officer. Central to the deliberations of the group was the necessity to remain aloof from direct State funding. There are two important points which emerge from the report. Firstly, iwi would be expected to contribute substantially to the Congress, and an initial sum of $5000 per iwi was proposed. Secondly, funding from other sources could be sought to supplement these iwi contributions. It was emphasized that, if Congress were to remain independent, it must also be financially independent of the State.

A Finance Committee, as recommended in *Discussion Paper No. 7*, was to be established to consider this matter further, to explore alternative avenues for funding, and to consider the possibility of developing an investment portfolio from which future funding might be derived. Meanwhile, iwi were asked to cover travel, accommodation, and other expenses incurred by their delegates, and to make an early contribution of $5000. These recommendations were formally accepted.

During the meeting on this second day at Turangawaewae the first officers of the Congress were appointed.

The erstwhile Taskforce Chairman, Mr Apirana Mahuika, was elected as

Figure 33: Apirana Mahuika, December 1987 (*Personal source*)

Congress Chairperson, while Te Atawhai (Archie) Taiaroa became his deputy. Professor Mason Durie assumed the position of Congress Secretary and Mr Stephen Asher was voted in as Treasurer. It was further decided that a Congress Executive, as outlined above, would be empowered to continue the establishment work of Congress. Accordingly, names of iwi delegates were called for and a meeting date and venue were agreed upon: the meeting was held on 11 August 1990 at Tākitimu Marae, Wairoa.

Congress Activities

Executive Hui

Meetings of the National Māori Congress Executive are by definition large. Even if only one delegate per affiliated iwi attended, numbers would exceed sixty; indeed, official attendance at all Executive hui thus far has never dropped below one hundred delegates and observers.[39] Lacking adequate funds to establish a permanent base, and not wishing to overburden any particular member iwi, Executive meetings are hosted by a different tribe at a different marae venue each time (see Table 12).

Relocating for each Executive hui allows broader participation in Congress business. (Figure 34 shows the locations of National Māori Congress Executive meeting venues.) Māori from the host region, irrespective of tribal origin, will attend to see what the Congress is all about. This level of casual participation, while occasionally requiring some issues to be revisited, allows the Congress to remain aware of the issues facing Māori in different areas. Also, delegates are not continually faced with the prospect of major travel arrangements to attend hui. Any location, no matter how central, will require some delegates to travel long distances. Shifting the venue facilitates a degree of proximity to different delegates for each hui.

Travelling to new locations for each meeting, which came to be held at two-monthly intervals, has had a further positive aspect. It has enabled iwi to exercise their privilege to demonstrate their hospitality—a demonstration which has been gratefully and enthusiastically accepted by delegates. The splendour of marae and the bounty of each host rohe has added a further dimension to the demanding tasks in which delegates have engaged. Na reira, ngā iwi kainga o ia rohe, o ia rohe, tēnā rawa atu koutou. Ko tēnei te tino mihi kia koutou e manākitia mai te kaupapa o te Kotahitanga, a, e whangaitia hoki te taha wairua, te taha hinengaro, me te taha tinana o mātou e takahia ana ngā huarahi o ngā mōtu. Tēnā koutou, tēnā koutou, tēnā rawa atu koutou katoa.

The first meeting of the National Māori Congress Executive was held at the request of Mrs Lena Manuel at Tākitimu Marae in Wairoa. At this gathering, attended by 178 Executive members, Congress delegates, and observers, the Executive formally selected the convenors for seven of its committees. At that time, the Executive was still developing procedures and processes for the conduct of its affairs and, similarly, the constitution of Congress committees had not yet been finalized.

Following discussion regarding the selection of committee convenors and members, it was resolved that the convenor and at least two members of each committee should be iwi delegates, and that an option of co-opting additional members as required would be useful. To enable the committees to be called together with a minimum of travelling and inconvenience, members would ideally live close to each other. It was decided, therefore, that convenors would select their committees from those who offered assistance and could readily attend meetings. (Table 12 shows the names of the first seven committee convenors.)

One extremely important issue, raised at Wairoa, that proved contentious, was the definition of iwi. Te Iwi Morehu spokesperson, Morgan Kawana, had early in the meeting requested formal membership in Congress of the Rātana movement. Their position—that although they are not an iwi they still desired membership—sparked considerable debate. Kawana expressed the view that it was untenable for their Tumuaki, Mrs Te Reo T. W. R. Hura, to be a

Table 13: NMC Executive hui

Venue	Date	Attendance
Turangawaewae Marae, Ngāruawāhia	14–15.7.90	310 (37 iwi)
Tākitimu, Marae, Wairoa	11.8.90	178
Te Tii Marae, Te Tii (Te Taitokerau)	6.10.90	103 (29 iwi)
Te Tokanganui-a-Noho, Te Kuiti	1.12.90	145 (30 iwi)
Whareroa Marae, Tauranga Moana	16.2.91	102 (27 iwi)
Ngapuwaiwaha Marae, Taumarunui	13.4.91	244 (30 iwi)
Takapuwahia Marae, Titahi Bay	22.6.91	123 (30 iwi)
Taupō-Nui-A-Tia College, Taupo	20.7.91	223 (33 iwi, 4 Rōpu Māori)
Owae Marae, Waitara	7.9.91	126 (27 iwi)
Murihiku Marae, Invercargill	16.11.91	121 (22 iwi)
Wāhi Pa, Huntly	7.3.92	196 (30 iwi)
Raukawa Marae, Otaki	30.5.92	96 (31 iwi)
Waipatu Marae, Hastings	11.7.92	298 (40 iwi)
Ruamatā Marae, Rotorua	3.10.92	118 (31 iwi)
Orākei Marae, Auckland	13.2.93	83 (31 iwi)

Bold type indicates Full Congress Hui, NMC Executive hui appear in plain type

Figure 34: National Māori Congress executive hui

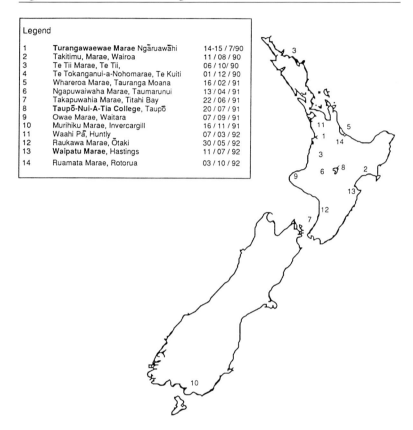

Legend

1	**Turangawaewae Marae** Ngāruawāhi	14-15 / 7/90
2	Takitimu, Marae, Wairoa	11 / 08 / 90
3	Te Tii Marae, Te Tii,	06 / 10/ 90
4	Te Tokanganui-a-Nohomarae, Te Kuiti	01 / 12 / 90
5	Whareroa Marae, Tauranga Moana	16 / 02 / 91
6	Ngapuwaiwaha Marae, Taumarunui	13 / 04 / 91
7	Takapuwahia Marae, Titahi Bay	22 / 06 / 91
8	**Taupō-Nui-A-Tia College**, Taupō	20 / 07 / 91
9	Owae Marae, Waitara	07 / 09 / 91
10	Murihiku Marae, Invercargill	16 / 11 / 91
11	Waahi Pā, Huntly	07 / 03 / 92
12	Raukawa Marae, Ōtaki	30 / 05 / 92
13	**Waipatu Marae**, Hastings	11 / 07 / 92
14	Ruamata Marae, Rotorua	03 / 10 / 92

President of Congress without the formal participation of Te Iwi Morehu. Opinion on the matter was, it transpired, somewhat divided. Some delegates insisted that the Congress must remain strictly iwi-based, while others felt that Te Iwi Morehu must be allowed a role in the Congress. A view not expressed, but containing a possible avenue for resolution of the matter, would have been that Te Iwi Morehu could be identified as an iwi for the purposes of Congress representation and thus brought into the new movement. No resolution was found at that time, and the matter was forwarded to Dr Tamati Reedy and the Constitution Committee to work through.

The related issue of how Congress defined 'iwi' was also deemed appropriate for discussion by that committee. Congress had not at that time, and indeed still has not, issued a clear, unequivocal statement on what constitutes an iwi. While it may seem unusual that an iwi-based organization does not define exactly what an iwi is, the position is defendable. Congress itself is defined and empowered by iwi to advance and assist iwi development. The matter of how iwi organize themselves and choose to express their iwitanga has always been an internal issue. What right would an external body or collective body have to intrude upon this essential freedom?

The possibility of membership for large Taura Here Rōpu[40] based in urban areas arose from consideration of the correspondence. While the philosophy was expressed that Congress membership should be as inclusive as possible rather than exclusive, the view that Taura Here should operate through the iwi structures in their home areas was also advocated. No immediate resolution emerged, and the matter was also delegated to the Constitution Committee.

On 6 October 1990, the Executive met at Te Tii marae in Te Taitokerau. During that hui, further issues were placed before the Constitution Committee for incorporation into their discussions. The issue of proportional representation, raised by Ngāpuhi, required careful consideration. Two schools of thought emerged as a result of the debate. The initial suggestion was that large iwi[41] were responsible to and for greater numeric proportions of the Māori population, and ought accordingly to have a greater mandate within the Congress structure. Less populous iwi were obviously disinclined to accept that proposal. Tino rangatiratanga would be undermined if a pro rata basis was used to determine iwi franchise within the Congress, and large powerful iwi would dominate and thus alienate less numerous iwi. A further issue of the accuracy and appropriateness of the statistics was also raised.

Over the course of several Executive hui, the names of respected kaumātua were presented by their iwi as persons who might provide presidential leadership of the Congress. It became clear, however, that it would be inappropriate to either reject or include nominees without serious deliberation. To include any would be to include all. To decline might possibly be seen as a slur upon them and their iwi. Clearly the desire for kaumātua to be given a suitable avenue for participation and the need to benefit from their wisdom and experience had to be addressed. The Constitution which was eventually adopted at Taupō on 20 July 1991 attempted to incorporate all of these points. (Figure 35 outlines the result of suggestions *vis-à-vis* Congress structure.)

A number of patterns were emerging from the discussions at early Executive meetings. The first was that issues, once raised, should be discussed by iwi at their own hui so that delegates could return to the table with a clear perception of iwi views. A second feature was that rangatiratanga and the mana of iwi were not easily overridden by the desire for united action. Many of the issues debated concerned the relationships between each member iwi—how they would interact with their peers and protect their own

Figure 35: NMC Membership structure (derived from Appendix A, National Māori Congress Constitution)

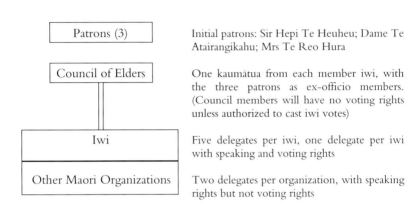

Patrons (3)	Initial patrons: Sir Hepi Te Heuheu; Dame Te Atairangikahu; Mrs Te Reo Hura
Council of Elders	One kaumātua from each member iwi, with the three patrons as ex-officio members. (Council members will have no voting rights unless authorized to cast iwi votes)
Iwi	Five delegates per iwi, one delegate per iwi with speaking and voting rights
Other Maori Organizations	Two delegates per organization, with speaking rights but not voting rights

positions. Considerable jockeying for position was evident, and on occasion this threatened the concept of kotahitanga. Over time, however, as Congress developed, iwi came to feel more secure. The desire to dominate proceedings was replaced with a sense of the value of collective action, and the Congress became an open forum to discuss views and adopt, where appropriate, unified approaches. Improved communications within and between iwi, enhanced by an increasingly cooperative mood, created fewer and fewer delays, and allowed detailed and informed discussion and debate to proceed.

Much of the time spent at the first few Executive hui was devoted to minutiae. How and when the various necessary structures and personnel, functions, and systems would be established and coordinated was debated and approved. A set of standing orders was developed by the Treasurer, Mr Stephen Asher, on behalf of the Operations Committee, and the mechanics of unity continued to develop.

Executive meetings have become more streamlined, and a broad range of issues have been tabled for discussion. Matters have ranged from participation in general elections and the nature of the relationship with the Crown, to the ownership of genetically modified organisms and the development of a national Māori sporting body.[42] Education, housing, employment, recent legislation, liable parent contributions, fishing quotas, telecommunications, and scores of other momentous and more prosaic issues have been raised and debated at Executive meetings. While unanimous resolutions have not been forthcoming on all of these issues, it is clear that iwi appreciate the opportunity to raise matters, and welcome the advice of other rangatira

Māori. A system of referral to committees has rapidly emerged to enable concise opinions, effective action, and fruitful discussion to take place. Consequently, Executive meetings devote much of their time to receiving and discussing Committee reports.

The mechanisms for and the nature of participation in and with central and local government has regularly entered into the deliberations of the Congress Executive.

Relationship with the State

As early as 10 March 1990 the Whakakotahi Taskforce had been advised by iwi who met at Turangi that day that select committee procedures were an inappropriate mechanism for ascertaining Māori opinion on legislative matters that impact on Māori.[43] That hui also pronounced that the Rūnanga Iwi Bill in its current form was unacceptable to iwi. On 19 May 1990, a further hui-a-iwi was convened at Massey University to discuss the Official's Report on the Rūnanga Iwi Bill. In a submission to the Select Committee, developed at that meeting, the Taskforce called for a joint working party to be established to consider any further submissions on the bill. The idea that Māori should participate equally with the State in legislative arrangements enacted for and on behalf of Māori was not new, but its emergence in Taskforce deliberations set the tenor for future Congress relations with the State. These two instances point to a developing perception among iwi of how matters relating to interaction with the Crown ought to be conducted.

The Rūnanga Iwi Bill itself had an important influence on the formation of Congress and also upon its perception of how it would interact with the Crown and its agencies. An analysis of the bill and the context of reform from which it emerged are therefore vital to understanding the Congress position and how it developed.

Briefly, as a result of two discussion documents circulated by Māori Affairs Minister, Koro Wetere, in 1988,[44] a three-stage plan was developed to replace the paternalistic Department of Māori Affairs with supposedly more suitable structures. They were to provide iwi with mechanisms to deliver services to their people and to facilitate a closer working relationship between iwi and Government, both nationally and locally. Some of these services were those formerly transacted by the Department of Māori Affairs, whereas others encompassed employment, housing, social welfare, and justice.

The creation of Manatū Māori, with a responsibility for policy development and overview prerogative, was the first stage. This was completed on 1 July 1990, when the Ministry under John Clarke (Ngāti Porou) became operational.

The second stage occurred in two phases. The first required the disestablishment of both the Board of Māori Affairs and the Department of Māori Affairs to make way for a new structure. This was done on 30 September 1990.[45] The second phase of stage two was the establishment of the Iwi Transition Agency (Te Tira Ahu Iwi). The Agency was charged with developing and strengthening iwi authorities, and was given a five-year period in which to accomplish the necessary tasks. It became operational on 1 October 1990.

The Rūnanga Iwi Act was the third stage. It ostensibly empowered iwi to deliver State-funded services, and created mechanisms for the establishment of iwi authorities with whom agents of State would be required to consult.

The role that these devolutionary policies played in the establishment of Congress, while not overt, is nonetheless clear. Government had shifted the basis of interaction with Māori. It moved from a perception of Māori as a unitary ethnic group towards recognition of discrete tribal authorities, and a perceivable increase in tribally based political activity occurred. This in itself was relatively positive, and the resurgence of tribalism prompted in part the latest manifestation of kotahitanga. There were, however, a number of negative concerns over the Rūnanga Iwi Bill itself.

One concern was the Crown motive behind these activities, and the increasing competition between iwi to secure resources was also seen by rangatira Māori as being potentially harmful. An equally threatening potential lay in internal dissension within iwi over issues of authority for that iwi. A further danger was that the devolution process itself would create status and non-status iwi and give the Crown an opportunity to minimize total input into Māori affairs by advancing only those groups which were able and willing to adhere to State directives. Finally, allowing the State to enact legislation by which iwi would be defined held the seeds of possible State prescription of traditional Māori constructs. Once enactment was deemed appropriate and accepted by Māori, the State would be in a position to amend legislation regarding the constitution of iwi finally achieving the domination of rangatiratanga by kāwanatanga.

The denunciation of the bill as it stood was premised upon those concerns and was to have an immediate effect on the development of Congress. As stated earlier, Wira Gardiner, formerly at least lukewarm to the Congress idea, was now firmly against it. Accordingly, he issued instructions to his staff to distance themselves from the Whakakotahi movement. Some delegates to the Taskforce were unable to continue participation, which hampered operations to some degree.

Gardiner's directive had its most serious impact upon the Rūnanga Iwi Working Party nominated at the hui-a-iwi convened at Massey University on 19 May 1990. The Working Party was to formulate a comprehensive collective response to the Official's Recommendations on the bill, and was composed of eleven leading Māori professionals, including several lawyers. The Taskforce had been instructed to solicit the necessary funding for their activities from the Iwi Transition Agency. The funding was not forthcoming and the Working Party never accomplished its task.

At the hui held in Turangi on 10 March 1990, the notion of direct consultation with the Crown was voiced. As a result, a delegation of twenty kaumātua, led by Sir Hepi Te Heuheu, met with the then Prime Minister, Rt. Hon. Geoffrey Palmer, on Friday 4 May 1990 at 11.45 a.m. In considering the make-up of this delegation, iwi were insistent that the Prime Minister be made aware that those whom he would be hosting were the leaders of their people, just as he was the leader of his people. Congress has since extrapolated this idea of speaking to the Crown at appropriate levels, and is currently considering a discussion paper on the subject.

The paper[46] written by Whatarangi Winiata was requested at the Executive meeting held at Owae Marae, Waitara on Saturday 7 September 1991. It proposed possible guidelines for the participation by Congress in Crown bodies. Congress was increasingly numbered among those organizations considered as appropriate sponsors for nominees to Crown organizations such as the recently established Crown Research Institutes. Congress had begun to ask itself whether such participation adequately reflected its own perceptions of how interaction with the State ought to be conducted. Having a single or even two representatives on any given panel dominated by the majority culture and answerable to the Crown has implications both for the individual(s) concerned and for the partnership outlined in the Treaty of Waitangi.

A lone Māori voice, even one backed by a nationally representative Māori organization, is effectively marginalized on boards of control which operate under and according to tikanga Pākehā. All such boards adopt a one-member-one-vote philosophy to decision-making which effectively eliminates any opposition premised upon cultural bases and advocated by a minority membership.

At another level, the British Crown entered into a partnership with iwi in February 1840, and has since delegated its share of that partnership to the New Zealand Parliament. Iwi, however, remain in possession of their tino rangatiratanga, and Congress is obliged by its Constitution and on behalf of iwi to ensure that no diminution of tino rangatiratanga results from its actions. Participation in Crown bodies would, therefore, most appropriately be undertaken by a body similar to the Crown body, but drawn from iwi and provided with an equivalent resource base. The iwi-derived entity must have an equal say in the outcomes of board debates.

The Winiata paper suggests the following guidelines that Congress could use as a basis for participation in Crown bodies:

(a) all appointments from Congress are to be made by Congress; Congress is not to be purely recommendatory for someone else to make the appointments,

(b) one of the Congress appointees is to be co-convenor, if not convenor,

(c) each body will be viewed as comprising appointees from tikanga Māori (those persons appointed by Congress) and representatives of other tikanga,

(d) if called for on any particular issue, voting is to be by tikanga: a majority of those representing tikanga Māori and a majority of those from all other tikanga as a group will be required for a decision,

(e) budgetary decisions and financial controls will be the joint responsibility of the Crown and Congress or their respective appointees, and

(f) where decisions are to be made on the recommendations or other aspects of the works of the body in question, those decisions shall be made jointly by Congress and the Crown.

Similarly, Congress is developing a position whereby counterpart bodies and officers within the State hierarchies are dealt with by individuals or groups of similar status from within the Congress.

The Winiata paper suggests that the following relationships could be suitable:

Crown	Congress
Governor-General	Congress Presidents
Parliament	Full Congress
Cabinet	Congress Executive
Ministers	Congress Officers
Chief Executives and Permanent Heads	Committee Convenors

This scenario, or a similar one, would ensure that discourse with the Crown and its agents would be conducted at levels compatible with Congress's perception of itself.

The inadequacy of submission writing as a means of expressing the partnership laid out in the Treaty of Waitangi prompted Congress convenors to develop a policy whereby the Crown and Congress both receive the results of select committee inquiries and together amend legislation.

The need for Congress to assume a proactive stance in its deliberations led to calls for spontaneous reaction to State policies to cease. To this end, eight goals that Congress would pursue over the twelve months of July 1991–July

1992 were adopted at the first annual Congress meeting in Taupō.[47] These goals, however, in no way preclude Congress from assuming a position as needed for legislative developments during this period.

The Eight Goals of Congress

Concern was expressed at Taupō during the second hui-a-tau of the National Māori Congress that unless Congress set its own agenda it could easily become completely preoccupied responding to government priorities. While some government priorities were also seen as being priorities for Māori, the sum total of Congress activity should not be prescribed by the State. Congress decided to seize the opportunity to be innovative and to develop a set of policies and programmes to accelerate Māori advancement.

In selecting its goals, Congress was mindful of its current reality. Despite being a focused and representative Māori organization capable of developing sound Māori policies, it has neither unlimited resources nor the advantage of full-time paid researchers. Consequently, Congress accepted eight identified goals suggested at Owae Marae in Waitara on 7 September 1991 as areas for priority action for its next twelve months of operation. Further, it was recommended that for each goal a taskforce be appointed to advance the objectives so that by mid-1992 substantial progress will have been made. These goals are included as Table 14.

Table 14: The eight goals

1	A Policy for Māori Employment
2	A Māori Education Authority
3	Iwi Development Banks
4	A Māori International Identity
5	Constitutional Rearrangements
6	An Extended Congress Membership
7	A Congress Secretariat
8	A National Identity for Congress

Goal One: A Policy for Māori Employment

Rationale: Māori unemployment had reached an unacceptably high level: 25 per cent of the potential Māori workforce was unemployed (more in many rural areas). Relief was unlikely under the government policies of the time, and strategies to address unemployment were not included on political agendas. The proposed Kiwi cards were not acceptable alternatives to jobs, and the absence of a clear national policy for the promotion of full employment would continue to disadvantage Māori.

The objective of goal one, then, is to develop policies and strategies for full Māori employment. An Employment Committee, convened by Rongo Wetere, was subsequently appointed at Murihiku Marae, Invercargill, on 16 November 1991 to undertake this goal. The tasks were to:

- review the current national position of Māori employment
- analyse economic factors associated with full Māori employment
- locate opportunities for job growth and critique government policies
- prepare detailed discussion papers with options and strategies to radically improve Māori employment.

To date, the focus of the Committee's activities has been on developing a network for iwi consultation and liaison, and securing funding to appoint a full-time employment officer. While some innovative approaches to job creation have resulted, there has been no evidence of any real impact at the macroeconomic level.

Goal Two: A Māori Education Policy

Several groups, including Rūnanga Mātua, Tino Rangatiratanga, the New Zealand Māori Council, and the Ministry of Māori Development, have expressed an interest in a Māori Education Authority.

The idea has also been raised at Congress, although couched in terms of an iwi-driven and independent authority. While to some extent the proposal represented a vote of no confidence in present State-controlled educational systems, it goes further than that by linking education with positive Māori development, language revitalization, and tino rangatiratanga.

The Congress Education Committee is already addressing the issue, but it was asked to make this objective a priority to ensure that positive action resulted. In preparing a detailed paper for Congress by July 1992 it was asked to consider the views of iwi, the advantages and disadvantages of various models, the aims, objectives, and management of an iwi education authority, costs and funding, international experience, submissions from government, and practical implementation. If there is agreement on the final recommendations then the Education Authority should be actively promoted by Congress. There was sufficient agreement at the Waipatu hui to endorse the concept of iwi education authorities, and work to establish them continues.

Goal Three: Iwi Development Banks

At the Congress Executive Meeting held at Te Kuiti on 1 December 1990, the Finance Committee tabled a paper on iwi development banks. A motion was passed that the Executive of Congress ask the Finance Committee, in consultation with iwi, to enter into discussion with the Māori Development Corporation (its shareholders and senior management), the Treasurer, the Ministers of Finance and Māori Affairs, and others, as appropriate, to explore the possible establishment of Iwi Development Banks (IDBs) including a reserve bank, to fill a serious gap in the financial infra-structure of Aotearoa/New Zealand by 30 June 1991 and report back with recommendations to the next meeting of the Executive.

The Finance Committee made some progress in this matter but, given the current state of the Māori economy and the failure of the Porter Project[48] to address the Māori situation, the need for a network of iwi development banks is even stronger.

It was recommended, therefore, that the Finance Committee give priority to that objective and present a detailed paper to Congress on the relative merits, aims and objectives, implementation, management, funding, and other implications by March 1992. A hui to advance this goal was held in March 1992 and positive steps towards the creation of Iwi Development Corporations have resulted.

Goal Four: An International Māori Identity

Several independent Māori delegates attended the Ninth Session of the United Nations Working Group on Indigenous Populations at Geneva in July 1991. The absence of an official Congress delegation was noted and Congress was urged to attend the 1992 session as well as the Earth Summit in Brazil in June 1992. The Earth Summit was seen by the Congress as particularly pertinent as it was concerned with indigenous populations and environmental protection. The International Committee investigated a Māori presence overseas in some detail and is actively pursuing options to ensure that Māori, as distinct from the New Zealand Government, are represented in an appropriate manner. As a result of the Committee's efforts, National Māori Congress delegates were present at both the aforementioned international forums and were represented by Dr Tamati Reedy at the United Nations Year of the World's Indigenous Peoples Conference in November 1992. In his well-publicized address, Reedy commented on the Sealord Fisheries settlement, presenting a view opposed to the agreement. It should be said that, whereas some members of the Congress held a similar view to that espoused by Reedy, a considerable number of affiliated iwi were and are supportive of the agreement. Indeed, it is often the case that the National Māori Congress must tread a moderate path on many issues, as membership maintains its right to express independent views on several issues.

Two matters were highlighted late in 1991 as requiring attention. These were:

- the development of an official international status for Congress
- the facilitation of Congress delegations to attend appropriate international conferences.

With regard to the first matter, it is possible for Congress to obtain non-governmental organization (NGO) status within the United Nations, and preliminary enquiries have been made with Sir Paul Reeves in New York. At the time of writing, however, Congress has moved away from seeking representation as an NGO. As detailed above, the second matter has progressed well.

Goal Five: Constitutional Rearrangements

In its first year of operation, Congress became acutely aware of the lack of any firm understanding about the position of Māori in New Zealand's constitutional arrangements. Government has received Congress delegations but has declined to afford them any particular constitutional status, except perhaps in the Railcorp negotiations.[49] In any event, there is no consistent government approach to the question of Māori representativeness, nor are there any guarantees that Māori will be involved in relevant decision-making.

The Congress Executive had already discussed constitutional matters; at Te Kuiti there was support for extensive parliamentary reforms and the introduction of a Senate, while at Taumarunui dissatisfaction with current electoral procedures led to a wide-ranging debate about greater Māori autonomy and revised constitutional conventions. The 1992 referendum on electoral reform further highlighted the need for constitutional reform in Māori. It is seen as significant that none of the options presented dealt directly with Māori representation. Many within Congress felt that because the changes were effectively superficial little benefit was to be derived from participation in the referendum. Progress, however, is still needed on the constitutional position of Māori in Aotearoa, hence the continuing importance of goal five. The objective of goal five, then, is to promote a change in New Zealand's constitutional arrangements in order to give due recognition to the position of Māori.

A taskforce convened jointly by the convenors of the Justice and Constitution Committees was appointed to realize this objective. Its function is to review current constitutional arrangements, obtain the views of iwi, develop options for new arrangements, establish a National Commission on Constitution Reform, and set a timetable for reforms to be implemented.

The taskforce was asked to have an overall strategy in place by December 1991 and to have the Commission established by July 1992. Since then, there has been a shift in focus away from the Commission idea and, partially as a result of current comments during the referendum debate, the notion of a Māori parliament has again emerged as a Kotahitanga objective. The question of a separate Māori parliament was discussed vigorously in January 1993 at the Ngāti Porou Indigenous Peoples Conference (1–7 January 1993).

Goal Six: Increased Congress Membership

In line with Article Three of the Congress Constitution adopted at Taupō on 20 July 1991, Congress has prepared a strategy to enter into discussion with other Māori organizations. These discussions will concentrate largely on the terms under which such organizations might participate in Congress. While Congress membership is essentially iwi-based, there are obvious advantages in Congress becoming a national forum for all Māori debate so that major national Māori issues can be resolved by Māori. Congress is taking an active role in negotiating with other Māori organizations and with those iwi who have not yet indicated an interest in Congress.

A taskforce, co-convened by Archie Taiaroa and Tamati Reedy and drawn from the Kaumātua Council, is being established to address uncertainty about the nature and function of Congress within Māori society. The immediate aim of this group is to establish contact with iwi who are yet to join Congress, and to negotiate with other Māori organizations over possible participation in Congress and the shape that this might take. The objectives are to:

• identify the appropriate groups
• arrange a consultation schedule
• prepare options for membership within Congress
• consult with those groups, and
• recommend conditions of membership to Congress.

This work has been ongoing and has formed an essential aspect of future Congress activity. Again, there has been a shift in emphasis, and increased cooperation with both the Māori Women's Welfare League and the New Zealand Māori Council has resulted. Currently the three bodies are working together in housing, electricity, and health.

Goal Seven: A Congress Secretariat

The work of Congress has expanded and is expected to continue to do so. Consequently, the need for a full-time secretariat with a permanent office has emerged as an important priority. There was sufficient work to warrant the appointment of a senior executive officer and an administrative assistant. However, those needs had to be balanced against the costs and the demands that they would place upon member iwi. Congress had accumulated a pool of funds during its first year of operation, but these would be rapidly depleted if a secretariat were established immediately. Some iwi had already suggested that membership fees should be lowered, and there was a degree of uncertainty about income for 1991–92.

Nonetheless, the situation had to be faced and it was recommended that the Operations Committee, together with the Convenor of the Finance Committee, prepare a plan to meet the objective of establishing a Congress Secretariat. The first step in this process has been made, and funding for an administrative assistant to work with the Congress Secretary for up to two years was approved at Murihiku Marae in Invercargill. Mr Mike Walsh (Ngā Rauru) took up a twelve-month appointment as administrative assistant to Secretary Mason Durie in February 1992. February 1993 saw the appointment of Mr Tuwhakairiora Williams (Te Whakatōhea and Ngāti Porou)[50] as Chief Executive Officer to the Congress. His role is to develop and administer the Congress Secretariat and to coordinate Congress activities. Immediately, a staff of two is seen as sufficient for the Secretariat, but it is hoped that further expansion will be possible to allow for a policy analysis and research capability to be realized.

Longer-term arrangements are still required and the Operations Committee are exploring further options.

Goal Eight: A National Identity for Congress

Rationale: The public profile maintained by Congress had been relatively low. More deliberate thought was needed to institute strategies for the promotion of a positive image for Congress. Initially this was to be aimed at particular groups and concentrated upon unaffiliated iwi. The possibility existed that misinformation and resulting suspicion might arise. Further, there was a need to address the developing curiosity and genuine interest both among Māori and in the broader New Zealand community. All Congress delegates would be required to play some part in the process by ensuring that at least their own iwi were accurately informed about Congress, its activities, and its intentions.

Where special groups were concerned, specific approaches were deemed necessary. The Committee convenors, for example, arranged a well-attended presentation for all senior government executives which was held at the Plaza International Hotel in Wellington on 1 November 1991. Quality information was prepared and disseminated, and a concise outline of Congress aims, ambitions, activities, and affiliations was delivered by the convenors. Feedback from participants was in the main positive and several departmental heads are seeking further contact with Congress. It was proposed that a further gathering be arranged during 1992 to inform State-owned enterprises executives and possibly private corporations, but as yet the hectic schedule confronting Congress has precluded such a gathering.

Other Goals

The eight goals are neither an exclusive nor a comprehensive list of proactive alternatives for Congress. Each of the committees have their own goals and others will arise over time. The eight goals identified and the strategies considered for their advancement were to ensure that Congress-initiated activities do not become submerged as other business arises. Although other urgent issues could and should be promoted by the Congress, a need to focus specifically upon at least a few clear-cut tasks was deemed essential.

Cooperation with Other Māori Authorities

Increasingly, the National Māori Congress is moving towards a greater level of cooperation with other national Māori organizations on issues of major importance to Māori development and well-being. Building on the joint submission on the Resource Management Bill that emerged from a hui held at the Airport Hotel, Wellington, on 22 May 1991, the Congress, the Māori Women's Welfare League, and the New Zealand Māori Council have began working together on the purchasing of a Māori housing portfolio.

The rationale for this purchase was outlined to the Congress Executive in a memorandum from the convenor of the NMC Housing Committee, Mr Tom Moana. [51] Essentially, the minimalization of State involvement in non-governmental issues, as manifest in recent devolutionary policies, is expanding to including housing. Government intends to withdraw from direct provision of mortgage financing, and, by July 1993 both Te Puni Kokiri and the Housing Corporation will cease mortgage lending. Further, the Housing Corporation's rental business is to become a State-owned enterprise and will be competing with the private sector. Inevitably, this will lead to an elimination of income-related rental subsidies, and eventually to a disposal of State rental properties.

Proportionately, fewer Māori own their own homes than non-Māori. Many are currently State tenants. Higher rentals, diminishing assistance, endemic discrimination in the private rental sector, and a perception of Māori as high-risk mortgagees will combine to further erode Māori housing standards. The need for proactive Māori involvement in housing is becoming increasingly necessary. While details of the negotiations between the national Māori bodies and the Government are yet to be made public, the wisdom of a joint approach to housing issues is obvious and likely to prove beneficial.

A Māori Health Authority

Congress cooperation with the MWWL and the Council is also evident in the health sector. In a climate of considerable reform, the need for a suitable body to advocate on behalf of iwi and Māori was clear. Such a body, Te Waka Hauora o Aotearoa, was formally launched at 4.00 pm on Wednesday, 24 February 1993, in the boardroom of Kensington Swan, Wellington.

The notion of a Māori health authority can be traced back to the Congress hui held at Waitara on 7 September 1991 when, following discussion on the health reforms, a realization emerged that Māori might be disadvantaged in the absence of a strong coordinated Māori influence on the whole process. The matter was more clearly stated at Takapuwahia marae in Porirua on 13 April 1992 during a hui called by the Ministerial Advisory Committee on Māori Health. [52] The hui was convened to discuss iwi participation in the health reforms and to promote discussion on options for improved Māori health. Representatives from the National Interim Provider Board, the Public Health Commission, the Health Reforms Directorate, and the Department of Health outlined the reforms and the new structures and gave iwi a progress report on the implementation of the new order.

In an address from the Committee's Chairperson, Dr Mason Durie, the possibility was raised of a Māori health authority whose role might be to negotiate with government and to act as an advocate for Māori in the new competitive health arena. The need for a strong central organization to balance the proposed regional health authorities was also pointed out. While the possibility that the authority might act as an umbrella organization for Māori health-care plans was mooted, this was not perceived as a primary function of the organization. As a result of these discussions, it was resolved that the issue ought to be developed further by the Māori Women's Welfare League, the Congress, and the New Zealand Māori Council, jointly.

Consequently, at the annual general meeting of the MWWL at Kaitaia on 10 May 1992, the matter was debated; the health committee of the NZMC discussed the proposal at a special hui on 24 May 1992 at Otāwhao on the Te Awamutu College marae; and the Congress Executive also explored the idea at their hui in Otaki on 30 May 1992. On 23 June 1992 the Māori Council hosted both other national organizations, again in Te Awamutu, to advance the health authority question. At that hui six fundamental questions were raised in a paper prepared by Dr Durie. These were:

• why have a Māori health authority (MHA)?
• what aims should a MHA have?
• how should a MHA relate to the State?

- how should a MHA relate to other Māori bodies?
- what should the status of a MHA be?
- how should a MHA be structured and funded?

Each question was then discussed.

Why?

While several Māori groups [53] and individuals [54] have an input in the health arena, their efforts tend to be isolated when there is no single, coordinated body to provide a clear focus for the development of Māori health policies. Potentially, conflicting advice to Ministers and administrators might arise. This in turn may result in negligible or even negative outcomes for Māori. Additionally, iwi have began to develop their own health plans, and at local and regional levels are starting to have some influence. An MHA, if it were sufficiently representative, authoritative, and informed, could provide a national focus for Māori input into health policies and their implementation. This would allow an effective, coherent, and consistent health system for Māori to develop.

Aims

Among the aims discussed at Te Awamutu, the advancement of Māori health, the formulation of Māori health policies, the provision of a national focus, and the provision of assistance for iwi health programmes found most favour. The possibility that the MHA might act as a conduit for funding to Māori health providers also received some support, especially as economies of scale are an important aspects of the health reforms.

Relationship to the State

Two options were put before the hui at Te Awamutu regarding possible positions which might be adopted in relation to the State. The first expressed the opinion that, if interaction with the State was to be couched in terms of a partnership, then the MHA ought not be a part of the State. An independent MHA could be Māori-driven should be Māori-funded, and must be accountable to Māori people. An independent MHA might be contracted by State agencies to provide policy advice and facilitate consultation with Māori service-users. Eventually the partnership might well extend to the provision of health services for and by Māori. Contracts could be made with the Minister or other providers, the MHA acting as a purchaser of health services either on behalf of specific iwi and iwi collectives, or for Māori in general.

A second option would be to have the MHA established as a part of the State health system. Structured as a section of the Department of Health or similar to a regional health authority, the MHA would be funded from the Vote: Health and be responsible to the Minister to provide policy advice and to ensure an effective use of health resources for and by Māori.

Relationship to Other Māori Organizations

The MHA would need to have regard to health initiatives already in train under the auspices of iwi or other Māori organizations, and take due care not to undermine or usurp existing arrangements. Instead, the MHA should support other bodies and be free to act on their behalf when asked. For this reason the MHA would require a level of independence both from iwi and other national organizations, as well as suitable ties to ensure both representativeness and accountability.

Status

A number of options were considered at the hui including: an agency of State model; a subcommittee of one or other national Māori body; a coordinating committee comprised of and responsible to a number of national Māori bodies; a fully autonomous structure.

While no substantive responses emerged at that time, the three bodies established a nine-person taskforce to pursue the matter further.[5] The taskforce called a national hui-a-iwi at Manuāriki near Taumaranui on Saturday 5 September 1992.

Generally, the proposal to establish a new national body to known as Te Waka Hauora a Aotearoa was well received by the hui, although matters of detail were debated strongly. Perhaps the most contentious issues were the selection process for members for Te Waka Hauora, and how various Māori health interest groups would be represented. In response to the general enthusiasm of those gathered and in order to address concerns raised, it was decided to appoint an interim board of directors for a twelve-month period. Initially, three interim directors were nominated and they were asked to develop a process for the selection of the other board members. The inaugural directors were Mason Durie (NMC), Maanu Paul (NZMC), and Areta Koopu (MWWL).

The three directors held their first meeting in Rotorua on 15 September 1992, and Maanu Paul agreed to act as Chairperson of the interim board. The directors, working with and drawing on the experience of the Waka Hauora taskforce, called for nominations from iwi for candidates for the board of directors in October of that year and selected six further members for the board in line with the mandate received at Manuāriki.

A fuller board was subsequently announced when Te Waka Hauora was formally launched. A range of experience and expertise was evident. Board

members were:
- Maanu Paul: (Chairman); Ngāti Manawa, Ngāti Moewhare
- Maryanne Baker: Ngāti Hine
- Elizabeth Cunningham: Ngai Tahu
- Mason Durie: Rangitāne, Ngāti Raukawa
- Linda Erihe: Te Ati Haunui a Paparangi, Ngāti Apa
- Areta Koopu: Aitanga a Hauiti, Ngāti Kahu
- Cyril Martin: Ngāti Porou
- Eru Pomare: Ngāti Toarangatira, Te Āti Awa
- Joe Williams: Ngāti Pukenga.

Te Waka Hauora has the potential to deliver sound policy advice and to act as a national focus for Māori health. What is uncertain is its capacity to maintain credibility and strength by being so clearly separated from the three sponsoring national organizations. In light of this concern, Te Waka Hauora must in time either seek a mandate directly from Māori people or effect more transparent relationships with its sponsors.

It is too early to conclude that the combined force of the three national bodies will be more effective in terms of Māori advancement than the independent efforts of all three. However, the willingness to cooperate displayed in the above examples augers well. Surely, the diverse membership which each organization brings to a combined arrangement will more closely approximate Māori at large. Additionally, the impact on the Crown of such a representative triad will be considerable and, if harnessed, beneficial.

A decision by the Congress to work in concert with other organizations appeared to depart from an earlier position which had allowed for other national bodies to be part of Congress. For now at least, there was an implicit acknowledgement that the Māori position, insofar as it could be, would be best represented by more than one national focus.

Conclusion

Essentially, the National Māori Congress is an indigenous response to 150 years of colonialism. The foregoing analysis of the emergence and development and the goals and aspirations of the movement can be summed up in the phrase 'autonomous Māori development'. That is to say, the advancement of Māori as an ethnic entity which is undertaken according to a Māori perception of the future, cast in a framework developed by Māori, and accountable only to the constituent Māori groups comprising Congress. In a recent New Zealand Planning Council publication, *Te Puna Wairere*, Manuka Henare considers the relationship between tino rangatiratanga and development.[56]

In that article he itemizes four indicators of tino rangatiratanga which he regards as relevant to development. The first of these, 'full control of a geographical area', addresses the traditional conception of iwi as being related to a definable tract of land. For him, a geographical area includes not only the land and sea, but all the possessions and resources of a region. 'Self-sufficiency in daily life' is the second hallmark of an autonomous people. The individual members of a group have not only the necessary access to the means of production that enable the development of their lifestyle, but perhaps also the motivation to strive to attain that lifestyle. Thirdly, the 'commitment by a people to building up a complex economy'. Herein lies the heart of the matter. In Aotearoa, Māori must have the freedom to decide how development will occur, where it will lead, and what outcomes will constitute the indicators of success. Henare's fourth and final point is that 'political independence' is attained as a result of integrating these first three aspects.

Congress could be measured against these indicators, and this suggests that Congress may well achieve its ambition to advance all Māori. With regard to the first of Henare's indicators, Congress is committed to the notion of rangatiratanga as expressed by iwi. Fundamental to that commitment is the notion of mana whenua. Regarding indicator two, the goal of Congress is to promote iwi development, and in this way the self-sufficiency of individuals. Goals one and two outlined above indicate some of the mechanisms which Congress is adopting to promote self-sufficiency. The work of the Finance Committee on iwi development banks and the establishment of an Employment Committee indicate the desire of Congress to build up a complex economy in line with Henare's third indicator, while the sum total of these and other initiatives should produce the political independence of the Congress.

To conclude this section on the National Māori Congress it is necessary to place the Congress in perspective with regard to the three themes developed in this book. All of the three themes, 'He Whakaminenga o Ngā Hapū', 'He Iwi Tahi Tātou', and 'He Paihere Tangata' are relevant to the Congress. Some of the case studies are useful as they display similar characteristics to the Congress and suggest possible scenarios whereby it might lose its way and fail in its mission. Others give clear and powerful warnings on how the State has manipulated Kotahitanga sentiments in the past and subsequently diffused them. Yet others are models of effective and ongoing mechanisms for the assertion of Mana Māori Motuhake, and highlight areas in which Congress might find strength.

Most relevant is the theme 'He Whakaminenga o Ngā Hapū'. The promotion of tribal integrity and the seeking in unity of a means to combat external threat clearly parallel the latest Kotahitanga movement. Perhaps the most important and striking lesson for Congress is the need to avoid a preoccupation with Crown machinations and assertions of power. In the opinion of this commentator, Pāremata Māori lost its way through its distraction with attaining a legislative mandate from Parliament. Congress needs to focus on the mandate derived from its constituent iwi and the phrase in the Constitution which states:

The Power of existence of Congress *derives solely from iwi* and no other source.

Government and the resources at its disposal provide an attractive and ongoing allure to Congress and its members. No doubt if and when Congress becomes sufficiently influential, and this may already be happening, the Crown will proffer inducements to it that, while outwardly most palatable, may ultimately prove detrimental. Congress ought to consider instituting measures to ensure that it and the iwi and the individuals the comprise it are protected from the pernicious advances of the State.

The theme 'He Iwi Tahi Tātou' also provides a useful model with which to gauge Congress. A number of useful and seemingly autonomous structures have been offered to Māori in the decades since contact with Europeans was first made. Most are couched in terms of protection and are premised by European concepts such as sovereignty, democracy, and egalitarianism. They were all, however, subject to legislative review and to the dictates of Treasury. With remarkable regularity, whenever macroeconomic pressures or political expedience required it, funding levels were either cut back or maintained at an insupportably low level. Further, in almost every instance, the power of veto was retained by the Crown, and in fact final decision-making was seldom in Māori hands. Even when Māori did have an input at an administrative level, the selection of personnel was not conducted by iwi, nor by their representatives, but by servants of the Crown.

Under the theme 'He Iwi Tahi Tātou', Māori were seldom perceived as members of iwi, but rather, in line with the imperative to amalgamate and assimilate, were seen as an ethnic unity. Differences between Māori were ignored as they tended to complicate and highlight the difference between Pākehā and Māori, and did not lend themselves to ready assimilation.

Another mechanism illustrated in that theme was the use of selected Māori leaders, some of whom received compensation for their efforts to provide validation for the Crown structures. While these rangatira were undoubtedly striving toward the advancement of their people, it can be seen that they were misguided in perceiving the State structures as vehicles for rangatiratanga and the exercise of Mana Motuhake. Congress must remain aware of the Crown's tendency to isolate and appropriate Māori leaders.

The third theme, 'He Paihere Tangata', emphasizes the advantages that accrue when a firm goal provides the basis for unity. The case studies considered in that theme, which have proved effective and enduring, were all underlined by a clearly perceived goal. In developing the eight-goal approach to 1992 outlined above, Congress is proceeding down a path which holds promise for success. The need for Congress to set and pursue its own agenda emerges strongly from this theme.

The example of the Māori Women's Welfare League also contains an important illustration for Congress. Part of its success has been its ability to provide a range of activities that allows all interested parties an avenue for participation whatever their background, skills, and interests may be. Another feature of the League, apart from its proactive approach, is the breadth of membership at the base level and the penetration into the whānau that this provides. Congress can benefit greatly by the example contained in this theme.

Endnotes

1.   Sir Hepi Te Heuheu underlines in this statement the necessity for independent Māori action rather than government sponsorship.
2.   For example, Te Rūnanga a Turanganui a Kiwa, which represents three iwi: Te Aitanga a Māhaki, Rongowhakaata, and Ngāi Tamanuhiri. The inclusion of this group highlights the fact that at its inception the National Māori Council allowed its membership to determine the criteria for defining the status as iwi.
3.   The recommendations appear as Appendix 9.
4.   The Whakakotahi Taskforce first met on 10 January 1990 and remained active until the establishment of Congress on 14 July 1990. Further details are included later in this chapter.
5.   Published in 1989, the Labour Government's *Principles for Crown Action on the Treaty of Waitangi* contains five principles derived by the Crown to address Treaty issues. The fourth, 'The Principle of Cooperation', p. 14, contains notions of reasonable cooperation and partnership.
6.   Introduced into the House late in 1989, the Rūnanga Iwi Bill was the third phase in the restructuring of the Department of Māori Affairs.
7.   Part III of the eventual Act, pp. 18–27.
8.   It must be noted that no obligation was placed on these agents of State to act upon iwi concerns so raised, nor were they required to respond to iwi-initiated consultation.
9.   His proposal, dated 3 March 1989, modified to 10 March, is contained in the unpublished records of the Whakakotahi Taskforce.
10.   I. A. Puketapu had been the Secretary of Māori Affairs from November 1977–December 1983: G. V. Butterworth and H. R. Young, (1990), *Māori Affairs: A Department and the People Who Made It*, Mānatu Māori, Wellington, p. 124. He was the second Māori to hold the position.

11. The three-phase plan is outlined in more detail later in this book.

12. Sir Hepi, the seventh leader of Ngāti Tuwharetoa to bear the name Te Heuheu, is descended from Mananui (Tukino II), tuakana of Iwikau. See J. Te H. Grace, (1959), *Tuwharetoa: The History of the Maori People of the Taupo District*, A. H. and A. W. Reed, Auckland, p. 462.

13. National Māori Leadership Hui, 23 and 24 June 1989, Waihi Marae.

14. At least a further one hundred people attended this hui as observers. Apologies were received from twenty-three Māori leaders, including the Governor-General, Sir Paul Reeves.

15. While the record does not include the names of iwi or bodies represented, at least thirty distinct groups can be identified. In a press release issued by the hui it was stated that fifty tribes were represented.

16. Bishop Mariu is the first Māori to be ordained as a Bishop in the Catholic Church.

17. National Māori Leadership Hui, 23 and 24 June 1989, Waihi Marae.

18. A highly respected and influential rangatira from Ngāti Hine. Sir James led the 28th (Māori) Battalion, June 1945, chaired the Tai Tokerau Māori Trust Board, and was a patron of the Kohanga Reo movement. He died on 2 April 1989.

19. The architects of Pāremata Māori, the Rātana movement, and the Kīngitanga movement also had those objectives in mind.

20. The need to inform and solicit response from iwi has indeed formed a central component in the operations of both the Taskforce and of the Congress. While time-consuming, the opportunity for iwi representatives to consult their people has consistently been recognized as a prerequisite for adequate Māori consultation. Although this convention necessitated the deferral of decision-making at early hui, the result has been the development of an efficient communication structure and a heightened awareness of the need to hold iwi deliberations prior to Congress Executive hui.

21. Convened by the then Minister of Māori Affairs, Koro Wetere, the Māori Economic Summit Conference sought to maintain the momentum of Māori development. See: G. V. Butterworth and H. R. Young (1989), *End of an Era: The Departments of Māori Affairs 1840–1989*, Manatū Māori, Wellington, pp. 28–9; and G. V. Butterworth and H. R. Young, *op cit.*, pp. 117–19 for details of this conference and its outcome.

22. *He Tirohanga Rangapū* appeared in April 1988, suggesting the immediate abolition of the Department of Māori Affairs. *Te Urupare Rangapū* modified this proposal and led to the establishment of the Iwi Transition Agency and a five-year handover period.

23. This concern over the relationship between the Congress and its membership has remained important and is reflected in the Constitution adopted at Taupo, as well as in the conventions which have been developed through successive Executive hui. The recent negotiations with the Crown aimed at formulating a process for the disposal of surplus Railway Corporation land are illustrative. Three groups—the Tainui Trust Board, Ngāi Tahu, and Ngāti Whakaue—were already involved in negotiations with the Crown and expressed a desire to stand aside from this arrangement. This position has been respected by the Congress and has not affected participation by these iwi in other Congress-related activity.

24. This action was brought by the New Zealand Māori Council concerning the effect of section 9 of the State-Owned Enterprises Act 1986 on the sale of State assets:

see F. Hackshaw—(1990), 'Nineteenth Century Notions of Aboriginal Title and their Influence on the Interpretation of the Treaty of Waitangi', in I. Kawharu (ed.), (1989), *Waitangi: Māori and Pākehā Perspectives of the Treaty of Waitangi*, Oxford University Press, Auckland, pp. 116–17—for details of the case and its effect, and J. B. Ringer (1991), *An Introduction to New Zealand Government*, Hazard, Christchurch, pp. 91–101 for an overview of the structure and function of State-owned enterprises.

25.   The Whakakotahi Taskforce convened two hui-a-iwi to discuss the Rūnanga Iwi Bill, 10 March 1990 at Turangi and 19 May 1990 at Massey University. The resource management legislation was discussed at the Airport Hotel, Wellington, 22 May 1991.

26.   These issues were among those dealt with by the Whakakotahi Taskforce, and were the subject of considerable debate in the months leading up to the National Māori Congress First Annual Conference.

27.   *Hui Whakakotahi Proceedings*, p. 31.

28.   Minutes of the Inaugural Taskforce Meeting held on Saturday 13 January in the Waiariki Room, THC Tokānu Hotel.

29.   These are listed in the bibliography as *Taskforce Discussion Papers 1–7. Taskforce Discussion Paper No. 1*, written by Mr George Asher, dealt with the Rūnanga Iwi Bill and provided valuable information on its possible effects should it be enacted in that form.

30.   The objectives suggested by the Taskforce were contained in *Taskforce Discussion Paper No 7* as Recommendation 4(a), while the guiding principles appeared in the same paper as Recommendation 4(b).

31.   The Constitution ratified at Taupō on 20 July 1991 includes provision for the inclusion of other Māori organizations, and provides for alterations to the membership structure to be made, Article 3 (a) (iii) and (e). See also Figure 34.

32.   *A Collective Submission on Supplementary Order Paper No. 22, Resource Management Bill*, May 1991, is an example of cooperation between the New Zealand Māori Council, the Māori Women's Welfare League, and FOMA.

33.   Māori Ecumenical Council established in 1982, a section of the National Council of Churches which was formed in the early 1940s.

34.   The Federation of Māori Authorities was formed as a result of work done by Sir Hepi Te Heuheu, who was constituted as a taskforce to investigate the possibility of forming a national organization for Māori landholding bodies following the 1985 Hui Taumata. Consisting mainly of section 438 Trusts (established under the Māori Affairs Act 1953), Māori land incorporations (constituted under the Māori Incorporations Act 1967), and Māori Trust Boards, FOMA was formed at a hui in Rotorua in 1986. FOMA has an executive body of ten and is administered by Kelvin Sanderson, who was appointed as chief executive officer in 1990.

35.   Convened jointly by Ken Mair of the Post Primary Teachers Association and Bill Hamilton of the New Zealand Education Institute, the inaugural hui of Tino Rangatiratanga was held at Rotorua Lakes High School on 8–9 July 1990.

36.   During the hui-a-iwi convened to discuss the Rūnanga Iwi Bill on 10 March 1990 at Turangi, Ngāti Kahungunu expressed a minority opinion. Accordingly, the final resolution of that meeting was altered to incorporate their opinions: *Proceedings of the Hui to Discuss the Rūnanga Iwi Bill*, (March 1990).

37.   Recommendation 6, *Taskforce Discussion Paper No. 7*.

38.   Recommendation 7, *Taskforce Discussion Paper No. 7*, Congress officers were to be elected at the inaugural hui.

39. Attendance registers are circulated at each venue; often, however, the dynamics of marae hui preclude full records from being obtained. It is likely that official figures represent 75–90 per cent of actual attendance.

40. An appellation applied to multi-tribal bodies established to meet the needs of Māori domiciled away from their traditional rohe. Originating from the Rūnanga Iwi Bill, the term denotes a link back to the home areas. Te Rūnanga Raki Pae Whenua, based on Auckland's North Shore and representing 11,000 Māori, lodged a formal request for membership.

41. According to the recent Department of Statistics work-force survey, Ngāti Porou and Ngāpuhi were the nation's most numerous iwi.

42. It was suggested after the Australian victory in the Rugby World Cup that this matter should, for the sake of national pride, be given some priority.

43. *Proceeding of the Hui to Discuss the Rūnanga Iwi Bill* (March 1990), p. 25, which resulted from a hui held at Turangi.

44. *He Tirohanga Rangapū* and *Te Urupare Rangapū* were taken around marae in April and November of 1988, respectively.

45. See the Iwi Transition Agency corporate plan, *Ko te Kaupapa Nui* (1990), p. 9.

46. 'Participation by Congress in Crown and/or Crown/Congress Bodies' (16 September 1991).

47. These goals (Appendix 11) were suggested at Taupō, and were adopted at Waitara on 7 September 1991.

48. In 1991, the Government sponsored a macroeconomic development project, the Porter Project, which drew on New Zealand commercial expertise.

49. As a result of Congress Justice Committee activity, an agreement has been reached with New Zealand Rail (NZR) on the disposal of surplus NZR land holdings.

50. Approval for Mr Williams's appointment was given by the Congress Executive hui held at Orākei Marae on 13 February 1993.

51. Written and circulated on 15 February 1992, the memo was discussed at the NMC Executive hui held at Waahi marae on 7 March 1992.

52. The advisory committee was established in August 1989 and in anticipation of Te Waka Hauora after August 1992, when its three-year term expired.

53. As well as the MWWL, the NMC, and the NZMC, the Women's Health League, the National Council of Māori Nurses, and Te Kohanga Reo Trust are all concerned with Māori health. The Department of Health has a Māori policy unit and both Te Puni Kokiri and Te Ohu Whakatipu (Ministry of Women's Affairs) provide advice to their Ministers on health matters.

54. This happens particularly where individual Māori are selected to health boards. For example, the National Interim Provider Board, the National Advisory Committee on Core Health and Disabilities Services, the Public Health Commission, and three of the four regional health authorities all had or have at least one Māori member, appointed by the Minister of Health, sometimes after consultation.

55. Each body put forward three members for the taskforce. They were: MWWL— Aroha Rereti-Crofts (League President), June Robinson, and Betty Hunapo; NZMC—Tom Moana, Kuini Harris, and Wairete Walters; NMC—Aroha Biel (Tapuika me Waitaha), Matire de Ridder (Turanganui ā Kiwa), and Selwyn Katene (Ngāti Toarangatira).

56. Manuka Henare (1990), 'Development: Sovereignty or Dependency?', in *Puna Wairere: Essays by Māori*, New Zealand Planning Council, Wellington, pp. 42–3.

Chapter Eight
Conclusions

In this book three themes have been used to explore Māori political unity at a national level and to provide a framework for consideration of the National Māori Congress. The first theme, 'He Whakaminenga o Ngā Hapū', concentrated upon kotahitanga engendered through independent Māori action and stimulated by the effects of colonization. Three case studies were employed to illustrate Māori attempts to maintain, develop, and reassert Mana Māori Motuhake. They all reflected a developing sense of sovereignty and nationhood among iwi and were founded by Māori leaders who subsumed, at least partially, the deep-seated imperative to maintain, enhance, and defend the mana of their hapū and iwi within the philosophy of kotahitanga. A conclusion reached in this book, in fact, is that kotahitanga was developed by rangatira in order to fulfil their obligations to protect and advance their people.

Legislative impediments to forestall Māori participation in mainstream political activities, early franchise restrictions, and the subsequent inception of inadequate representation in national, provincial, regional, and local governments provided one impetus for kotahitanga. Ironically, although Māori sought alternative avenues through united action to express their political aspirations, that action was often directed at obtaining a share of power. By recognizing the mandate of Parliament and seeking its validation for their own structures, they provided the Crown with a means to diffuse Māori initiatives. The succession of rūnanga and councils analysed in theme two provides ample evidence of that fact.

Further, the preoccupation with attaining State recognition so often proved to be frustrating and restraining. The energies of many talented and influential Māori leaders were focused upon a goal that was inevitably shaped by the whims of the majority. In contrast, the example set by Tāwhiao, whereby he withdrew from political intercourse with the State, ultimately had within it the seeds of success, albeit in the early years at some considerable price. A conclusion in this book is that Mana Māori Motuhake must be founded on Māori institutions if its goals are to be realized. A further conclusion is that the aims of Mana Māori Motuhake have always been in

190

conflict with deliberate and continued European attempts to entrench their own social, economic, cultural, and political mores in Aotearoa and also with the State's determination to avoid any serious discussion of sovereignty or its constitutional relationship with Māori.

The second theme, 'He Iwi Tahi Tātou', explored some of the responses developed by various agents of the Crown to destroy or, failing that, to control Māori nationalism. A recurrent theme of countering Māori expressions of sovereignty through State-prescribed and -funded structures is clearly evident. By granting limited autonomy to some representatives of selected iwi and delegating to them responsibility for certain functions of State, successive administrations, jealous of their own political power, have successfully extinguished effective Māori participation in the governance of the nation.

Financial domination consistently emerged as a significant factor in the manipulation of Māori aspirations. First, monetary inducements in the form of stipends and salaries were offered to some key Māori leaders to draw them into State schemes. Once a level of support had been obtained, usually to the detriment of structures determined by Māori, funding was then either reduced to or maintained at an inadequate level. The economic strangulation of Pākehā-inspired and administered institutions deliberately hampered Māori involvement in the social, political, cultural, and economic life of the nation.

Premised upon the egalitarian notion of majoritarianism, European structures supplanted indigenous preferences under a guise of equity and fairness. In line with the fundamental precepts of amalgamation and assimilation, the Crown adopted a paternalistic attitude to Māori affairs. Rather than encourage or even allow Māori to adapt or create their own structures, the holders of kāwanatanga have instead imposed their own self-serving institutions upon iwi. It can be concluded that if Māori are to eventually share in the benefits of modern society then a policy of proactive, independent action must be adopted. Further, arguments amassed in this book lead to the conclusion that the State's preferred option over the years has been one of assimilation—pseudo-national Māori institutions being constructed to speed that process.

The Kotahitanga movements discussed in this book under theme three, 'He Paihere Tangata', are testimony to the strengthening of Māori independence. The Māori Women's Welfare League, although developed under the auspices of the Department of Māori Affairs, has continued to set its own agendas, and has concentrated upon instituting mechanisms to advance its members, rather than entering into undue conflict with the Crown. The Rātana movement developed and flourished outside mainstream socio-religious institutions, and eventually infiltrated the political heartland of the nation. The Māori War Effort Organisation, even though a Crown agency operating under exceptional circumstances, focused upon specific goals and enabled effective united action to occur. These three case studies lead to the conclusion that unity of action among Māori people, derived from a shared cultural background, has in fact provided a sound basis for unity at a national level, and at the same time significantly influenced government policy.

If the current Kotahitanga movement, the National Māori Congress, is to achieve its goals, then much can be learned from the lessons of the past. Principally, unless Congress resists the very strong temptation to align itself with the State for short-term advantages, it runs the risk of abandoning its own agenda in favour of the State's inconsistent Māori policies. Secondly, it must adopt a position of proactive policy development and implementation, and avoid *ad hoc* responses to the initiatives of Government. Whereas it will be important to monitor and perhaps censure the Crown in the latter's perambulations, an undue focus on the machinations of Government, on select committee hearings, and on bureaucratic restructuring could inadvertently lead Congress to devote its entire energies to meeting Crown deadlines and priorities.

Whereas it is important to enter into a relationship with the Crown, that relationship must be firmly based upon the agendas of confederated iwi. If Congress allows the State to enact provisions for its operation then it becomes subject to the perusal and control of a party that should more appropriately be seen as a partner.

The strength of Congress is that its mana derives from its membership, and not from an external third party. Validation by an external body, national or international, may in fact be the *coup de grâce*.

Kotahitanga has no single goal. It has at times sought to strengthen iwi, and at other times to embrace Māori as individuals. It has focused on both an independent Māori nation and more effective Māori participation in mainstream political activity. It has been concerned with the social and economic advancement of Māori people as well as the retention and development of a traditional and evolving culture. It has appeared in response to particular threats and challenges, but has also arisen directly from the vision of Māori leaders.

Kotahitanga has not been uniform or static. Some Kotahitanga movements have emphasized the continuing independence of Māori institutions, others have recognized the importance of Māori institutions as a step towards assimilation, while still others have created new Māori institutions to retain some common thread of Māoritanga that can be expressed in an urbanized society. All Kotahitanga movements have had to grapple with the changing nature of Māori politics and both the rekindling and strengthening of new and traditional alliances. Where kotahitanga has embraced the autonomy of its members, recognizing their diversity and incorporating those differences as a strength, it has flourished.

In the ongoing evolution of Māori political unity, the National Māori Congress has emerged as a body with the potential to incorporate several aspects of kotahitanga. Its ultimate contribution to the position of Māori in Aotearoa will depend heavily upon its ability to steer a balanced course between contemporary national and international realities, the aspirations and dreams of its members, and the manner in which Māori people themselves remain its anchor stone.

Ko te tangata ke te puna o te Kotahitanga.[1]

Endnote

1.   Unity is not an end in itself, it must be beneficial to people, without whom it cannot succeed.

Appendix One
He Wakaputanga O Te Rangatiratanga O Nu Tirene/Declaration of Independence in New Zealand

Māori Text

1. Ko matou, ko ngā tino Rangatira o nga iwi o Nu Tirene i raro mai o Haurake, kua oti nei te huihui i Waitangi, i Tokerau, i te ra 28 o Oketopa, 1835. Ka wakaputa i te Rangatiratanga o to matou wenua; a ka meatia ka wakaputaia e matou he Wenua Rangatira, kia huaina, 'Ko te Wakaminenga o nga Hapu o Nu Tirene'.

2. Ko te Kingitanga, ko te mana i te wenua o te wakaminenga o Nu Tirene, ka meatia nei kei nga tino Rangatira anake i to matou huihuinga; a ka mea hoki, ekore e tukua e matou te wakarite ture ki tetahi hunga ke atu, me tetahi Kawanatanga hoki kia meatia i te wenua o te wakaminenga o Nu Tirene, ko nga tangata anake e meatia nei e matou, e wakarite ana ki te ritenga o o matou ture e meatia nei e matou i to matou huihuinga.

3. Ko matou, ko nga tino Rangatira, ka mea nei, kia huihui ki te runanga ki Waitangi a te Ngahuru i tenei tau i tenei tau, ki te wakarite ture, kia tika ai te wakawakanga, kia mau pu te rongo, kia mutu te he, kia tika te hokohoko. A ka mea hoki ki nga tauiwi o runga, kia wakarerea te wawai, kia mahara ai ki te wakaoranga o to matou wenua, a kia uru ratou ki te wakaminenga o Nu Tirene.

4. Ka mea matou, kia tuhituhia he pukapuka, ki te ritenga o tenei o to matou wakaputanga nei, ki te Kingi o Ingarani, hei kawe atu i to matou aroha; nana hoki i wakaae ki te Kara mo matou. A no te mea ka atawai matou, ka tiaki i nga Pakeha e noho nei uta, e rere mai ana ki te hokohoko, koia ka mea ai matou ki te Kingi kia waiho hei Matua ki a matou i to matou tamarikitanga, kei wakakahoretia to matou Rangatiratanga.

Kua wakaaetia katoatia e matou i tenei ra, i te 28 o Oketopa 1835, ki te aroaro
o te Rehirenete o te Kingi o Ingarani.

English Text

1. We the hereditary chiefs and heads of the tribes of the Northern parts of
   New Zealand, being assembled at Waitangi, in the Bay of Islands, on this
   28th day of October 1835, declare the Independence of our country,
   which is hereby constituted and declared to be an Independent State,
   under the designation of the United Tribes of New Zealand.
2. All sovereign power and authority within the territories of the United
   Tribes of New Zealand is hereby declared to reside entirely and
   exclusively in the hereditary chiefs and heads of tribes in their collective
   capacity, who also declare that they will not permit any legislative
   authority separate from themselves in their collective capacity to exist, nor
   any function of government to be exercised within the said territories,
   unless by persons appointed by them, and acting under the authority of
   laws regularly enacted by them in Congress assembled.
3. The hereditary chiefs and heads of tribes agree to meet in Congress at
   Waitangi in the autumn of each year, for the purpose of framing laws for
   the dispensation of justice, the preservation of peace and good order, and
   the regulation of trade; and they cordially invite the Southern tribes to lay
   aside their private animosities and to consult the safety and welfare of our
   common country, by joining the Confederation of the United Tribes.
4. They also agree to send a copy of this Declaration to His Majesty the King
   of England, to thank him for his acknowledgement of their flag, and in
   return for the friendship and protection they have shown, and are
   prepared to show, to such of his subjects as have settled in their country, or
   resorted to its shores for the purposes of trade, they entreat that he will
   continue to be the parent of their infant State, and that he will become its
   Protector from all attempts upon its independence.

Agreed to unanimously on this 28th day of October, 1835, in the presence of
His Britannic Majesty's Resident.

(Here follow the signatures or marks of thirty-five hereditary chiefs or
heads of tribes, which form a fair representation of the tribes of New Zealand
from the North Cape to the latitude of the River Thames.)

English witnesses
(Signed)

Henry Williams, Missionary, CMS
George Clarke, CMS
James C. Clendon, Merchant
Gilbert Mair, Merchant

Note: After 1835, other Chiefs supported the Declaration. We have included their names.

Appendix Two
Te Tiriti o Waitangi/The Treaty of Waitangi

The Māori Text

Ko Wikitoria, te Kuini o Ingarani, i tana mahara atawai ki nga Rangatira me Nga Hapu o Nu Tirani, i tana hiahia hoki kia tohungia ki a ratou o ratou rangatiratanga, me to ratou wenua, a kia mau tonu hoki te Rongo ki a ratou me te ata noho hoki, kua wakaaro ia he mea tika kia tukua mai tetahi Rangatira hei kai wakarite ki nga tangata Māori o Nu Tirani. Kia wakaaetia e nga Rangatira Māori te Kawanatanga o te Kuini, ki nga wahi katoa o te wenua nei me nga motu. Na te mea hoki he to komaha ke nga tangata o tona iwi kua noho ki tenei wenua, a e haere mai nei.

Na, ko te Kuini e hiahia ana kia wakaritea te Kawanatanga, kia kaua ai nga kino e puta mai ki te tangata Māori ki te pakeha e noho ture kore ana.

Na, kua pai te Kuini kia tukua a hau, a Wiremu Hopihona, he Kapitana i te Roiara Nawa, hei Kawana mo nga wahi katoa o Nu Tirani, e tukua aianei amua atu ki te Kuini; e mea atu ana ia ki nga Rangatira o te Wakaminenga o nga Hapu o Nu Tirani, me era Rangatira atu, enei ture ka korerotia nei.

Ko Te Tuatahi

Ko nga Rangatira o te Wakaminenga, me nga Rangatira katoa hoki, kihai i uru ki taua Wakaminenga, ka tuku rawa atu ki te Kuini o Ingarani ake tonu atu te Kawanatanga katoa o o ratou wenua.

Ko Te Tuarua

Ko te Kuini o Ingarani ka wakarite ki nga Rangatira, ki nga Hapu, ki nga tangata katoa o Nu Tirani, te tino Rangitiratanga o o ratou wenua o ratou kainga me o ratou taonga katoa. Otiia ko nga Rangatira o te Wakaminenga, me nga Rangatira katoa atu, ka tuku ki te Kuini te hokonga o era wahi wenua e pai ai te tangata nona te wenua, ki te ritenga o te utu e wakaritea ai e ratou ko te kai hoko e meatia nei i te Kuini hei kai hoko mona.

Ko Te Tuatoru

He wakaritenga mai hoki tenei mo te wakaaetanga ki te Kawanatanga o te Kuini. Ka tiakina e te Kuini o Ingarani nga tangata Māori katoa o Nu Tirani. Ka tukua ki a ratou nga tikanga katoa rite tahi ki ana mea ki nga tangata o Ingarani.

(Signed) William Hobson,
Consul and Lieutenant Governor

Na, ko matou, ko nga Rangatira o te Wakaminenga o nga Hapu o Nu Tirani, ka huihui nei ki Waitangi. Ko matou hoki ko nga Rangatira o Nu Tirani, ka kite nei i te ritenga o enei kupu, ka tangohia, ka wakaaetia katoatia e matou. Koia ka tohungia ai o matou ingoa o matou tohu.

Ka meatia tenei ki Waitangi, i te ono o nga ra o Pepuere, i te tau kotahi mano, e waru rau, e wa tekau, o to tātou Ariki.

The English Text

Her Majesty Victoria Queen of the United Kingdom of Great Britain and Ireland regarding with Her Royal Favour the Native Chiefs and Tribes of New Zealand and anxious to protect their just Rights and Property and to secure to them the enjoyment of Peace and Good Order has deemed it necessary in consequence of the great number of Her Majesty's Subjects who have already settled in New Zealand and the rapid extension of Emigration both from Europe and Australia which is still in progress to constitute and appoint a functionary properly authorised to treat with the Aborigines of New Zealand for the recognition of Her Majesty's Sovereign authority over the whole or any part of those islands—Her Majesty therefore being desirous to establish a settled form of Civil Government with a view to avert the evil consequences which must result from the absence of the necessary Laws and Institutions alike to the native population and to Her subjects has been graciously pleased to empower and to authorise me William Hobson a Captain in Her Majesty's Royal Navy Consul and Lieutenant Governor of such parts of New Zealand as may be or hereafter shall be ceded to her Majesty to invite the confederated and independent Chiefs of New Zealand to concur in the following Articles and Conditions.

Article The First

The Chiefs of the Confederation of the United Tribes of New Zealand and the separate and independent Chiefs who have not become members of the

Confederation cede to Her Majesty the Queen of England absolutely and without reservation all the rights and powers of Sovereignty which the said Confederation or Individual Chiefs respectively exercise or possess, or may be supposed to exercise or to possess over their respective Territories as the sole Sovereigns thereof.

Article The Second

Her Majesty the Queen of England confirms and guarantees to the Chiefs and Tribes of New Zealand and to the respective families and individuals thereof the full exclusive and undisturbed possession of their Lands and Estates Forests Fisheries and other properties which they may collectively or individually possess so long as it is their wish and desire to retain the same in their possession; but the chiefs of the United Tribes and the individual Chiefs yield to Her Majesty the exclusive right of pre-emption over such lands as the proprietors thereof may be disposed to alienate—at such prices as may be agreed between the respective Proprietors and persons appointed by Her Majesty to treat with them in that behalf.

Article The Third

In consideration thereof Her Majesty the Queen of England extends to the Natives of New Zealand Her royal protection and imparts to them all the Rights and Privileges of British subjects.

W. Hobson
Lieutenant Governor

Now therefore We the Chiefs of the Confederation of the United Tribes of New Zealand being assembled in Congress at Victoria in Waitangi and We the Separate and Independent Chiefs of New Zealand claiming authority over the Tribes and Territories which are specified after our respective names, having been made fully to understand the Provisions of the foregoing Treaty, accept and enter into the same in the full spirit and meaning thereof: in witness of which we have attached our signatures or marks at the places and the dates respectively specified.

Done at Waitangi this Sixth day of February in the year of Our Lord one thousand eight hundred and forty.

Appendix Three
Resolutions of Kohimārama Hui

Resolutions adopted by the Hui at Kohimārama on Friday 10 August 1860*

Resolution One
'That this conference takes cognizance of the fact that several chiefs, members thereof, are pledged to each other to do nothing inconsistent with their declared recognition of the Queen's sovereignty, and of the union of the two races; also to discountenance all proceedings tending to breach the covenant here solemnly entered into by them.'
Proposed: Paikea
Seconded: Te Manihera Ruia

Resolution Two
'That this conference is of opinion that the project of setting up a Māori King in New Zealand is a cause of division and strife, and is fraught with troubles to the country.'
Proposed: Wiremu Nero Te Airaitaia
Seconded: Hamiora Matenga Tu

Resolution Three
'That this conference having heard explained the circumstances which led to the war at Taranaki, is of opinion that the Governor was justified in the course taken by him; that William King te Rangitake himself provoked the quarrel, and that the proceedings of the latter are wholly indefensible.'
Proposed: Winiata Pekamu Tohi Te Ururangi
Seconded: Te Manihera Ruia

Resolution Four
'That the conference deprecates in the strongest manner the murders of unarmed Europeans committed by the natives now fighting at Taranaki.'
Proposed: Wiremu Tamihana
Seconded: Manihera Matangi

Resolution Five

'That this conference desires to thank the Bishop of New Zealand for his kindness in allowing them the use of the buildings at Kohimārama.'
Proposed: Tamihana Te Rauparaha
Seconded: Mete Kingi

Resolution Six

'That this conference desires to thank his Excellency the Governor for his goodness to the Māori people; that is, for his constant kindness and love to them; and also for granting them this great boon, the 'runanga', whereby they are enabled to express their views, and propose measures for the settlement of the difficulties which arise among the native people.'
Proposed: Wiremu Paten Whitirangi
Seconded: Ramiora Matenga Tu

Resolution Seven

'That this conference desires to thank their friend Mr McLean for his great exertions on their behalf, and for his kindness to the natives of this island of New Zealand.'
Proposed: Te Makarini Te Oka
Seconded: Tamihana Te Rauparaha

(There follow the 'signatures' of 106 rangatira.)

We agree to these Resolutions, with the exception of one, which is not clear, and from which we dissent, viz.:

Resolution Three

'That this conference having heard explained the circumstances which led to the war at Taranaki, is of opinion that the Governor was justified in the course taken by him; that William King te Rangitake himself provoked the quarrel, and that the proceedings of the latter are wholly indefensible.'

This is the Resolution from which we dissent.
Signed
Wiremu Tamihana Te Neke
    Te Manihera Matangi
    Epiha Karoro

Witness to Signatures
   Henry T. Clarke
   Resident Magistrate
   Bay of Plenty

★ From *Great Britain Parliamentary Papers* (1861) 12, pp. 129–30. Names of those proposing and seconding each resolution were taken from pp. 119–20 of the same volume.

Appendix Four
Treaty of Waitangi Hui Signatories, 1892

The names of the following rangatira and their iwi/rohe were recorded in *Ngā Korero o te hui o te Whakakotahitanga i tu ki te Tiriti o Waitangi* on 14 April 1892.

Wihapi Pakau: ....Ngāti Awa
Wiparata Te Kakakura: ....Ngāti Toa; Te Āti Awa, Taranaki
Tamihana Te Hoia: ....Ngāti Raukawa, Otaki
Meiha Keepa Te
   Rangihiwinui: ....Whanganui; Nga Rauru; Rangitane; Muaupoko
Te Mana o Tawhaki: ....Ngawaiariki; Ngāti Apa, Turakina
Te Maraku: ....Ngāti Tuwharetoa; Ngāti Tekohera, Taupo
Hoani Nahe: ....Ngāti Maru; Ngāti Tamatera; Ngāti Pukenga;
Ngāti Paoa, Hauraki
Hamiora Mangakahia: ....Moehau, Whangapoua, Whitianga, Harataunga
Akapita Tetewe: ....Ngai Terangi, Tauranga
Eru Teuremutu,
Matenga Taiwhanga,
Hori Taiawhio: ....Te Arawa (katoa katoa)
Te Ramaapakura: ....Ngāti Awa, Whakatane, Te Teko
Paora Taia: ....Whakatohea; Te Whanau Apanui, Opotiki
Tuta Nihoniho,
Apiata Te Hame: ....Ngāti Porou, Timata mai Tikirau tae noa ki
Tokaataiau
Wipere Timikara: ....Turanga katoa me te Urewera
Hoani Kehua: ....Kahungunu; Mahia, Nuhaka, Whakaki
Tamihana Huata,
Kerei Teota: ....Kahungunu; Wairoa, Waiau, Waikare,
                                  Whakapunake, Mohaka
Hekengarangi, Peni Te Ua,
Mohi Teatahikoia,
Wi Rangirangi, Peni Tepuna: Kahungunu; Waikari, Patea, Hineuru, Te
                                    Whanganui a Orotu, Ahuriri
Tunuiaranga: ....Kahungunu; Wairārapa, Heretaunga
Timoti Te Whuia,
Hoani Maaka: ....Ngai Tahu; Ngāti Mamoe, Te Waipounamu
Heta Paikea, Hauraki: ....Ngāti Whatua, Kaipara
Taurau Kukupa,
Mari Te Hautakiri,

Wiremu Pomare,
Pomare Kingi, Tito,
Pouaka Parere,
Netana Patuawa, Rikihana: .... Te Parawhau; Te Rarawa; Tekoroa; Ngāti
                                                    Whatua; Whangarei, Mangakahia, Waiora,
Opunake
Hapakuku Maetara,
Wiki Tepa, Toi: .... Ngāti Korokoro; Waimamaku
Pere Riwhi, Re Te Tai: .... Whirinaki Te Hikutu, Hokianga
Kohipara Mohi,
Wikitahi Wairama,
Kereama Pihi: .... Ngāti Hau; Omanaia
H. M. Tawhai,
Raniera Wharerau,
Heta Te Tuhi Waipapa,
Hemi Papkura: .... Waima, Pairama, Tetihi, Utakura
Miti Kakau, Hori Karaka,
Tawhiti, Piripi Rakena: .... Ngāpuhi; Rarawa, Mangamuka
Temaunga, Hone Papahia,
Herewini Te Toke,
Heremia Tawake,
Te Wharemate: .... Rarawa; Waihou, Whakarapa, Orongotea,
Whangape
Timoti Puhipi: .... Rarawa; Ahipara, Kaitaia, Te Awanui,
Karaponia
Eparaima Kapa,
Hare Tehara, Iraia Peti,
Tane Haratua, Hone Ngapua,
Wiremu Katene,
Maihi Kawiti: .... Ngāpuhi; Pewhairangi

Appendix Five
Native Rights Bill 1894*

The 'Native Rights Bill' presented to the General Assembly by Hone Heke (MHR for Northern Māori) in 1894

An Act to empower the Aboriginal Natives of New Zealand to enact Laws for the Government of themselves and their Lands and other Property.

Whereas the legislation heretofore in force relating to Native lands and the powers of Native Lands Courts, and relative to property and rights of the aboriginal inhabitants of New Zealand, have been found to be and are inadequate and unjust, whereby the progress of a great part of the colony has been retarded, and the said aboriginal natives have been subject to great wrongs and grievances for which they have now no remedy: And whereas, by reason of the matters aforesaid, the said aboriginal natives have suffered much loss in lands and moneys and otherwise: And whereas it is to the benefit of both the European and aboriginal inhabitants of New Zealand that the said aboriginal natives and their lands and other property should be governed by laws enacted by themselves:

Be it therefore enacted by the General Assembly of New Zealand in Parliament assembled, and by the authority of the same, as follows:—

1. The Short Title of this Act is 'The Native Rights Act, 1894'.

2. A Constitution shall be granted to all the persons of the Māori race, and to all persons born of either father or mother of the Māori race who are or shall be resident in New Zealand, providing for the enactment of laws by a Parliament elected by such persons.

3. Such laws shall relate to and exclusively deal with the personal rights and with the lands and all other property of the aboriginal native inhabitants of New Zealand.

Bills Thrown Out, 1894, Government Printer, Wellington.

★ From W. David McIntyre and W. J. Gardiner, *Speeches and Documents on New Zealand History* (Oxford University Press, London), pp. 164–5.

Appendix Six
*King Tawhiao's Constitution, 1894** †

. . . notice to the 'Hapus and Tribes of New Zealand, from the tail to the head of Maui's fish, crossing the sea of Raukawa (Cook's Straits) to Te Waipounamu, that the following laws have been adopted by the Māori Kauhanganui (Convention), and assented to by King Potatau Tawhiao under his Royal seal and sign manual.'

1. That he has been pleased to appoint Taua Taingakawa Te Waharoa (son of the King-maker William Thompson) to be Premier of the Māori kingdom of Aotearoa.
2. That the Kauhanga (Convention) of manukura (nobles) and matariki (commoners) shall assemble on the 2nd of May in each year.
3. That the Convention shall then assemble before the Prime Minister and submit their deliberations (laws) to King Tawhiao on his throne.
4. Special provision will be made for those chiefs who may hereafter join the King movements that they shall be equal with the Europeans.
5. On 2nd May in each year returns will be published . . . of the amount raised by the Poll Tax of 2s. per head, and careful statements given showing the just and equitable expenditure of the same. . . .
6. Every Act of the Assembly must be confirmed by King Tawhiao by affixing the seal of the kingdom.
7. The leasing of land under the King's authority is assented to.

Sub-section (1) provides that land may be leased for a term not exceeding 22 years including kore-kore or 'lean' years; (2) Each year is divided in three 'quarters' of four months, and rents all payable at end of each quarter, unless arranged differently between the contracting parties; (3) Any breach of agreement shall be followed by instant eviction and determination of the lease; (4) All metals—gold, silver, iron, copper, coal, road metal, clay for bricks or pottery—to belong to the State; (5) Leases only give the lessee power to graze stock and cultivate; (6) Arrangements may be made by which all metals, &c., can be acquired by the lessee; (7) The King reserves power to make public roads through such leased land, also for purpose of working any of the aforesaid metals; (8) Nothing growing on the land, such as timber and flax, shall be affected by the preceding sub-sections.

Clause 8.—Part 1 defines various classes of land, such as land which has not been affected by European laws. Claimants must apply to the Premier of the Kingdom for ascertainment of individual or tribal rights. Part 2—Native lands which have been dealt with by the European Native Land Court, being lands inherited by the Māoris from their ancestors, can be dealt with under the laws of the Kingdom. Part 3—For judgements and rehearings for lands dealt with by European laws special provision by regulations will be made.

Sub-section 1.—Lists of Māori owners' names to be given, &c., inclusive of halfcastes. It shall not be lawful for any halfcaste or halfcastes to set aside Māori rights or customs, nor to assume supreme control of the land; (2) halfcastes are defined as consisting 'only of those persons who are peaceful and law-abiding, who will not bring trouble and ruin upon their mother race;' (3) the Māori Government to have full power to enquire into and adjust any dispute or trouble of whatever kind. The European Government may take part in any such enquiry should it so desire, and it makes written application to, and obtains permission from, the Māori Premier.

Part 4.—Single individuals will not be permitted to force on surveys. Permission must be obtained from the Prime Minister after the whole of the reputed owners or tribe have expressed their convenance.

Part 5.—Defines Crown lands . . . lands which have been Crown granted, but since placed by the Māori owners under the King's protection. Māoris or Europeans having claims thereto must apply to the Premier in order to prevent confusion.

Sub-sections 1 to 4 provide for dealing with such lands in a 'spirit of truth and justice.' Where lands the lawful property of others have been wrongfully Crown-granted, such grants will be annulled. Then follow a number of amendments relating to the leasing of Crown-granted lands which have not been dealt with by Europeans.

Part 6.—Deals with gifts of lands, and with land placed by the owners under King Tawhiao's sovereignty.

Part 7.—Lands given to the missionaries for school endowments. Where the trusts have not been fulfilled, the area shall be assumed to be no more than five acres in each case, residue to revert to original owner.

Part 8.—Disputed lands not to be dealt with till all troubles connected therewith have been decided by the Māori tribunals.

9. Public lands to be dealt with under clauses 1 and 6.

10.   Provides for the appointment of magistrates within the Māori kingdom, to uphold the laws, keep the peace, settle all disputes as to persons, live stock property, offences, &c.

Laws as to marriage, under the ancient customs and manners of the Māori race.—
(1) If the parents, brothers, and the hapū generally, consent to the marriage of a girl with the man of her choice, the union shall be binding in law, without further ceremony. (2) If one or more of the parents or relations object to a marriage, then full enquiry shall be made to endeavour to remove reason of objection; but the wish of the majority must be final. (3) Under these laws it shall not be lawful for a Māori women to marry a pakeha. Should the woman still cling to her European spouse, she may be given her own way, but she will henceforth be deemd 'a child of the night,' and an outcast from the native race; such being ancient Māori custom. (4) No licenses shall be granted to individuals to perform the marriage ceremony.

Part 2.—Settlement of Europeans on the land.—It shall not be lawful for the owners of such land to locate Europeans upon any land whatever unless sanction is first obtained. Any natives so offending will be punished in the event of trouble and loss coming upon the European.

11.   Makes regulations for printing the Paki o Matariki.

12.   For the appointment of a capable person as editor, Government printer, &c.

13.   The Government of the Māori kingdom have assented to the establishment of licensed stores in Māori districts under King Tawhiao's authority, but the sale of ardent spirits is strictly prohibited.

The names of ten chiefs are gazetted as Justices of the Peace in certain districts, 'all being good men and true.'

A number of chiefs notify that they have banded together to prevent the sale of spirits, and agree to fine every person breaking this agreement £5.

Issued by order of the Prime Minister of the Māori Kingdom.

(Sd.) T. T. Rawhiti.

The Evening Post, Wellington, 30 May 1894

★ From W. David McIntyre and W. J. Gardiner, *Speeches and Documents on New Zealand History* (Oxford University Press, London), pp. 165–8.

† A translation published in a Wellington newspaper of the constitution for the 'Kingdom of Aotearoa' adopted by the Kauhanganui. First published in *Te Paki o Matariki*, the gazette of 'The Independent Royal Power of Aotearoa', Maungākawa, 12 April 1894.

Appendix Seven*
The Māori Councils Act 1900

'An Act to confer a Limited Measure of Local Self-government upon Her Majesty's Subjects of the Māori Race in the Colony', 18 October 1900.

WHEREAS reiterated applications have been made by the Māori inhabitants of those parts of the colony where the Māoris are more or less domiciled and settled, forming what is known as Māori centres and surroundings, for the establishment within those districts of some simple machinery of local self-government . . .

BE IT THEREFORE ENACTED . . .

3. The Governor may proclaim any district a Māori district . . .

6. For every Māori district established under this Act there shall be a Council consisting of the official member and of not less than six or more than twelve members to be elected from among the Māoris of such-and-such a district as hereinafter provided; and the number of members shall be fixed by the Governor on the establishment of the district; and it shall be lawful for the Governor, by Proclamation, to subdivide any such district into convenient sections, and to appoint and declare the number of such members to be elected for each such section. . . .

8. In every Māori district established under this Act the Stipendiary Magistrate at the chief town within such district, or such other person as the Governor may from time to time appoint, shall be ex officio a member of such Council. . . .

15. It shall be the duty of the Council to formulate, and from time to time report to the Governor upon, a general plan that would be acceptable to the Māoris of the district, and be best adapted for the purposes following; that is to say,—

    (1.) For ascertaining, providing, and prescribing for the observance and enforcement of the rights, duties, and liabilities, amongst themselves, of tribes, communities, or individuals of the Māori race, in relation to all social and domestic matters.

    (2.) For the suppression of injurious Māori customs, and for the substitution of remedies and punishments for injuries in cases in which compensation is now sought by means of such customs.

(3.) For the promotion of education and instruction, both ordinary and technical, and the conduct and management of Native schools.

(4.) And generally for the promotion of the health and welfare and moral well-being of the Māori inhabitants of the district. . . .

And it shall be the duty of the Council to collect and tabulate facts and statistics in relation to, and to report to the Governor upon, the following matters:—

(1.) The general health of Māori inhabitants of the district, the causes of death as far as it is possible to ascertain them;

(2.) The movement of the population, the extent of consanguineous connections or marriages and their effect, and the extent of the absorption of the Native race by inter-marriage with Europeans;

(3.) The number of persons engaged in industrial pursuits and the nature of such pursuits, the extent of land cultivated or under pasture, and the number and nature of stock depasturing thereon;

(4.) Any other matters that the Council may deem necessary in order that the Governor may know from time to time the condition of the Native race, the fluctuations of population, the causes of decrease of population if there is a decrease, any influences that may be at work to ameliorate the condition of the race, and the progress that may be made towards the adoption of healthier habits and pursuits.

16.   It shall be lawful for the Council of any Māori district constituted under this Act to make, and from time to time vary or revoke, by-laws respecting all or any of the matters following, that is to say,—

[Health. Cleansing of houses. Common nuisances, Drunkenness. Tohungas. Meeting-houses. Dogs. Branding of cattle, &c. Eel-weirs. Oyster-beds, &c. Burial grounds. Recreation-grounds. Hawkers, Smoking. Gambling. Water-supplies. Sanitation. Diseases of animals.] . . .

17.   The Council shall have power to appoint from among the Māoris of any Māori kainga, village, or pa a Committee of not less than three or more than five, who shall be called the Village Committee (Komiti Marae), and who shall, subject to the Control of the Council, order the abatement or removal of any nuisance, or the destruction of rubbish likely to prove detrimental to the Māori inhabitants of any Māori town, village, or pa; who shall enforce the proper sanitation of all whares or other buildings. . . .

29.   A general Conference of delegates from the Councils may be held annually.

New Zealand Statutes, 1900, 64 Vict., no. 48, pp. 252–60.

★ From W. David McIntyre and W. J. Gardiner, *Speeches and Documents on New Zealand History* (Oxford University Press, London), pp. 168–70.

Appendix Eight
Taskforce Recommendations to the Hui Whakakotahi

Taskforce recommendations to the Hui Whakakotahi, Turangawaewae Marae, 14 July 1990—from *Whakakotahi Taskforce Discussion Paper No. 7*, 17 June 1990.

Recommendation 1
That a National Māori Congress be established without further delay.

Recommendation 2
That each iwi appoint five delegates, these delegates to make up the membership of Congress.

Recommendation 3
That a Constitution for Congress be developed over the next twelve months and that in the meantime Congress be guided by a set of objectives and principles.

Recommendation 4 (a) Objectives
The Congress objectives shall be:
1) The advancement of all Māori People;
2) The exercise, by each iwi, of tino rangatiratanga;
3) The provision of a national forum for iwi representatives to address economic, social, cultural, and political issues within tikanga Māori;
4) The promotion of constitutional and legislative arrangements that enable Māori people to control their own right to development and self determination.

Recommendation 4 (b) Principles
In meeting the above objectives, the Congress shall be guided by:
1) The philosophy of whakakotahi based on the shared traditions and aspirations of all Māori people;

2) The principle of Māori mana motuhake which recognises the right of Māori people to decide their own destiny;
3) The principle of tino rangatiratanga in which is embodied the mana and autonomy of each iwi in respect of their own affairs;
4) The principle of paihere tangata acknowledging the strengths that accrue when people are joined together in the pursuit of common goals;
5) The articles of the Treaty of Waitangi.

Recommendation 5
That iwi participating in Congress accept responsiblity for funding Congress activities.

Recommendation 6
That at the Hui Whakakotahi the Congress Presidents be appointed by the Hui to lead Congress.

Recommendation 7
That at the inaugural meeting of Congress, delegates should elect from the membership the following officers:
• Congress Chairperson
• Deputy Chairperson
• Congress Secretary
• Treasurer.

Recommendation 8
That a Co-ordinating Group made up of one delegate from each iwi be established at the inaugural meeting of Congress.

Recommendation 9
That a body to be known as the Congress Executive be delegated authority to act on behalf of Congress, the Executive to include:
• The Presidents
• Congress Chairperson
• Deputy Chairperson
• Congress Secretary
• Treasurer
• The members of the Co-ordinating Group.

Recommendation 10
That at the first meeting of the Congress Executive, a convenor from the Congress Executive and a minimum of four members from the Congress

membership should be appointeed to each of the following committees:
- A Constitution Committee
- An Operations Committee
- A Finance Committee
- A Communications Committee
- A Legislation Committee
- A Government Review Committee
- A Justice Committee
- An International Committee.

Appendix Nine
National Māori Congress Constitution*

Preamble

Guided by the philosophy of *whakakotahi* based on the shared traditions and aspirations of all Māori people; and
Accepting the principle of *Māori Mana Motuhake* which recognises the right of Māori people to decide their own destiny;
Reaffirming the principle of *tino rangatiratanga* in which is embodied the mana and autonomy of each iwi in respect of their own affairs; and
Recognising the principle of *paihere tangata* acknowledging the strengths that accrue when people are joined together in the pursuit of common goals; and
Honouring the Treaty of Waitangi.

We the United Iwi/Tribes of Aotearoa and Te Waipounamu hereby establish *The National Māori Congress.*

The power of existence of Congress derives solely *from iwi* and no other source.

Constitution

The National Māori Congress shall be recognised by the statement of principles contained in the Preamble.

The National Māori Congress shall be administered in a manner consistent with the following Articles:
Article One—Name
Article Two—Objectives
The objectives of National Māori Congress shall be:
1 To provide a national forum for iwi to address issues affecting Māori people;

2 To promote the exercising by each iwi, of tino rangatiratanga;

3 To provide a forum which advances iwi nationhood;

4 To promote constitutional and legislative arrangements that enable Māori people to control their own right to development and self determination;

5 To monitor Government policy and legislative arrangements and its development and implementation insofar as such legislation/policy affects or impacts upon iwi, Māori institutions or organisations, and Māori;

6 To advance, coordinate and promote a unified national iwi position/ view/response on foreign policy matters, not only to the New Zealand Government, but internationally;

7 To carry out such administrative, financial, investment, or other function or activity as may be considered necessary or desirable;

8 To carry out all functions economic, social, cultural and political in accordance with the Articles of the Treaty of Waitangi;

9 To assist iwi in the developing and monitoring legislation by the Government that affects iwi, Māori institutions or organisations, and Māori;

10 To advance all Māori people.

★   From *Te Whakakotahitanga o Nga Iwi o Aotearoa me Te Waipounamu/ The National Māori Congress: Hui A Tau, Tauponui A Tia, 20 Hongongoi 1991*, p. 34.

Appendix Ten
The Eight Goals

1 A Policy for Māori Employment
The objective for this goal is to develop policies and strategies for full Māori employment.

2 A Māori Education Authority
The main objective for this goal is to establish an iwi education authority for Māori.

3 Iwi Development Banks
The objective is to establish a network of iwi development banks and a reserve bank.

4 A Māori International Identity
The Goal 4 objectives are therefore for Congress to obtain the status of an NGO under the United Nations and to be represented at Brazil and Geneva in 1992.

5 Constitutional Re-Arrangements
The objective is to promote a change in New Zealand's constitutional arrangements in order to give due recognition to the position of Māori.

6 An Extended Congress Membership
The objective is to enter into discussion with Māori organisations regarding participation in Congress.

7 A Congress Secretariat
The objective is to establish a Congress Secretariat.

8 A National Identity for Congress
The objective is to actively promote a national identity for Congress.

Other Goals

These eight goals are not an exclusive or comprehensive list of goals. Committees will have their own goals and others will arise during the course of the year, some urgently. The purpose for identifying these eight is to ensure that Congress-initiated activities do not become submerged as other business arises. A case could be made for many more priorities to rank alongside those that are identified in this paper. But an equal case could be made to insist that Congress remain realistic, thorough in all its activities, and committed to expending energy only where it will have the greatest effect.

Appendix Eleven
Participation at Rātana Hui Rangatira

The following list of iwi, rūnanga, and Māori organizations has been derived from the official record of the Rātana Hui Rangatira, held on 12 August 1989. They are grouped as

- iwi
- taurahere roopu
- rūnanga
- other Māori organizations.

Iwi

Atihaunui a Paparangi
Hauraki
Muaupoko
Ngā Rauru
Ngā Uri a Uenukukopako
Ngāi Tahu
Ngāi Tai
Ngāi Te Rangi
Ngāruahine
Ngāti Apa
Ngāti Awa
Ngāti Hauā
Ngāti Hauā Hinekehu
Ngāti Kahungunu
Ngāti Kahungunu ki Heretaunga
Ngāti Kahungunu ki Te Wairoa
Ngāti Koata
Ngāti Kuri
Ngāti Maniapoto
Ngāti Mutunga
Ngāti Pahauwera
Ngāti Porou
Ngāti Pukenga
Ngāti Ranginui
Ngāti Raukawa
Ngāti Raukawa Trust Board
Ngāti Ruanui
Ngāti Taharua
Ngāti Tahu/Whaoa
Ngāti Tama
Ngāti Tama a Waho
Ngāti Tamatera
Ngāti Tarawhai
Ngāti Toarangatira
Ngāti Tupoho
Ngāti Wai
Ngāti Whātua
Rangitane
Rangitane ki Manawatu
Tai Poutini
Tainui
Tamaupoko
Taranaki Tuturu
Te Arawa/Ngāti Pikiao
Te Arawa/Tapuika

Te Arawa/Tuhourangi
Te Arawa/Waitaha
Te Āti Awa
Tuwharetoa/Te Atua Reretahi
Te Aupouri
Te Whanau a Apanui
Te Iwi o Wharekauri
Tūhoe
Tukorohe
Tuwharetoa
Tuwharetoa ki Kawerau
Whakatohea
Whangaehu

Taurahere Roopu
Ngā Mata Waka Tūhoe
Ngā Matawaka Otautahi
Ngāpuhi Whanui ki Tamaki
  Makaura
Ngāti Awa ki Poneke
Ngāti Porou ki Murihiku
Ngāti Porou ki Tamaki
Rūnanganui Taurahere ki te
  Whanganui a Tara
Taurahere Rūnanga o te Upoko o
  te Ika
Te Aupouri ki Tamaki Taurahere
Te Whanau Apanui ki Poneke

Rūnanga
Te Kakano o te Whanau
Te Pakakohi
Te Rangatahi o Tamaki
Te Rarawa
Te Rūnanga o Muriwhenua
Te Rūnanga o Ngāpuhi
Te Rūnanga o Ngāti Porou
Te Rūnanga o Raukawa
Te Rūnanga o te Ika a Maui
Te Rūnanga o Turanganui a Kiwa
Te Rūnanga o Whaingaroa
Te Rūnanga Rangatahi o Taranaki
Te Rūnanga o Muriwhenua
Te Rūnanganui o Ngāti
  Kahungunu
Te Rūnanganui o Te Ika Whenua
Te Rūnanganui o te Tauihu o te
  Waka a Maui

Other Bodies
Board of Māori Affairs
Kotahitanga Church Society
Manatū Māori
Ministry of Māori Affairs
Māori Women's Welfare League
Māori Education Foundation
New Zealand Planning Council

Bibliography

28 Māori Battalion Association, (1990), *Golden Jubilee 1940–1990: The Māori Battalion Remembered, Te Hokowhitu a Tumatauenga*.

Adams, P. (1977), *Fatal Necessity: British Intervention in New Zealand 1830–1847* (Auckland University Press/Oxford University Press, Auckland).

Anderson, A. (1983), *When All The Moa Ovens Grew Cold: Nine Centuries of Changing Fortune for the Southern Maori* (Otago Heritage Books, Dunedin).

Anderson, A. (1989), 'The Last Archipelago: 1000 Years of Maori Settlement in New Zealand', in David Green (ed.), *Towards 1990: Seven Leading Historians Examine Significant Aspects of New Zealand History* (GP Books, Wellington), 1–19.

Asher, G. and Naulls, D. (1987), *Maori Land: Discussion Paper No. 29* (New Zealand Planning Council).

Beaglehole, J. C. (ed.). (1955), *The Journals of Captain James Cook*, Vol. 1 (Cambridge).

Beattie, H. (1920), 'Nature Lore of the Southern Maori', in *The Proceedings of the New Zealand Institute* 52: 53–77.

Beattie, H. (1990), *Tikao Talks: Ka Taoka o te Ao Kohatu: Treasures from the Ancient World of the Maori* [1939] (Penguin, Auckland).

Belich, J. (1989), *I Shall Not Die* (Allen and Unwin/Port Nicholson, Wellington).

Best, E. (1924), *Maori Religion and Mythology, Part I* (Government Printer, Wellington).

Best, E. (1952 edn), *The Maori As He Was* (Government Printer, Wellington).

Best, E. (1974), *The Maori School of Learning: Its Objects, Methods, and Ceremonial* (Government Printer, Wellington).

Binney, J. (1968), *The Legacy of Guilt. A Life of Thomas Kendall*, (Auckland University Press/Oxford University Press, Auckland).

Binney, J. (1987), 'Maori Oral History, Pakeha, Written Texts: Two Forms of Telling History', *New Zealand Journal of History*, 21: 16–28.

Bolitho, H. (1921), *Rātana: The Maori Miracle Man: The Story of his Life: The Record of his Miracles* (Geddis and Blomfeld, Auckland).

Bowden, R. (1979), 'Tapu and Mana: Ritual Authority and Political Power in Traditional Maori Society', *Journal of Polynesian History*, 14: 50–61.

Brewster, B. (1987), *Te Moa: The Life and Death of New Zealand's Unique Bird* (Nikau, Nelson).

Brookfield, F. M. (1989), 'The New Zealand Constitution: The Search for Legitimacy', in I. H. Kawharu (ed.), *Waitangi: Māori and Pākehā Perspectives of the Treaty of Waitangi* (Oxford University Press, Auckland), 1–24.

Buck, Sir Peter H. (1926), 'The Value of Tradition in Polynesian Research', *Journal of the Polynesian Society*, 35: 181–203.

Butterworth, G. V. and Young, H. R. (1989), *End of an Era: The Departments of Māori Affairs 1840–1989* (Manatū Māori/Te Tira Ahu Iwi, Wellington).

Butterworth, G. V. and Young, H. R. (1990), *Māori Affairs: A Department and the People who Made it* (Manatū Māori/Te Tira Ahu Iwi, Wellington).

Cairns, K. (1972), 'Papawai and the Maori Parliament', in *New Zealand Heritage*, 61: 1697–701.

Caughley, G. (1988), 'The Colonisation of New Zealand by the Polynesians', *Journal of the Royal Society of New Zealand*, 18: 245–70.

Cody, J. F. (1956), *28 (Maori) Battalion: Official History of New Zealand in the Second World War 1935–45* (War History Branch, Department of Internal Affairs, Wellington).

Colenso, W. M. (1880), 'On the Vegetable Food of the Ancient New Zealanders before Cook's Visit', *The Proceedings of the New Zealand Institute*, 13: 3–38.

Condliffe, J. B. (1971), *Te Rangihiroa: The Life of Sir Peter Buck* (Whitcombe and Tombs, Christchurch).

Cowan, J. (1983 edn), *The New Zealand Wars and the Pioneer Period*, Vol. 1 (Government Printer, Wellington).

Dalziel, R. (1989), 'Towards a Representative Democracy: 100 Years of the Modern Electoral System', in David Green (ed.), *Towards 1990: Seven Leading Historians Examine Aspects of New Zealand History* (Government Printer, Wellington), 49–64.

Davidson, J. (1983), 'Maori Prehistory: The State of the Art', *Journal of the Polynesian Society*, 92: 291–307.

Davidson, J. (1984 edn), 'The Polynesian Foundation', in W. H. Oliver (ed.), *The Oxford History of New Zealand* (Oxford University Press, Auckland), 3–27.

Davidson, J. (1984), *The Prehistory of New Zealand* (Longman Paul, Auckland).

Department of Justice (1989), *Principles for Crown Action on the Treaty of Waitangi* (Department of Justice, Wellington).

Department of Māori Affairs (1988), *He Tirohanga Rangapū: He Whakawhitiwhiti Whakaaro (Partnership Perspectives)* (Department of Māori Affairs, Wellington).

Deaprtment of Māori Affairs (1988) *Te Urupare Rangapū: Te Rarangi Kaupapa (Partnership Response)* (Department of Māori Affairs, Wellington).

Department of Statistics: Te Tari Tatau, *New Zealand Official 1990 Yearbook: Te Pukapuka Houanga Whaimana o Aotearoa*, 94th edn (Department of Statistics, Wellington).

Doak, W. (1984), *The Burning of the Boyd*, (Hodder and Stoughton, Auckland).

Downes, T. W. (1918), 'Notes on Eels and Eel-weirs', *The Proceedings of the New Zealand Institute*, 50: 296.

Durie, E. T. and Orr, G. (1990), 'The Role of the Waitangi Tribunal and the Development of a Bicultural Jurisprudence', *New Zealand Universities Law Review*, 14 (1): 62–81.

Durie, M. H. (1989), 'Congress of Māori Leadership', 18 July 1989, unpublished paper.

Elsmore, B. (1985), *Like Them That Dream* (Tauranga Moana, Tauranga).

Elsmore, B. (1989), *Mana From Heaven: A Century of Maori Prophets in New Zealand* (Moana, Tauranga).

Ensor, S. and Rountree, K. (1984), *An Introduction to New Zealand Prehistory: A Maori Studies Resource Book and Planning Guide for Teachers* (Auckland Museum Education Service, Auckland).

Fox, A. (1978), *Tiromoana Pa, Te Awanga, Hawke's Bay Excavations 1974–5* (Department of Anthropology, Otago University, Dunedin).

Firth, R. (1972 edn), *Economics of the New Zealand Maori* (Government Printer, Wellington).

Gorst, J. E. (1975 edn), *The Maori King, or, The Story of Our Quarrel with the Natives of*

New Zealand (Capper, Christchurch).

Grace, J. Te H. (1959), *Tuwharetoa: The History of the Māori People of the Taupo District* (A. H. and A. W. Reed, Auckland).

Great Britain Parliamentary Papers Vol. 3, 'Correspondence and Papers Relating to New Zealand 1835–42'(Irish Universities Press, Shannon).

Great Britaian Parliamentary Papers Vol. 8 (Irish Universities Press, Shannon).

Great Britain Parliamentary Papers Vol. 12, 'Correspondence and Papers Relating to the Maori Uprising in New Zealand 1861', 84–7, 95–117 (Irish Universities Press, Shannon).

Green, D. (ed.) (1989), *Towards 1990: Seven Leading Historians Examine Significant Aspects of New Zealand History* (GP Books, Wellington).

Gudgeon, C. (1908), 'The Maori Tribes of the East Coast', *Journal of the Polynesian Society*, 4: 17.

Gustafson, B. (1986a), *The First Fifty Years: A History of the National Party* (Reed Methuen, Auckland).

Gustafson, B. (1986b), *From the Cradle to the Grave: A Biography of Michael Joseph Savage* (Reed Methuen, Auckland).

Haast, Julius (1872), 'Moas and Moahunters', *The Proceedings of the New Zealand Institute*, 4: 67–9.

Hackshaw, F. (1989), 'Nineteenth Century Notions of Aboriginal Title and their Influence on the Interpretation of the Treaty of Waitangi', in I. H. Kawharu (ed.), *Waitangi: Maori and Pakeha Perspectives of the Treaty of Waitangi* (Oxford University Press, Auckland), 92–120.

Hakaraia, Te Hope Huia (1986), 'Mana Motuhake: The Nature of its Business', *Tu Tangata*, No. 32.

Hamer, D. (1988), *The New Zealand Liberal Party: The Years of Power, 1891–1912* (Auckland University Press, Auckland).

Hanson, A. (1989), 'The Making of the Maori: Cultural Invention and Its Logic', *American Anthropologist*, 91: 890–902.

Hawkes, J. (1955), *Early Britain* (William Collins, London).

Henare, M. (1990), 'Development: Sovereignty or Dependency?', in *Puna Wairere: Essays by Maori* (New Zealand Planning Council, Wellington), 39–47.

Henderson, J. M. (1963), *Rātana: The Origins and the Story of the Movement* (Polynesian Society, Wellington).

Henderson, J. M. (1965 edn), 'The Rātana Movement', in J. G. A. Pocock (ed.), *The Maori and New Zealand Politics: Talks from an NZBC Series with Additional Essays* (Blackwood and Janet Paul, Auckland and Hamilton), 61–72.

Henderson, J. M. (1972 edn), *Rātana: The Man, the Church, the Political Movement* (A. H. and A. W. Reed/Polynesian Society, Wellington).

Hobbes, T. (1968, 1988 edns), *Leviathan*, with introduction by C. B. Macpherson (Penguin, London).

Hohepa, P. W. (1964), *A Maori Community in Northland* (Department of Anthropology, University of Auckland, Auckland).

Hohepa, P. W. (1978), 'Maori and Pakeha: The One People Myth', in M. King (ed.), *Tihe Mauri Ora: Aspects of Maoritanga* (Methuen, Auckland), 98–111.

Horsfield, A. and Evans, M. (1988), *Te Minitatanga mo ngā Wāhine: Māori Women in the Economy* (Ministry of Women's Affairs, Wellington).

Jones, P. Te Hurinui (1968), 'Maori Kings', in E. Schwimmer (ed.), *The Maori People in the Nineteen Sixties* (Longman Paul, Auckland), 132–74.

Kawharu, I. H. (1968), 'Urban Immigrants and Tangata Whenua', in E. Schwimmer (ed.), *The Maori People in the Nineteen Sixties* (Longman Paul, Auckland), 174–86.

Kawharu, I. H. (ed.) (1989), *Waitangi: Maori and Pakeha Perspectives of the Treaty of Waitangi* (Oxford University Press, Auckland).

Kelly, L. G. (1990 edn), *Tainui: The Story of Hoturoa and his Descendants* (Pukapuka, Onehunga).

Kelly, L. G. (1951), *Marion du Fresne at the Bay of Islands* (A. H. Reed, Auckland).

King, M. (ed.) (1977 edn), *Te Ao Hurihuri: The World Moves On* (Hicks Smith/ Methuen, Auckland).

King, M. (1977), *Te Peua* (Hodder and Stoughton, Auckland).

King, M. (ed.) (1978), *Tihe Mauri Ora: Aspects of Maoritanga* (Methuen, Auckland).

King, M. (1981), *New Zealanders at War* (Heinemann, Auckland).

King, M. (1983), *Māori: A Photographic and Social History* (Heinemann, Auckland).

King, M. (1984 edn), 'Between Two Worlds', in W. H. Oliver (ed.), *The Oxford History of New Zealand*, (Oxford University Press, Auckland), 279–301.

Kingsbury, B. (1989), 'The Treaty of Waitangi: Some International Law Perspectives', in I. H. Kawaharu (ed.), *Waitangi: Māori and Pākehā Perspectives of the Treaty of Waitangi* (Oxford University Press, Auckland), 121–57.

Kupenga, V., Rata, R., and Nepe, T. (1990), 'Whaia Te Iti Kahurangi: Māori Women Reclaiming Autonomy', in *Puna Wairere: Essays by Maori* (Wellington).

Latukefu, S. (1970), 'King George Tupou I of Tonga', in J. W. Davidson and D. Scarr (eds), *Pacific Island Portraits* (A. H. and A. W. Reed, Wellington and Auckland).

Lyons, D. P. (1975), 'An Analysis of Three Maori Prophet Movements', in I. H. Kawharu (ed.), *Conflict and Compromise* (A. H. and A. W. Reed, Wellington).

McCulloch, B. (1984), *Prehistoric New Zealand and its People* (Canterbury Museum, Christchurch).

McHugh, P. G. (1989), 'Constitutional Theory and Māori Claims', in I. H. Kawharu (ed.), *Waitangi: Maori and Pākehā Perspectives of the Treaty of Waitangi* (Oxford University Press, Auckland), 25–63.

McIntyre, W. D. and Gardner, W. J. (1971) (eds), *Speeches and Documents on New Zealand History* (Clarendon, Oxford).

Mackay, J. A. (1949), *Historic Poverty Bay and the East Coast, NI, NZ: A Centennial Memorial* (J. G. Mackay, Gisborne).

McLintock, A. H. (1958), *Crown Colony Government in New Zealand* (Government Printer, Wellington).

McNab, R. (ed.) (1908), *Historical Records of New Zealand*, Vol I (Wellington).

Mahuika, A. (1977 edn), 'Leadership: Inherited and Achieved', in M. King (ed.), *Te Ao Hurihuri: The World Moves On* (Hicks Smith/Methuen, Auckland), 62–85.

Mahuika, A. and Durie, M. H. (1991), An Address to the New Zealand Council of Trade Unions, Wellington, 8 October 1991.

Mahuika, A. and Durie M. H. (1991), 'Information Brief for Iwi: Joint Working Party: Arrangements in Recent Surplus Crown Railway Properties and Treaty of Waitangi Claims', unpublished paper.

Mahuta, R. (1978), 'The Māori King Movement Today', in M. King (ed.), *Tihe Mauri Ora* (Methuen, Auckland), 33–41.

Makura, W. (1892), *Nga Korero o te hui o te Whakakotahi i tu ki te Tiriti o Waitangi* (Wiremu Makura, Auckland).

Manatū Māori (1991), *Nga Take i neke ai te Māori: Māori Mobility* (Manatū Māori,

Wellington).

Manatū Māori (1991), *Te Aka Kumara: He Raranga Ingoa hei Whakaputanga atu: Directory of Contacts for Consultation* (three volumes) (Manatū Māori, Wellington).

(1984), *Maori Economic Devlopment Summit Conference Proceedings 1984* (Government Printer, Wellington).

Māori Land Court, Manatu Māori, Te Tira Ahu Iwi (1990), *Rūnanga Iwi Act* (Wellington).

Mariu, J. (1988), 'Māori Women's Welfare League Healthy Lifestyles Programme', in *Proceedings of the Nutrition Society of New Zealand*, 13: 95–98.

Marsden, M. (1977 edn), 'God, Man, and the Universe', in M. King (ed.), *Te Ao Hurihuri: The World Moves On* (Hicks Smith/Methuen, Auckland), 143–63.

Marsden, S. (1908), 'Copy of a Letter dated June 4, on the Need for a Maori King', in *Historical Records of New Zealand*, 1: 627.

Matthews, R. H. (1911), 'Reminiscences of Maori Life Forty Years Ago', *The Proceedings of the New Zealand Institute* 43: 598–605.

Metge, J. (1976), *The Maoris of New Zealand: Rautahi*, 2nd edn, (Routledge, Kegan and Paul, London).

Mulgan, R. (1989), *Māori, Pākehā, and Democracy* (Oxford University Press, Auckland).

National Māori Congress, National Maori Leadership Hui, 23 and 24 June 1989, Waihi Marae.

National Māori Congress, Te Whakakotahitanga o Nga Iwi o Aotearoa me Te Waipounamu/The National Maori Congress: Hui A Tau, Tauponui A Tia, 20 Hongongoi, 1991.

National Māori Congress, *A Collective Submission on Supplementary Order Paper No 22 Resource Management Bill*, May 1991.

New Zealand Planning Council (1990), *Puna Wairere: Essays by Maori* (NZPC, Wellington).

Ngata, A. T. (1928), 'Anthropology and the Government of Native Races in the Pacific', *The Australasian Journal of Psychology and Philosophy*, 6: 1–14.

Oliver, W. H. (ed.) (1984 edn), *The Oxford History of New Zealand* (Oxford University Press, Auckland).

Oliver, W. H. (ed.) (1990), *The Dictionary of New Zealand Biography, vol. 1* (Bridget Williams/Department of Internal Affairs, Wellington).

Olssen, E. and Stentson, M. (1989), *A Century of Change: New Zealand 1800–1900* (Longman Paul, Auckland).

Orange, C. (1980), 'The Covenant of Kohimārama: A Ratification of the Treaty of Waitangi', *New Zealand Journal of History*, 14: 61–79.

Orange, C. (1987a), *The Treaty of Waitangi* (Allen and Unwin/Port Nicholson, Wellington).

Orange, C. (1987b), 'An Exercise in Maori Autonomy: The Rise of the Maori War Effort Organisation', *New Zealand Journal of History*, 21: 156–72.

Owens, J. M. R. (1974), *Prophets in the Wilderness: The Wesleyan Mission to New Zealand 1819–27* (Auckland University Press/Oxford University Press, Auckland).

Owens, J. M. R. (1984 edn), 'New Zealand Before Annexation', in W. H. Oliver (ed.), *The Oxford History of New Zealand* (Oxford University Press, Auckland), 28–53.

Parsonson, A. (1984 edn), 'The Pursuit of Mana', in W. H. Oliver (ed.), *The Oxford*

History of New Zealand (Oxford University Press, Auckland), 140–67.

Pocock, J. G. A. (ed.) (1965), *The Maori and New Zealand Politics: Talks from an NZBC Series with Additional Essays* (Blackwood and Janet Paul, Auckland and Hamilton).

Pool, I. (1991), *Te Iwi Maori: A New Zealand Population Past, Present and Projected* (Auckland University Press, Auckland).

Ramsden, E. (1946), 'Old Papawai: A Pa Carved out of Virgin Bush', *The Evening Post*, Monday 30 December: 10.

Raureti, M. (1978), 'The Origins of the Rātana Movement', in M. King (ed.), *Tihe Mauri Ora* (Methuen, Auckland), 42–59.

Reed, A. H. and Reed, A. W. (eds) (1969 edn), *Captain Cook in New Zealand* (A. H. and A. W. Reed, Wellington).

Reed, A. W. (1977), *Treasury of Maori Exploration: Legends Relating to the First Explorers of New Zealand* (A. H. and A. W. Reed, Wellington).

Renwick, W. (1990), *The Treaty Now* (GP Books, Wellington).

Rickard, L. S. (1963), *Tamihana, The Kingmaker* (A. H. and A. W. Reed, Wellington).

Ringer, J. B. (1991), *An Introduction to New Zealand Government* (Hazard, Christchurch).

Ritchie, (1965), 'The Grass Roots of Māori Politics', in J. G. A. Pocock (ed.), *The Maori and New Zealand Politics: Talks from an NZBC Series with Additional Essays* (Blackwood and Janet Paul, Auckland and Hamilton), 80–6.

Ross, J. O. (1980), 'Busby and the Declaration of Independence', *New Zealand Journal of History*, 14: 83–9.

Royal Commission on Electoral Reform (1986), *Report of the Royal Commission on the Electoral System: Towards a Better Democracy* (State Services Commission, Wellington).

Salmond, A. (1975), *Hui: A Study of Māori Gatherings* (Reed/Methuen, Auckland).

Salmond, A. (1983), 'The Study of Traditional Maori Society', *Journal of the Polynesian Society*, 92 (3): 309–31.

Salmond, A. (1991), *Two Worlds: First Meetings between Māori and Europeans* (Viking/ Penguin, Auckland).

Schwimmer, E. (ed.) (1966), *The World of the Maori* (A. H. and A. W. Reed, Wellington).

Schwimmer, E. (1968a), *The Maori People in the Nineteen Sixties* (Longman Paul, Auckland).

Schwimmer, E. (ed.) (1968b), 'The Maori and the Government', in *The Maori People in the Nineteen Sixties*, (Longman Paul, Auckland), 328–51.

Schwimmer, E. (1990), 'The Maori Hapu: A Generative Model', *Journal of the Polynesian Society*, 99 (3): 299–317.

Sharp, A. (1990), *Justice and the Māori: Māori Claims in New Zealand Political Argument in the 1980s* (Oxford University Press, Auckland).

Sigley, D. (1974), 'The YMP', in M. Te Aranga Hakiwai (ed.), *Te Aranga o Te Aute: Ta te Rangatira Tana Kai he Korero ta te Ware he Muhukai* (Pukehou), 22–36.

Sinclair, K. (1959), *A History of New Zealand* (Penguin, Auckland).

Sinclair, K. (1965), 'The Maori in Politics, 1840–67', in J. G. A. Pocock (ed.), *The Maori and New Zealand Politics: Talks from an NZBC Series with Additional Essays* (Blackwood and Janet Paul, Auckland and Hamilton), 14–21.

Sinclair, K. (1991), *Kinds of Peace: Maori People after the Wars, 1870–85* (Auckland University Press, Auckland).

Sissons, J. (1988), 'Rethinking Tribal Histories', *Journal of the Polynesian Society*, 97: 199–204.

Sorrenson, M. P. K. (1963), 'The Maori King Movement', in R. Chapman and K. Sinclair (eds), *Studies of a Small Democracy: Essays in Honour of Willis Airey* (Paul for University of Auckland, Hamilton), 33–55.

Sorrenson, M. P. K. (1965), 'The Politics of Land', in J. G. A. Pocock (ed.), *The Maori and New Zealand Politics: Talks from an NZBC Series with Additional Essays*, (Blackwood and Janet Paul, Auckland and Hamilton), 21–46.

Sorrenson, M. P. K. (1979), *Maori Origins and Migrations: The Genesis of Some Pakeha Myths and Legends* (Auckland University Press, Auckland).

Sorrenson, M. P. K. (1984 edn), 'Māori and Pākehā', in W. H. Oliver (ed.), *The Oxford History of New Zealand* (Oxford University Press, Auckland), 168–93.

Sorrenson, M. P. K. (1986), 'A History of Maori Representation in Parliament', in *Report of the Royal Commission on the Electoral System: Towards a Better Democracy*, (State Services Commission, Wellington) Appendix B.

Sorrenson, M. P. K. (1989), 'Towards a Radical Reinterpretation of New Zealand History: The Role of the Waitangi Tribunal', in I. H. Kawharu (ed.), *Waitangi: Māori and Pākehā Perspectives of the Treaty of Waitangi* (Oxford University Press, Auckland), 158–78.

Soutar, M. G. (1988), 'The Origins and Early History of Te Aitanga-A-Mate', unpublished paper.

Stafford, D. M. (1967), *Te Arawa: A History of the Arawa People* (Reed, Auckland).

Stirling, A. and Salmond, A. (1976), *Amiria: The Story of a Maori Woman* (A. H. and A. W. Reed, Wellington).

Stirling, A. and Salmond, A. (1980), *Eruera: The Teachings of a Māori Elder* (Oxford University Press, Auckland).

Stone, N. (ed.) (1987), *The Makers of English History* (Guild, London).

Taylor, Rev. R. (1974 edn), *Te Ika A Maui: New Zealand and its Inhabitants* (Wertheim and Macintosh, Auckland).

Taiapa, P. and Williams, Archdeacon H. W. (1955), trans., *Tuwhakairiora: Souvenir Booklet Commemorating the Opening of the House* (Te Rau, Gisborne).

Tawhai, Te Pakaka (1991), 'Aotearoa's Spiritual Heritage', in Donovan (ed.), *Religions of New Zealand* (Dunmore, Palmerston North), 11–19.

Te Awekotuku, N. (1991), *Mana Wahine Māori* (New Women's Press, Auckland).

Te Hurinui, P. (1959), *King Potatau: An Account of the Life of Potatau Te Wherowhero the First Maori King* (Polynesian Society/Roydhouse, Carterton).

Te Rangihiroa (Sir Peter Buck) (1977 edn), *The Coming of the Maori* (Maori Purposes Fund Board/Whitcoulls, Wellington).

Te Runanga ko Huirau (1989), 'Submission to the Select Committee on Maori Fisheries', unpublished submission.

Te Tira Ahu Iwi (1990), *Ko Te Kaupapa Nui A Te Tira Ahu Iwi 1990–1991: Corporate Plan of the Iwi Transition Agency* (Te Tira Ahu Iwi, Wellington).

Te Whakakotahi Taskforce, *Discussion Paper 1: Rūnanga Iwi Bill* (Whakakotahi Taskforce, Palmerston North).

Te Whakakotahi Taskforce, *Discussion Paper 2: Congress Principles and Objectives* (Whakakotahi Taskforce, Palmerston North).

Te Whakakotahi Taskforce, *Discussion Paper 3: Summary of Agreements from Rātana Hui Workshops* (Whakakotahi Taskforce, Palmerston North).

Te Whakakotahi Taskforce, *Discussion Paper 4: Congress Representation* (Whakakotahi

Taskforce, Palmerston North).

Te Whakakotahi Taskforce, *Discussion Paper 5: Congress Funding* (Whakakotahi Taskforce, Palmerston North).

Te Whakakotahi Taskforce, *Discussion Paper 6: Congress Structure* (Whakakotahi Taskforce, Palmerston North).

Te Whakakotahi Taskforce, *Discussion Paper 7: Taskforce Recommendations for the Establishment of a National Maori Congress* (Whakakotahi Taskforce, Palmerston North).

Te Whakakotahi Taskforce, 'Proceedings of the Rātana Hui held on 12 August 1989' (Department of Māori Studies, Massey University, Palmerston North).

Te Whakakotahi Taskforce, 'Proceedings of the Hui to Discuss the Rūnanga Iwi Bill, 10 March 1990'.

Te Whakakotahi Taskforce, 'Commentary on the Officials Report to the Māori Affairs Select Committee on the Rūnanga Iwi Bill' (Department of Māori Studies, Massey University, Palmerston North).

Te Whakakotahi Taskforce, 'Minutes of the Inaugural Taskforce Meeting held on Saturday 13 January in the Waiariki Room, THC Tokaanu Hotel'.

Te Whakakotahi Taskforce, 'Minutes of the Whakakotahi Taskforce held on Sunday 25 February at the Tuwharetoa Māori Trust Board Office, Turangi'.

Te Whakakotahi Taskforce, 'Minutes of the Whakakotahi Task Force held on Sunday 25 March at the Bridge Lodge, Turangi'.

Te Whakakotahi Taskforce, 'Minutes of the Whakakotahi Task Force held on Sunday 29 April at the Bridge Lodge, Turangi'.

Te Whakakotahi Taskforce, 'Minutes of the Whakakotahi Task Force held on Sunday 20 May at the Manu Flights, Palmerston North'.

Te Whakakotahi Taskforce, 'Minutes of the Whakakotahi Taskforce held on Sunday 17 June at the Bridge Lodge, Turangi'.

Tremewan, P. (1990), *French Akaroa* (University of Canterbury Press, Christchurch).

Turei, M. (1911), 'Tuwhakairiora', *Journal of the Polynesian Society*, 20: 1.

Waitangi Tribunal (1983), *Wai 6, Report of the Waitangi Tribunal on the Motunui, Waitara Claim* (Waitangi Tribunal, Wellington).

Waitangi Tribunal (1987), *Wai 9, Report of the Waitangi Tribunal on the Orakei Claim* (Waitangi Tribunal, Wellington).

Waitangi Tribunal (1988), *Wai 22, Report of the Waitangi Tribunal on the Muriwhenua Fishing Claim* (Waitangi Tribunal, Wellington).

Waitangi Tribunal (1991), *Wai 27, The Ngai Tahu Report 1991* (Waitangi Tribunal, Wellington).

Walker, R. J. (1989a), 'The Flowering of Kotahitanga', *NZ Listener*, 29 July: 23–4.

Walker, R. J. (1989b), 'The Treaty of Waitangi as a Focus of Māori Protest', in I. H. Kawharu (ed.), *Waitangi: Maori and Pākehā Perspectives of the Treaty of Waitangi* (Oxford University Press, Auckland), 263–99.

Walker, R. J. (1990), *Ka Whawhai Tonu Matou: Struggle Without End* (Penguin, Auckland).

Ward, A. (1973), *A Show of Justice: Racial Amalgamation in Nineteenth Century New Zealand* (Auckland University Press/Oxford University Press, Auckland).

Wards, I. M. (1968), *The Shadow of the Land: A Study of British Policy and Racial Conflict in New Zealand 1832–1852* (Historical Publications Branch, Department of Internal Affairs, Wellington).

Williams, D. V. (1989), 'Te Tiriti o Waitangi—Unique Relationship Between

Crown and Tangata Whenua?', in I. H. Kawharu (ed.), *Waitangi: Māori and Pākehā Perspectives of the Treaty of Waitangi* (Oxford University Press, Auckland), 64–91.

Williams, D. V. (1990), 'The Constitutional Status of the Treaty of Waitangi: An Historical Perspective', *New Zealand Universities Law Review*, 14 (1): 9–36.

Williams, H. W. (1921), *The Ministry of Healing and Rātana and His Work* (Poverty Bay Herald, Gisborne).

Williams, H. W. (1971), *A Dictionary of the Maori Language*, 7th edn, 1844, W. Williams, Pahia (Government Printer, Wellington).

Williams, J. A. (1969) *Politics of the New Zealand Maori; Protest and Cooperation* (University of Auckland/Oxford University Press, Auckland).

Williams, J. A. (1965), 'The Foundation of Apirana Ngata's Career, 1891–1909', in J. G. A. Pocock (ed.), *The Maori and New Zealand Politics: Talks from an NZBC Series with Additional Essays* (Blackwood and Janet Paul, Auckland and Hamilton), 55–61.

Williams, J. (1989), 'Towards a Treaty Driven Society: New Perspectives on the Treaty of Waitangi' (The New Zealand Planning Council).

Wilson, J. (1990), 'The Maori Struggle for Mana Motuhake', *New Zealand Historic Places*, 30: 26–30.

Winiata, W. (1991), 'Participation by Congress in Crown and/or Crown/Congress Bodies', unpublished paper.

Legislation

New Zealand Constitution Act 1853, 'An Act to Grant a Representative Constitution to the Colony of New Zealand', 15 & 16 Victoria, cap. 72, 30 July 1852.

State-Owned Enterprises Act 1986.

Treaty of Waitangi Act 1975.

Cases

Worchester v. *Georgia* (1832) 31 US (6 Pet.) 350.

Index

Marupo 84
Mason, H. G. R. 102, 103
Massey University ix, 169, 171
Massey, William 92
Mataatua 149
Matamata 49
Matangi, Te Manihere 78
Matiria 47
Matthews, R. H. 20
Matua, Henare 63, 65, 86
Maunga 21
Maungākawa 73 58, 59, 61
Maungapohatu 50
Maungatautari 51
Mawhete, Rangi 101, 103, 126
Mead, H. M. 146
Ministry of Māori Development 174
Moehau 51
Moetara 84
Moko, Pita 123
Morehu 118
Murihiku 16, 20
Murihiku Marae 166, 174, 178
Muriwhenua 20–2

Nahe, Hoani 67
National Māori Congress ix, 140–86,
    190, 216–19
National Māori Leadership Hui ix
National Service Department 102
National Party 141
Native Circuit Court Judges 81
Native Circuit Courts Act 63, 81
Native Councils Bill 1860 81
Native Department 102, 103
Native Districts 81
Native Districts Regulation Act 63,
    81
Native Land Act 1865 63
Native Lands Act 1888 66
Native Magistrate 81
Native Minister 64, 102, 103
Native Representation Act 61
Native Rights Bill 1894 69, 205
Native Secretary 63
Native Territorial Rights Act 63
Nene, Tamati Waka 82–4
Nera 49
New Leinster 32

New Munster 32
New South Wales 31
New Ulster 32
New Zealand Government Act
    1846 33–4
New Zealand Māori Council 76,
    102–8, 143, 145, 147, 151, 174
New Zealand Planning Council 183
New Zealand Settlements Act
    1863 57
Ngā Koata e Whā 123
Ngāpuhi 29, 47, 66, 84, 93, 167
Ngā Rauru 46
Ngāi Tahu 17, 22–3, 50, 90, 146, 147
Ngāi Te Rangi 29, 51, 87
Ngāi Tūhoe 50, 62, 68
Ngapua, Hone 67
Ngapuwaiwaha Marae 165
Ngāruawāhia 51, 52, 57, 60, 165
Ngata, Sir Apirana Turupa 90, 92–3,
    95, 96, 97, 98, 100, 124
Ngāti Apa 50, 87, 118
Ngāti Apakura 48
Ngāti Awa 50, 87, 146
Ngāti Hauā 29, 49, 51, 52, 59
Ngāti Kahungunu 50, 63, 64, 65, 90,
    147
Ngāti Koata 146
Ngāti Koroki 48, 51
Ngāti Mahuta 44, 46, 51
Ngāti Mamoe 90
Ngāti Manawa 50
Ngāti Maniapoto 51, 52, 56, 57
Ngāti Maru 51
Ngāti Matakore 51
Ngāti Parakiore 58
Ngāti Porou 20, 29, 50, 92, 170
Ngāti Raukawa ix, 45, 51, 87, 146
Ngāti Ruanui 51
Ngāti Ruanuku 20
Ngāti Tamatera 29, 51
Ngāti Te Whatuiapiti 42, 63, 65
Ngāti Toa 20, 50
Ngāti Whātua 66, 78
Ngāti Whakatere 51
Ngāti Whakaue 30
Ngongotahā (Te Arawa) 50
Non-signatory tribes 29–30
Normanby, Lord 11, 27, 28